Demons Within Schizophrenia and Maladaptive Daydreaming Disorder

Christian testimony of Danica Ked

DANICA KED

BALBOA.PRESS
A DIVISION OF HAY HOUSE

Balboa Press books may be ordered through booksellers or by contacting:

Balboa Press
A Division of Hay House
1663 Liberty Drive
Bloomington, IN 47403
www.balboapress.com.au
1 (877) 407-4847

Print information available on the last page.

ISBN: 978-1-5043-2146-4 (sc)
ISBN: 978-1-5043-2147-1 (e)

Balboa Press rev. date: 04/23/2020

CONTENTS

Acknowledgements

I'm a servant of Jesus Christ, and I want to thank the Lord and acknowledge him for delivering me out of Satan's kingdom and bringing me back into his marvellous light. I wrote this book to expose the unfruitful deeds of darkness and to inform you through my own personal experiences of what Satan can do to a true born-again Christian. Without the Lord's intervention, I most likely wouldn't have been able to write this testimony. I pray that this book opens your eyes to the truth.

The Lord Jesus once told me,"If you hear my words and do them, you will be saved."

I want to thank Joshua, my husband, for supporting me in publishing this book. Thank you for all your love and support.

To my two beautiful girls, Violet and Ruby, I just want to say thank you for helping Mummy through this horrible time. You both kept me going through it all. Thank you for all your hugs and kisses.

"You are writing something I don't want anyone to know. I warn you: I will get to you. I will kill you." He spoke in a subtle, smooth tone of voice, almost civil in conversation. It was loud and clear, and I knew I had just heard from the devil himself.

Chapter 1

GROWING UP

I was born in Sydney, Australia in the early 1980's. Growing up in Australia was a fun time for me. I grew up on a dead-end street, with our house being directly opposite the park grounds. In our street and surrounding streets lived kids our own age. We introduced ourselves and became friends. All of us grew up together, and we would often go over each other's houses and play games like soccer, volleyball, cricket, and tennis. We would fly kites in the open park and hang around each other and talk. At this stage, life was a breeze, and I didn't have a worry in the world.

During my childhood, my sister, Sally, and I decided to visit a friend who lived a few doors down from us. Some of the neighbourhood kids were over too. As we were inside their garage, they secretly brought out a Ouija board, also known as a spirit board. Sally and I didn't participate in this game. However, we hung around and watched. Our friends sat down in a circle around the board and brought out a glass cup. They all breathed into the glass cup and placed it on the board. I saw how the glass lifted off the board while each person placed a finger on it. A spirit had entered the glass, causing it to hover over the board game. When they asked the spirit questions, the glass would hover over "yes" or "no" or move to each letter and spell out a word. At this stage, I didn't know what this game was. This game is from the occult, and being a Christian from birth, I had decided not to join in. This was the first demonic spirit I ever encountered.

One morning, when I was seven, I had had a seizure and wasn't able to respond to anyone. An ambulance was called and I was taken to the local hospital. At the hospital, I came back to myself recovering from the seizure. The doctors put me on medication. However, it hindered my ability to study. As a result, my year 2 teacher decided that I should be held back. My mother intervened in the school's decision and asked them to see how I would do in the following year. They accepted her request and allowed me to enter the next grade. Once I was taken off the medication, I was able to study well again. You see, if I had repeated the year, I wouldn't have met Joshua, my husband, and had our two children with him. My high school friend introduced me to him, and we ended up getting married.

When I was a young child, my parents, Emily and Luke, decided to put a cartoon on the television for us to watch. They thought it was innocent and did not see the underlying storyline of the film, which was filled with sorcery and evil. The cartoon was about a young boy who was possessed by an evil spirit. This young boy was evil, and the good guys stopped him by casting the spirit out of him. As a result, he became good. I remember how annoyed I became at the end of this cartoon. I hated it and wanted the evil character back. Something about this possessed boy made me like evil. He had power, and his mannerism was controlling. As a result, I was drawn towards him. This movie was the 1985s Care Bear movie and the evil boy was Dark Heart.

Our family grew up in a Christian household. We were of the Pentecostal faith until my father converted to the Message Believers. This church held the teaching taught by William Branham. These people claimed he was a prophet, and my father started following their doctrines.

The following information is from the website www.gotquestions.org

They believe (who are the Message believers) that William Branham, or "Brother Branham," was the final prophet to the church, in fulfilment of Malachi 4:5. Branham, who was quite influential in the heretical Latter Rain Movement, was to be the one to restore the church to the true apostolic faith.

William Branham was born in 1909 in Cumberland County, Kentucky. He says his parents told him that a light hovered over him in his cradle. He claims to have had a revelation from God at the age of 3. After a nearly fatal accident, he claimed to have heard a voice—another revelation from God—and at that point he began to seek God. He got involved in the Pentecostal movement and eventually was ordained as an Independent Baptist minister, although he endorsed the teachings of Oneness Pentecostalism. He claimed to have regular visions and revelations from God.

Branham began a healing ministry in 1946 and as a faith healer made a number of incredible, high-profile claims. In the mid-1950s, his following began to decline, and with the decline came more and more controversial and sensational teachings. In fact, Branham taught that members of denominational churches had taken the mark of the beast. There are a number of groups today that still follow William Branham. These range widely in belief in practice.

One group, "Branham Christ" goes so far as to say that Christ is the "Alpha" and William Branham is the "Omega" and that Jesus is the

"Only Begotten Son" and William Branham is the "First Begotten Son." It is clear from their official website that they see Jesus and Branham as equal if not equivalent. Another group believes that Branham will be resurrected first and then call for the return of Christ. Another group listens to the recorded messages of William Branham as their only teaching. And there is at least one group that has great respect for Branham's teachings but has attempted to correct them.

The teachings of William Branham are a bit jumbled and contradictory and difficult to categorize. But some of the most controversial doctrines are as follows: modalism (God exists as only one Person but reveals Himself in different modes), baptism in the name of Jesus only (believers baptized using the Trinitarian formula must be re-baptized), the serpent seed doctrine (Eve's sin in the Garden was having sex with the serpent), annihilationism (hell is not a place of everlasting punishment) the idea that the zodiac and the Egyptian pyramids are equal to written Scripture. On Christmas Eve 1965, William Branham died as a result of injuries in a car accident.

When I grew up inside this church I had mixed feelings. I watched my dad idolize William Branham so much that I felt like it was almost a form of worship. I only wanted Jesus as my Lord and Saviour. I grew angry at William Branham because of the way this church acted. After a while I began to resent William Branham and his teachings. William Branham has made big errors in his teachings, but I know that not everything he taught was incorrect.

On January 1964 Kenneth Hagin received a prophecy about William Branham.

The prophecy says, at the end of 65, he who now stands in the forefront of the healing ministry as a prophet will be taken out of the way. He'll make a false step and Satan shall destroy his life, but his spirit will be saved and his works will follow him. Ere 66 shall come, he shall be gone.

William Branham also received 7 prophetic visions in the year 1933.

Vision One

He saw in a vision that the dictator of Italy, Benito Mussolini, would invade Ethiopia and according to the voice, Ethiopia "would fall at his (Mussolini's) steps". However, the voice continued and prophesied a dreadful end of the dictator, for he would have a horrible death and his own people would literally spit on him.

Vision Two

The next vision indicated America would be drawn into a world war against Germany which would be headed up by the Austrian, Adolph Hitler. The voice predicted that this terrible war would overthrow Hitler and he would come to a mysterious "end". In this vision he was shown the Siegfried line where at a great toll of American lives would be exacted, but Hitler would be defeated.

It might be well to mention here that a subsequent vision relative to this war predicted that President Roosevelt would declare war against Germany and in so doing would eventually be elected for a fourth term.

Vision Three

The third part of the vision showed that though there were three ISMS, Fascism, Nazism, Communism in the world: that the first two would come to nothing, but that Communism would flourish. The voice admonished him to keep his eyes on "Russia" concerning future involvements, for Fascism and Nazism would end up in Communism.

Vision Four

The fourth vision that appeared to him was one in which there was predicted to be tremendous technological advances right after the war. This was symbolized by an egg shaped car with a plastic bubble roof, going down beautiful highways completely under perfect remote control. There was no steering wheel in the car and the occupants of the car appeared to be playing a game like checkers.

Vision Five

The fifth scene that appeared involved the character of womanhood around the world. In this scene there appeared the fast moral decay of women. Starting back when she received her liberty to enter into worldly affairs by means of the vote, she soon began to wear clothes that were too revealing. She cut off her hair and adopted the clothing of men. Finally the vision showed her all but stripped naked and she merely covered herself with a tiny apron about the size and shape of a fig leaf. With her womanhood de-valued a terrible moral decay came upon the earth and with it perversion even as set forth by the Word of God

Vision Six

Then there arose in the United States a most beautiful woman clothed in splendor, and great power was given to her. She was beautiful, but there was a hardness about her that defied description.

Beautiful as she was, yet she was cruel, wicked and cunning. She dominated the land with her authority; she had complete power over the people.

Vision Seven

The voice told him look once more. As he turned a great explosion rent the entire land, and left the land of America a smouldering ruin. As far as the eye could see there was nothing but craters, smoking piles of debris, and no humanity in sight.

Continuing my testimony, we attended a church every Sunday; my uncle Tim was the pastor. It was the smallest church I had ever seen. It only had a handful of members, and we were basically the only children attending. We were bored at church as children. Deep down, I wanted to attend my grandmother's church. It had children my own age, and I found it more interesting. It was meant to be one of the true churches, and God was present there. When I did attend my grandmother's church, a person would stand up and give prophecies. This person would speak out the prophecy as she received it, which edified the church. This fascinated me.

The Lord told this church through another prophecy to take up a three day fast, so he can reveal the sins that the church had amongst them. However, the church didn't listen to the prophecy, and didn't fast. However, the Lord still revealed the churches sins. Some of the church members were involved in motor vehicle theft. The Lord had also told the pastor through a prophetess that he was no longer going to lead the church. The pastor decided to move to Melbourne and the church slowly fell apart, until the church closed down and the congregation separated into other churches. Some of the members of this church started to attend a Slavic Assemblies of God church. This is where my grandmother also decided to attend.

I rarely prayed as a child, but one night I prayed, "Lord, could you give me wisdom like Solomon?" I don't know why I asked the Lord for wisdom. However, as I was growing up, the Lord opened my eyes to a lot of things. I even tried hard to avoid entering the world, until Satan drew me away from God.

In the early 1990s, my mother was diagnosed with motor neurone disease. She was in her early thirties when she became sick. My parents began seeking deliverance through prayer meetings and healing services; one day, a Christian brother prayed over her and received a vision. He told her that he saw an open grave and saw her being in the resurrection. She wanted to live out her life and did not want to pass away at such a young age. She hoped that God would heal her from the disease, but in 1993, my mother passed away at the age of thirty-two.

Grandmother May, was a big help to my parents. While my mother was sick, she often came over and took care of my father and three siblings. One morning, I woke up early and walked into my parents' bedroom; I laid down next to my mother as my father went to work. Shortly after, I woke up and walked out of the room, without looking at her. I didn't speak to her or say anything and just left the room; the only thing I can recall is looking at the clock, which read 6:00 a.m. This was the day she died.

I believe the Lord pulled me out of the room that day. I would've been extremely afraid to witness my mother's death. I got ready for school earlier than I normally would have. Usually, I would wait for my grandmother to wake me up, but that day was different. When my grandmother went to check on my mother, she yelled out in pain, and it shocked me. I remember running into my bedroom, covering my head, and crying out to God, "Please, Lord, no, no!" I knew my mother had passed away.

It was a horrible time for all of us, and it took me a long time to get over her death. For some unknown reason, I started to have memory loss. I can recall some memories, but a large part of my memory seems to have been completely erased.

As a child, I loved the Lord with all my heart, and I used to sing to the Lord. One of the songs I would sing was "In the Name of Jesus." I never listened to secular music, and my father taught me that evolution goes against God. He would give me creation magazines to read and showed us documentaries on creation versus evolution. The Bible teaches that the Lord created everything in six days and rested on the seventh day.

We once rented a movie with evil content throughout it. It was a very dark film for kids at the time, and I remember how the scenes shocked me. This movie was the Labyrinth. These types of films led me down a darker road in my life, and I started to watch horror films and supernatural television series like Buffy The Vampire Slayer, Charmed, Angel, True Blood. When I was a teenager, I used to record some of these shows behind my father's back. I really wanted to watch these shows, but I didn't want to risk my father stopping me. This was how I slipped away from God. And before I realised it, Satan had a hold on me.

Sometimes after church, we would go to my cousin's place. He owned a collection of these popular children's novels called, "Goosebumps." The storylines of these novels were all supernaturally themed. I would take one each time I visited him and read them. At that young age, it never occurred to me to stay away from such things, and no one stopped me from reading them, nor did they confiscate them.

My grandmother is a Christian who has left the world to serve the Lord. Grandmother May doesn't watch television or celebrate any holidays, and she prays and use to fast often. She also prays in tongues and is truly out of the world. She has had some influence over my life. However, we differ in doctrines. She holds the doctrines of "Jesus only" or "Oneness," and she always told me not to watch television. But as a young child, I ignored her complaining. One day, she told me a story of how her sister, my great-aunt Julie, was attacked by demons in her apartment. Aunt Julie wasn't a Christian at this stage, but after so many demonic attacks, she came to Christ. This story of how she was terrorised by demons stuck with me all my life. She saw a demonic-looking dwarf in her apartment and was tormented by demons. During these attacks, she asked a Christian brother to pray over her, as well as covering the house with oil. She was then set free from further attacks. God delivered her.

One day, we visited Great-Aunt Julie's place, and while on my visit, I looked up and saw this hole in the wall which was previously used as an electrical power point; live wiring was exposed. As I stared at it, I fell into a trance and felt the presence of a spirit, luring me towards this exposed hole to electrocute myself. Someone interrupted me and woke me out of this trance. This was the first time a spirit tried to kill me. I truly believe God helped me at that moment.

My cousin Samantha was haunted by a demon.

"I see a man following me when I go to sleep," she said, in a fearful tone.

It frightened her a lot. My mother's family had a history of the supernatural, both from the Lord and from the devil. I went to visit another cousin of mine named Felicity, and she revealed to me that her brother Tom had been haunted by a being at a young age.

"Tom sees a man at the edge of his bed at night," Felicity told me. "He stands at the bed with his arms together," she continued describing the man. "Tom is not able to see his face, just the back of his body."

I was horrified and quickly said, "It has to be a demon."

"No, Tom thinks it's just his mental health," she replied.

My grandfather Darren passed away a good number of years ago. He walked with the Lord as a Christian and received prophecies. Before the war broke out in his homeland, my grandfather was told by the Lord to leave the country. He obeyed God and left Yugoslavia with his family. One day during prayer, my grandfather received word from the Lord. "As many children as your daughter has, I will save them all," he said to my grandfather. Knowing about this prophecy growing up, it seemed like a normal thing to me, and I didn't appreciate the meaning behind it until now. This daughter was my mother, and the prophecy was about my siblings and me. The Lord told my grandfather that he was going to save us all. My brothers, however, slipped away from the Lord, but if this truly was from God, it will come to pass.

My great-grandfather John was the first member of our family who came to Christ. Before this, he was a Muslim, but he decided to convert to Christianity after a Christian man witnessed to him about Jesus. I couldn't imagine not growing up as a Christian, and I thank the Lord for this. God also healed a sick person through my great-grandfather.

My parents could not decide what to name my youngest brother. He did not have a name for about a month after he was born. God spoke to my mother in a dream and said, "Give this child the name Samuel." My parents both agreed and named him Samuel.

Grandmother May was raised a Christian but left God during her marriage. All of a sudden she had a severe stomach pain that made her very sick. She was scared and thought she would die from the severe stomach pain. She said, "Lord, if you heal me now, I will serve you all my life."

She felt the power of God heal her and instantly came back to the Lord that day; she has been serving the Lord ever since. She was given the gift of tongues later in her life.

At our childhood home, my older brother Paul, witnessed my mother's industrial sewing machine operating by itself. No-one had turned it on; Paul was fascinated by it. He decided to approach the machine. He reached out his hand and touched it. As soon as he laid his hand on the sewing machine it immediately stopped working. He told my grandmother about what he had experienced. Grandmother May responded to him and then told us all that the Lord was trying to reach out to Paul. I grew up believing that Paul really did get an experience from the Lord, but now I believe we were actually visited by demons.

I remember my youngest brother Samuel telling me in a stunned voice that he just seen a young boy inside his bedroom. Samuel said that this boy had appeared for a second and then vanished. He recognised that this boy was a relative of one of the neighbouring children that lived in the area. He was not deceased and was still alive. This was not a ghost, but a demon which came to my brother. My brother still to this day denies what he had seen and doesn't like to talk about it.

I remember something weird took place when I was a child, and it had to do with the front door. I wondered what was behind the door. A UFO came to mind. Was I remembering this right? I thought to myself. I recently asked my grandmother about this strange event, which took place one evening at our house, and she confirmed it to me.

She said, "One evening, Emily, Julie, and I were out in the backyard at your place when we witnessed a UFO fly one metre above the house." My grandmother attracted my attention with this and continued, "I saw a round circular disc with colourful lights flashing around it, and in the window were these green-looking beings."

My own memory of this was only the front door and our family racing to the front of the house, looking into the open park for an unidentified flying object.

One day, Grandmother May asked me, "Who is God?"

I quickly pondered my brain, and a song named "His Name Is Wonderful" came to mind. I answered, "Jesus!"

It's because of the lyrics to this song, which stated he was "Almighty God"; unfortunately, I denied the Father, not understanding the Lord God completely. Grandmother May never corrected me, because this was the answer she wanted to hear from me. As I started to read the Bible, I realised that Jesus is the Word of God who was manifested in the flesh. The Word was with God in the beginning, and the Word is God. Jesus is the Son of God, everlasting Father, and Almighty God because the Father and Jesus are one. The Bible also states that Jesus sits on the right hand of the Father, who is God.

"In the beginning was the Word, and the Word was with God, and the Word was God. The same was in the beginning with God. All things were made by him; and without him was not anything made that was made." (John 1:1–3KJV)

My grandmother was determined to make sure I knew that there was only one God, which is true, but as I came to Christ, I could see just how complicated the Lord was.

"For there are three who bear record in heaven, The Father, the Word and the Holy Spirit: and these three are one." (1 John 5:7KJV)

Chapter 2

MALADAPTIVE DAYDREAMING DISORDER

It all started to go extremely wrong at the age of eleven. I sat at church, not listening to the sermon, and suddenly had the ability to enter deep inside a dream world (which also is the spirit world).

I used to become extremely bored when it came to preaching, and I would pick up the Bible in church and read some of it to pass the time. I just couldn't pay attention to the preaching; my attention span was bad. I would try to focus, but I always ended up drifting away in my thoughts. I would also sneak out to the bathroom. One time, I looked into the mirror and said, "I don't want to go to church when I'm older." Church really annoyed me, and it felt like a waste of time. As I sat in church one Sunday afternoon, I saw this invisible thing come upon me, and from that moment on, I was able to daydream while awake in a very detailed and deep way. This fantasy world just came to me, and it would take me away from the word of God. This world started off as a childhood fantasy, but down the years, it became extremely dark and evil.

When I was a child, I was given a Barbie doll as a gift, and I kept it inside the box for a few years. Sometime after I started daydreaming, I decided to open the box and play with this doll in a sexual way; this opened the door to sin. This particular doll just suddenly appeared inside my fantasy world. After she entered my life, my storyline changed drastically. It was no longer a childhood fantasy that I was entering into. I quickly attached myself to her and used her to become the main character. I named her Blade Destiny Star, and she would take me into a very dark tunnel, deep into this dark world of demonic daydreaming.

This daydream world was semi-realistic. It was like watching a computer-animated film, in which you could interact with all the characters, just like using an avatar in a video game. I would use the characters which Satan gave me to interact with my character, and although I didn't create her, I used this main character to act out the scenes of the story. I had a lot of demonic influence with all the scenes and characters. I used to open my eyes and see into this world, and it would start up and just take off right in front of my eyes. I would then enter this world and go deep inside it, separating our reality from this fantasy world.

At this stage, I didn't realise that it was influenced by Satan. It was a world that I thought I created all by myself until recently, when God opened my eyes to what I was doing. I was using my imagination to help me move this dream world in the direction I wanted my story to head towards. However, I was daydreaming in a demonic world that I thought was just part of my mind, and me controlling this world that I thought I created.

One day, I asked myself this question: "How can you subconsciously design a world, using your mind with the help of your imagination, without thinking or making up any of these images?"

The images just come to me. People believe it's just your mind alone performing this task, but after daydreaming for twenty-two years, I can tell you that I never once came up with any of the actual daydreaming designs: the people I interacted with or the background or the colours. When I used my imagination, I would enter into the dream world. I did control a part with my mind. I would initiate the storyline, and then the images would come to me. I also controlled where I wanted to go, what I wanted to do, or who I wanted to see, and the scene would just appear in front of my eyes, allowing me to act out the desires of my heart in a detailed way or creating a detailed storyline that would always end up with evil or exciting twists within this state. However, Satan was the one who was giving me these images and controlling my fantasy world.

When you dream, are you just in your subconscious? This is what I used to think until recently. However, my experience in the dream world opened my eyes to the truth. Unless your dreams are from the Lord. Satan will and does control your dreams and imagination for his own schemes and purposes.

In the occult, people practice lucid dreaming.

Wikipedia describes lucid dreaming as a dream during which the dreamer is aware that they are dreaming. During a lucid dream, the dreamer may gain some amount of control over the dream characters, narrative, and environment.

There was a Christian testimony of a man who was an ex-lucid dreamer. This man stated that he would prepare himself to enter into this lucid dreaming state before he went to bed. I would like to explain, when a person is preparing themselves to enter into the lucid dreaming state. These people are allowing the devil to grant them their request. He makes it possible for them to be able to enter into such a state within a dream. When this man became fully aware of being inside a lucid dream. He would enjoy himself by flying around within the walls of the dreaming state. It felt as real as being in our reality. He also stated that he would look for a light switch as an anchor to know whether he was within the dream world or in the real world. He claimed that the light wouldn't switch on while he was inside the dreaming state. This Christian man claimed that demons would also entered into his lucid dreaming state, causing him to become fearful while lucid dreaming.

While another man, who I believe wasn't a Christian, claimed while he was within the lucid state had a series of dreams. In these dreams, he dreamt that he was driving his car when he had a car accident. From this scene he found himself in an apartment with a woman who he ended up having sex with. This woman was a evil spirit. When he awoke, he found himself kissing a demon. This demons form was invisible, but he felt his mouth being sexually kissed by this spirit. This demon entered into him causing him to become demon possessed, which put him into a sleep paralysis state. He was unable to move his body. This particular demon ended up yelling through him with a monstrous roar. The man expressed that he had never felt that much fear before, then when he was possessed by this evil spirit.

The Bible also tells us to cast down our imaginations, and it's clear that God doesn't like us using it. Daydreams usually reflect the heart and desires of a person. The heart is usually sinful and daydreams tend to play out what the heart desires.

"Casting down imaginations, and every high thing that exalteth itself against the knowledge of God, and bringing into captivity every thought to the obedience of Christ." (2 Corinthians 10:5KJV)

My daydream world was science fiction, mixed with drama, horror, supernatural themes, and action. It is hard to describe exactly, but imagine having a semi realistic computer-animated movie where you could talk to the characters in an interactive way and develop deep emotions towards each of them. It was a way of resting my mind through entertainment and also taking my mind off my own reality. I knew the difference and in no way confused the two. I understood that this was a fantasy world, and I entered into it almost every day.

I will describe my world which consumed my life for twenty-two years. I can't describe every detail, but I will explain my world to you and try my best to show you this is truly a demonic condition. The world knows this as maladaptive daydreaming disorder or excessive daydreaming, but the truth is Satan had a lot to do with this fantasy world; the way I received it, I felt it enter into me. I know now that I was interacting with evil, and they would take over some of my scenes and put such heavy satanic influence in them. It would be saturated with evil. This storyline began when I stopped playing with dolls; I opened my eyes and went into this world of fantasy.

Blade was the main character I controlled. She was pretty with a perfect body and was extremely fit. She had red hair and blue eyes and looked like my doll. She wore black clothes consisting of a black top that didn't cover her belly button and black leather pants and boots. Her transportation of choice consisted of a black motorcycle, which could convert into another vehicle. She was secretly a superhero. She was a half-human and half-alien being with a powerful human body that withstood any weapon on Earth.

Her biological father was a king from a light world who came to Earth. He looked human but had incredible power. He had a one-night affair with a human girl, and she became pregnant. He left Earth and returned back to his world without understanding that she was pregnant with his unborn child. Blade was the king's first child. The king had a ring of power which would automatically pass on to the true heir, and no one could take the throne except the first-born child, who was now lost on Earth. She was a crown princess of this world, who would one day rule half the universe. However, she was unaware of this fact.

As she was growing up, an evil immortal king called Tayten came across this princess, and he wanted to train her and use her to take over the light world. Her father still had no clue that she existed. King Tayten teleported into her room one day and took her to his world. He put a magical bracelet on her that would cause her pain if she misbehaved or rose against him; with his mind, he could control her with this bracelet. King Tayten was in war with the light world, and they would try to protect the universe from this evil king.

He trained Blade in martial arts and weapons of warfare; she could fly through the universe in a spaceship, battling against her own people because she was controlled by this evil king. Her father was shocked to find out he had a daughter and realised she was under the control of this evil king. They attempted to rescue her instead of killing her, but they failed. The soldiers who came to rescue her were killed in a horrific way by the king.

King Tayten was truly evil; he would kill people by means of torment and torture, like cutting their heads off with a blunt knife and performing human sacrifices with a dagger in an occult ritual. This was the scene that Satan took over: People knelt down to this king, and mass killings would take place through the form of human sacrifices. I also saw this king take my character and make her witness humans being eaten up alive by demonic creatures in an arena. He would drag my character and show her torment and even torture her. I also wanted to replay these scenes, I would repeat them inside this daydream world. By doing this I allowed Satan to control me and my fantasy world. The Demons would enter inside my daydream world, without understanding, I was interacting with them constantly.

The background story of King Tayten was that he came from Light Star and was a prince in this world, until his twin brother, King Porter, forced him to fight demonic-looking creatures with a few powerful soldiers. However, the soldiers were told to kill Prince Tayten because King Porter wanted to marry his brother's wife, Oracle, but to fulfil his wish, he needed to get rid of Prince Tayten. The soldiers surrendered him to the evil creatures and went back to their world. However, the evil creatures took him alive and predicted that he would be powerful, so they decided to keep him, tormenting him for ten years. Once he was released, Prince Tayten returned back to his world and informed his twin brother, King Porter, that the soldiers betrayed him. Not knowing that he was also betrayed by his twin brother, he ordered Prince Tayten's children into a room and killed them, placing the blame on him, using the excuse that he went insane after such torture from the demonic creatures over the ten-year period. The world and his ex-wife believed the king and sided against Prince Tayten.

They exiled him to an inescapable world, where he became sick. On his deathbed, an evil being came to Prince Tayten and offered him a deal for his soul, because he was filled with anger and wanted revenge. He sold his soul to this evil being; his eyes turned red, and he was given a power ring just like his twin brother's. This was when he became immortal. The evil being which he sold his soul to change the world he was exiled to into a beautiful world; he named it Darkness.

He claimed revenge and tortured his brother to death, while his ex-wife Oracle committed suicide. He took half of his followers back to his world to rule over them. He infected his followers with his blood, and they turned evil and received red eyes like his.

There were now two major races and two royal families, one from Darkness and the other from Light Star. King Tayten ruled over the universe until he finally lost control and Light Star recovered, separating from King Tayten and expanding their kingdom again by waging war against the kingdom of Darkness. When Tayten killed his brother, King Porter, his wife Oracle had a baby who the servants smuggled out to save the royal line. This child would have received the ring, and once Tayten lost control, the king would have returned to take his rightful place as ruler. Ten thousand years passed by when he discovered Blade on Earth and eventually ruled over her.

King Tayten was pure evil. He took advantage of my character; he raped Blade and forced her to drink blood and perform extremely evil deeds. I could feel darkness around me in this daydream world; the adrenalin pumped through my body while I interacted within this world. I would play secular music from my stereo system while I daydreamed, which enhanced my daydreaming and made it extremely addictive. I was being directed by Satan, he was the one leading me to do these types of acts and dragging me further into darkness. I was a willing participant. I forgot about Jesus Christ while under such a demonic state.

Blade was allowed to return back to Earth to live there. She could be summoned to this dark world and would open portals or touch a mirror to be transported there. My character would use a fire element as her power, and she would see people in danger and race off to save them while on Earth. King Tayten had black hair, red eyes, and a strong physique. His manner was pompous; he was in control, and no one could cross him. He was controlling and smart. He was a vampire alien who appeared as a rich gentleman with a psychopathic mindset; he wasn't the type of person to mess with. King Tayten wanted to rule the universe and claim the other powerful world under his rule. He was scary.

I was never able to come up with an ending for any of the stories. I would start again and twist a new storyline with a different view or scenario. I would initiate the story, but I never came up with the images. Each character had a different personality. My character's personality was very secretive and always tried to protect her identity. She was quiet but outspoken and was meant to be very intelligent.

This is the main storyline of my fantasy world. This world was entertaining and exciting, but it took me twenty-two years to see that this was truly Satanic. I was truly asleep and in darkness.

Just after I started to daydream, my father, siblings, and I were invited to visit my grandmother's church. A Christian man had a vision of our family and revealed to my father that we were all surrounded by flames. I was a little stunned but didn't think much of it at the time. I quickly forgot about what this man told us and didn't correct my life to what God wanted us to be. I was more concerned about daydreaming in this demonic world that Satan handed to me.

One time, Grandmother May invited this man to her house, so I decided to go there and meet him, as my grandmother lived directly behind my own house, separating us by only a gate. I became nervous because I thought God was going to reveal to him what I was doing. I didn't want to get caught and didn't want it to stop. I was happy to daydream because it entertained me, and I never wanted to give it up. God never revealed my secret to the man, but he left without asking God to deliver me. I now truly regret the mistake I made, as I could have been delivered from this condition. My family were all in serious trouble with God due to this vision, and at that time, we were not right with the Lord. Looking back now, I should have been afraid of this vision.

Being in high school didn't stop me from daydreaming. My friends talked about boys, parties, and other stuff quite often. However,

I didn't want to be involved in these types of conversations, so I escaped from reality and daydreamed instead. I was the nice quiet girl, who could hardly speak to another person without my nerves taking effect on my body. I also was suffering from anxiety. I found it hard to speak to others. I also was shy and didn't have the self-confidence that my friends had. However, my life in the dream world was the opposite. I was entertaining myself constantly and didn't want to live in the real world any longer. I found an escape, and it consumed my very existence.

During high school, I went away to camp, and one night, the girls and boys came together and decided to play a game called Light as a Feather, Stiff as a Board. The teenagers all chanted the words "Light as a feather, stiff as a board" while they had one finger from each hand underneath a person's body; this person had volunteered to be the one they lifted off the ground. As they were chanting these words, they seemed to lift this person effortlessly off the ground; they all seemed to enjoy performing this.

I decided not to play, knowing something wasn't right at the time but not realising what it was. I avoided this game and learned later on in life that it was an occult game. I'm sure that Satan gave them this ability to lift a person off the ground without effort. I had been avoiding these occult games that came into my life, but I was no better off; after I avoided this game and witnessed them doing it, I turned around and returned to my daydream world instead. I was not aware that the devil had a hold on me.

In my mid-teens, I was asked to be baptised while on a conference camp at a Message Believer convention. I was scared by this; deep down inside, I wasn't ready. I knew I was deep in sin, but I couldn't say no. Also, the elders of this church didn't ask us to confess our sins.

After I was baptised, I thought I would attempt to stop daydreaming and leave this world behind. I did stop daydreaming for a few days, but I became agitated. I began daydreaming again on the way back home from the camp.

Chapter 3

ACCIDENT PRONE

In my late teens, I travelled to a country town to visit family for one week. During the trip, my family and I went to this waterfall area. It looked like a rock pool with rocks surrounding it and the water flowing into the rock pool from the waterfall. Some of the teenagers, including my eldest brother Paul, decided to walk up to the top of the waterfall. I ended up following them, and while we were at the top of this waterfall, Paul accidentally put his foot out, which tripped me over.

As I fell down the waterfall on my belly, I tried for dear life to grab onto something, but couldn't. The rock was completely smooth, so there was nothing to hold onto. I called upon the name of Jesus, and suddenly, I was pushed over and landed inside a deep pool, halfway down the waterfall. I know that the Lord saved me that day.

For whosoever shall call upon the name of the Lord shall be saved. (Romans 10:13KJV)

Had I landed at the bottom of the waterfall, I would have certainly landed on the rocks, being seriously injured or even killed. As I climbed out of that rock pool and got to safety, I still did not repent and turn to the Lord with all my heart. I did love the Lord but couldn't give up these deep, dark sins that I kept hidden from people.

For five years, I held a nursing position at an aged-care facility. It was a hard job, and although it weighed heavily on my body, it was also a very rewarding job. Unsure of what I wanted to do after high school, I decided to complete a certificate in nursing with a close friend of mine. After completing this course, I decided to study science, completing a certificate in laboratory skills, and then commenced a diploma in laboratory technology (pathology testing). Soon after I enrolled in this programme, I happened to find the nursing job and was no longer able to study. In saying this, my heart was no longer into completing the course either, as I woke up one day and decided that science wasn't something I wanted to explore anymore.

As I looked after the patients at the aged-care facility, I met an elderly lady with schizophrenia. One time after giving her a shower, I witnessed her turning her head and telling off a few voices that she heard. She looked at me awkwardly and brushed it off. She never told me much about her experiences with these voices, but I could tell she wasn't happy when they spoke to her. Being an inexperienced nurse, I didn't know much about mental health at the time. I just thought she was hearing voices, and that was it. However, it wasn't until I went through a few things myself that I fully understood what these voices were.

I would work afternoon shifts at the aged-care facility; most of my work colleagues were young university students, studying to become registered nurses. I never thought much of what I wanted to become. Currently, I'm working as a receptionist in a chiropractic clinic. It's been a number of years since my days of working as a nurse.

One day at the aged-care facility, I was challenging a colleague about evolution. She argued with me, and I spoke back regarding my beliefs. I was witnessing to her about the accuracy of the Bible and how the Lord created everything. This was the second time I witnessed to another soul; my husband Joshua was the first one I witnessed to. I was a confused mess at the time, daydreaming secretly and then witnessing to the lost souls when deep down, I was lost too.

I believed in the Lord and stood by him and fought against evolution. I even gave her a video of a creationist documentary to show her a bit about what I believed. She watched the tape but dismissed the idea and added, "I read the Bible once, and I don't believe in the blood of Jesus."

She didn't like the idea of the Lord dying on the cross and his blood being shed for her. One morning, I had a dream which left me puzzled. Unaware at the time what Satan can do within a dream, I dreamt that I was in bed with this colleague; she was a lesbian in my dream. I dismissed the dream and went to work that same day to find out that she actually was. She revealed the news to all the staff that she started to date another female nurse. Satan had given me this dream before I even found out that she was a lesbian.

My biggest fear after my mother passed away was to see a dead person. I couldn't get over the idea that I was working within a facility where people I took care of passed away on a regular basis. I praise the Lord now that within a five-year period of working there, I never once had to deal with a patient's dead body. God had kept me from it; he knew I feared this the most. People had died on my shift, but I was never the one to attend to the body.

A year before I was married, I left Joshua's place and headed for home. On the way, I fell into a micro sleep while driving and crashed the car into a telegraph pole. I got out of the car with minor injuries, while the car was declared a write-off. Out of fear, I ended up lying to the police about the events of this car accident. I told them that I hit a pothole and lost control of the steering, which caused me to step on the accelerator. What a bad move on my end. I really regretted this lie and would love to remove it from my life. Before the accident, I remember I was driving the car and then just simply blanked out. As I hit the kerb, it woke me up just in time to see me hit the pole. I was stunned and just sat inside the vehicle until someone came to my rescue. I was taken to the local hospital and received a few stitches to my knee. After this event, I had the most realistic dream. In this dream, I was driving the car and experienced the car accident all over again. I woke up completely shaken by this, with a feeling like this accident was a warning call to me.

A few years later, after I had gotten married and had our first child Violet. Felicity invited me, my husband, and our eldest daughter Violet to her son's first birthday party. It was raining, and the roads were wet. I happened to be at the shops when Felicity called me. She told me not to come up to the party because of the wet conditions.

However, I said, "We'll come anyway."

As I went to pay at the cash register, I took notice of the radio, which was broadcasting the weather. I found it a bit creepy and thought it felt like a warning. It got my attention, like in a movie before something happens. When I arrived home, Sally also called me. She told me that she was not going to the party any longer because of the wet conditions. She suggested that we not go either, but we dismissed her suggestion and got into the car to make the two-hour trip.

Just before driving off, I asked Joshua, "Do you think we should still go because it's wet?"

He replied, "We'll take it easy and drive up slowly."

We were only fifteen minutes away from our destination when Joshua unexpectedly lost control of the car as he drove around a large bend. We crossed two empty oncoming lanes and ploughed the boot of our car into a tree. As he lost control, time seemed to slow down. As time slowed down, two thoughts entered my mind: The first thought was, my daughter is going to die. The second thought was to call out to Jesus to save us, which I did. I once again used his name. In my surprise, Violet, Joshua, and I all came out alive and without a scratch. At that moment, I developed a deep fear that I was going to hell. I started to think about my eternity, but still I didn't instantly repent and turn to the Lord.

One day, Joshua played a supernaturally themed cartoon for Violet to watch called, "Spirited Away." I didn't mind at the time, and I sat down with her and started to watch this cartoon. As I was watching a scene with spirits and demonic creatures, something hit me like a pile of bricks. It was God's wrath that fell over me. I panicked and immediately took the USB stick out of the television. I deleted the cartoon off it and also deleted the original file from the computer. Violet already was affected by it though. She only watched a small amount of the film but it had already made her very fearful. She was afraid of the bedroom door and kept on saying she was afraid of the swishing that the door made. I was concerned at what was happening because I didn't want her to feel that way. I hadn't realised at the time that Satan had affected her. These images on this movie were demonic and Satan is the one helping these animators produce such images.

I was upset and at this stage and was far from the Lord. I no longer attended church or read the Bible. However, I still loved him and would tell people that I was a Christian. I couldn't deny him or the faith.

One time Sally asked me to come back to Jesus. These words sunk deep into my heart, and I became sad. However, I couldn't come back to him because I was deep in sin by daydreaming the way I did. I was truly hurt and couldn't face him. I told her with a sad heart that I had my reasons why I couldn't come back to him. I was regretting my own words. I hated what I had just said. I could feel my tears building behind my eyes, and my throat went dry.

Chapter 4

WE ARE HERE

In 2014, I became annoyed with my daydreaming world; I was bored because I no longer had the ability to enter into King Tayten's kingdom within this dream state. It was like someone had put a hold on this world, enforcing it in my heart and mind not to seek after him. I believe this someone was God. The storyline became boring. Instead, I stayed up and watched nearly every supernatural television series that was out in 2014, until I came across one that made me very upset. I hated the ending, for it was far too dark and evil for me.

Angry and annoyed, I said, "That's it … I'm done!"

I decided then and there that I was no longer going to watch anything evil ever again. I sat on the couch and said, "Lord, can I come back home to you?"

I was tossing and turning; I wanted to return to the Lord but wasn't able to.

One night not long after this, I sat down and watched a documentary on television about a Christian church. The host of the show mocked the church because of their attitude towards the gay community and other issues. When they mentioned the Antichrist, I suddenly heard a voice speak to me, saying, "We are here."

The fear and power of the Lord God gripped me, so I immediately got on my knees and repented, turning away from all evil. I knew hearing those words caused me to repent. However, this wasn't the Holy Spirit which spoke to me, but a spirit. I believe this spirit was from the Lord.

I truly repented and turned back to God. I gave up imagining and I never went back to my dream world again. I removed the stereo away from my room and placed a Bible on my bedside table where it used to sit; I no longer watched secular movies or listened to secular music. I placed my supernatural television shows, movies, secular music, and anything associated with the world in the rubbish bin (except for an expensive mask which sat in a glass cabinet). Joshua didn't allow me to throw out some of the items; I told him that they were all his, as I didn't want to be associated with these items any longer.

As soon as I repented, I noticed that the Lord started giving me hymns, which just came to my mind. They were songs from my childhood that had been forgotten; I didn't remember them. Also, these songs were not attached to my own thoughts; they were floating thoughts. I wasn't the one thinking or playing these songs within my mind. The Lord had given them to me and was filling my mind with his songs of praise. I started to notice this and went online to look up the words to these songs. The first song that I received was "Just as I Am without One Plea," and the words touched my heart. All the songs I received gave me such hope. I started to read and listen to the Bible every day and started to pray and fast.

One morning, as I was awaking out of sleep, I heard these lyrics: "Burdens are lifted at Calvary. Jesus is very near." I recognised that these words came from the song "Burdens Are Lifted at Calvary." The Lord was telling me he is coming soon. I was so excited and tried to prepare my life away from the world and to praise God and listen to his word every single day.

On a separate day, I was trying to figure out who the Lord was. I still had some of the Jesus-only doctrines inside my head and could not admit to what the Bible was showing me about the Lord Jesus and our Father in heaven. I knew there was only one God, but I could see three which bared record in heaven. I started to cry with all my heart while I was cooking a meal for my family, telling the Lord, "I don't know you at all."

I decided to go and empty the rubbish bin; when I opened the front door, I saw the most perfect rainbow I had ever seen. It was so bright and clear. As I had opened the front door and spotted the rainbow, this incredible feeling of love and peace entered my body. In awe of such a presence, I soaked it all in and then showed my children the rainbow in excitement, explaining to them that this was a covenant the Lord gave to us to never flood the earth again.

When Violet was five, she woke up early one morning and went to the bathroom. The noise that she was making woke me up. I decided to get out of bed to check if she was fine. As I approached her, she stood still and said to me in a surprised voice, "Mum, I can hear a trumpet sounding like the one you showed me," referring to a lesson on the Jewish shofar, which I taught her earlier in the week.

It frightened me because it was a silent morning, and I thought that I was not ready to meet the Lord (even though I wanted the rapture to happen). It was a wake-up call for me, that I still wasn't ready to meet him. One of the doctrines I believed in at the time was the pre-tribulation rapture. Also I had asked the Lord that night during prayer if he could send me a sign to show me if what I had done was pleasing to him. You see, I had just posted up a YouTube video of my short testimony of how the Lord had pulled me out of maladaptive daydreaming disorder. I just wanted to make sure that the Lord had approved my work.

Violet then slept in my bed and heard what I believe were angels singing. She looked up and said, "Mum, I can hear singing."

I decided to do a fast for the Lord and ended up fasting for two days straight. On the second day of the fast, I heard a male voice say to me clearly, "Do a third day!" I now realise that it was an evil spirit pushing me to continue fasting for a third day. I never did fast for the third day, even though I really wanted to.

While I was driving home from my daughter's school, the Lord gave me the song, "I'm So Glad Jesus Set Me Free," and I started to sing it. When I got to the verse, "Satan had me bound but Jesus set me free," a woman who was in the opposite lane looked over at me and started to abuse me.

Our windows were both up. I looked at her and wondered why she was abusing me. I didn't do anything to her that I was aware of. Either she was annoyed at my calm and relaxed driving or demons had manifested through her. I just continued on singing and drove off. When I was singing this song, I did direct it to Satan that Jesus set me free.

Chapter 5

DREAMS

When I first came back to the Lord, I started receiving dreams. I realise that many Christians receive dreams; some are from the Lord, and others are from Satan. Here are a few examples of what our Father in heaven, Jesus, and the devil has given me within a dream.

One night, this dream came to me: I found myself on a wide, dark road full of people. All the people were running towards their destruction. Their destination was hell. At the edge of a cliff, I saw this image of Jesus; People dressed in black standing together with this Jesus. They were picking up their bows and arrows, and releasing their arrows into the crowd. To my relief, the arrows just missed me. The dream ended, and I heard a voice, knowing full well that it was our Lord Jesus speaking to me. The Lord said, "If you hear my words and do them, you will be saved."

I had another dream where I received a boot and heard these words: "This is a covenant between you and me." I was given a box of tissues and saw a light behind the boot. I really felt like God, our Father, sent me this dream, because I had a strong feeling of God's presence when I received it. The dream felt like I was given a promise. He was telling me in a way that I was going to cry, which was true. My future became extremely hard, which you will see why.

In another dream, I was in the backyard when a plane crashed onto our house, causing it to catch on fire. In the next scene, I saw Violet on fire and quickly told her to roll on the grass to extinguish the flame. As I was saying this, the fire also landed on my face and hands. The scene changed, and I found myself arguing in the kitchen with Joshua. From this scene, I ended up in hospital and saw Jesus standing next to me. He was my doctor, and I heard him say, referring to my youngest child Ruby, "She is safe." He showed me her cot; Ruby was sound asleep in it. At the time, I didn't know what this dream meant. This dream resembled my future. The Lord had sent me a warning in advance that disaster was around the corner. This dream had fulfilled itself and came to pass. Just as the Lord had shown me that night.

This nightmare was from Satan: I was outside in our front yard, and our small red car was parked on the lawn, like normal. I noticed I was my character Blade and felt like something was about to happen. I quickly swam out of the dream, calling on Jesus to get me out of there. I was so afraid because I knew the scene was set up for something to happen. The Lord helped me get out of this dream before anything took place.

In another dream, I was sitting in my grandmother's church. I saw a door on the left-hand side of me. It had light coming from it, and a cold wind was coming through the door. I saw a lady with short brown hair turn around and shiver in the cold, and the men of the church were trying to close this door. Then the scene changed as I began to hear secular music, and I asked them, "Who let this music into the church?"

They replied "The pastor did."

I saw the pastor standing at the front of the church and asked him, "Do you think you will make the rapture?"

This was when I woke up. I believe this was from the Lord. I believe all pastors should look at themselves and see if they have let too much of the world into the churches.

Another time, I dreamt I was outside in our backyard, and I had a few pieces of mixed coloured clothing sitting in a clothes basket, ready to hang up. I said, "By the time I hang these up, the Lord will return." This was from the Lord.

In another dream, I found myself in an elaborate room. As I stood in front of these massive doors, all of a sudden, fear gripped me. I saw how the doors shook violently, making a banging noise. Demons were behind these doors, wanting to enter through them to get to me. I was surrounded by the presence of evil, but suddenly, while in this dream state, I said, "I rebuke you in the name of Jesus." Immediately, the doors stopped banging, and I awoke out of my sleep. I realised it was God who allowed me to rebuke demons while dreaming, which left me amazed because this would be the first experience I had rebuking demons.

Another time, I dreamt I was by myself in a hotel room, and I went over to this bedside table. Right behind me appeared a white spirit, and with a loud voice, it reached out its hand and said "Come here." Fear struck me, so I shouted out, "I rebuke you in the name of Jesus," while still asleep. As I was awaking out of my sleep, I continued to repeat these words. I didn't want to go back to bed after this attack because I was so afraid, shaking from the experience.

On the news, I began to notice certain subjects highlighted, like the Hadron Collider from CERN. I felt this presence in the room as it drew me towards the television. This also happened to me while watching news converge of Israel's Prime Minister Benjamin Netanyahu, who spoke to the American Congress in 2015. At the time, I thought it was the Lord, but I now believe it came from the devil, which highlighted these events and drew me to the television and YouTube to look deeper into these things.

The Netanyahu speech controversy, explained by Zack Beauchamp from Vox, wrote the following:

"Prime Minister Benjamin Netanyahu's goal is to convince Congress to torpedo the US-led Iranian nuclear negotiations, which he thinks will result in a deal that hands Iran the bomb on a silver platter. He wants Congress to vote to impose new sanctions on Iran, which would kill the talks, and thus significantly alter US policy toward the Middle East."

I became hooked on YouTube and started to search on a daily basis for prophecies from the Lord Jesus, God, disasters, and so on. I have to explain why I believed that we could receive prophecies from our Lord: It was because God poured out his spirit onto us, as is stated in Acts 2:17–18:

"And it shall come to pass in the last days, saith God, I will pour out of my Spirit upon all flesh: and your sons and your daughters shall prophesy, and your young men shall see visions, and your old men shall dream dreams: And on my servants and on my handmaidens I will pour out in those days of my Spirit; and they shall prophesy."

I truly believed these people, because they were claiming to be Christians, but I didn't even think about the enemy and what they had done to the church of God. Some Christians are deceived by spirits because they hear a voice and believe it's from the Lord; they are not able to discern them, like the Bible states in 1 John 4:1–3:

"Beloved, believe not every spirit, but try the spirits whether they are of God: because many false prophets are gone out into the world. Hereby know ye the Spirit of God: Every spirit that confesseth that Jesus Christ is come in the flesh is of God: And every spirit that confesseth not that Jesus Christ is come in the flesh is not of God: and this is that spirit of antichrist, whereof ye have heard that it should come; and even now already is it in the world."

I didn't understand just how much the enemy could blind us, until I went on a particular YouTube channel set up by a woman named Anne, who believed she was hearing directly from our Lord Jesus Christ.

Chapter 6

FALLING AWAY

Anne appeared to be a Christian and claimed to be receiving prophecies from Jesus nearly every night. I know in our Christian walk, we can talk to our God directly, and he does respond to us through our very spirit. I'll give you a few examples: He can wake us up to go into prayer or to spend time with him before going off to a busy schedule. He can remind us of important things that we would forget otherwise. He can rebuke us if we step out of his will. This can happen several times a day; I've experience this first-hand. The Lord can speak directly through our mouth or even directly to us. He also can speak to us inside our dreams with a message or word. Other times, we need to seek the Lord earnestly with prayer. We also need to make sure that we are not deceived by an evil spirit. We need to discern who we are talking to. We do this by testing the spirits. However, the way Anne received her prophecies was through prayer. The Lord recently opened my eyes to the demon behind her messages. Anne would claim that this Jesus would come and spend time with her nearly every single night. Anne would then record the conversation she had with this spirit which claimed to be Jesus. Anne sounded like a genuine Christian; however, when you look deep into her doctrines and prophecies that she has posted up on her channel, you can see that they are completely false and unbiblical.

Unless God pulls you out of such a situation or you test the spirits to get an answer, you are trapped and serving the devil. Even if this person is told that they are receiving their prophecies from a demon, they won't believe you because they are hearing a voice and truly believe it is from the Lord.

When I went on her channel, I instantly fell away from the truth and fell asleep. My eyes became closed, and I was blinded by this false Jesus. For the first time in my life, I was drawn away from the true Jesus Christ.

I can now see how Christians are deceived by these channels. Those who are on such channels believe that these prophecies are coming from the Lord, but they are really receiving false prophecies from unclean spirits and doctrines taught by demons. I'm not saying every channel isn't from the Lord, and Christians do post up true messages from God. However, this particular channel was not from the Lord.

"Now the Spirit speaketh expressly, that in the latter times some shall depart from the faith, giving heed to seducing spirits, and doctrines of devils." (1 Timothy 4:1)

It all began when I was searching YouTube and accidently ended up in the middle of one of her videos clips. I automatically heard a third person in her message and was drawn towards it. This third person was a demon which gave her these messages. I heard the message and imagined a male voice loud and clear coming from her. My eyes twinkled away, and I was lost from that moment on. "Ice skating on

Saturn with the Lord Jesus," I heard her say through her message. Addiction set in, and I started to crave her messages every single day. Anne spoke a lot about the bride of Christ and marrying Jesus. She even had a detailed vision of her marrying the Lord Jesus and has also published a so-called Christian book called, The Chronicles of the Bride, regarding her experiences with this spirit. I want to explain that Satan can give you a vision.

As I viewed her videos, Satan and the devils attempted to brainwash me by using her information. This was the beginning of a battle which erupted between Satan, the demons, and me. I was so ignorant about demons that I wasn't even aware of what they were about to do to me until I experienced it.

Unaware that Satan had just entrapped me again with this channel, I began to experience the supernatural on a whole new level.

I was at home one day when my heart felt as if it was crushed into pieces. I was in agony and crying out in pain. A thought had entered my mind, telling me that Jesus had just broken my heart, like a boyfriend crushing his girlfriend's heart when they break up. I didn't understand that I was being attacked spiritually. I could see this occurring, but nothing registered inside of me that demons started to attack me.

Another evening, I decided to lie down on the couch, and this feeling of bliss came upon me. A tingling feeling entered my heart and spread throughout my body. I was on a blissful drug of pure bliss, and it felt incredible. I started to want this feeling and would seek it out on a daily basis; it would come to me and take me away into a state of pure bliss again and again. I didn't even realise who was behind this experience, as I lay there patiently waiting for this to happen. It was so pleasant, and I really enjoyed it. I was lured away by it. Satan was giving me this supernatural feeling.

"I am floating away," I told my sister Sally while on the phone to her.

She asked me, "Are you okay?"

I was all high from the experience and mumbled away a few other things to her. I didn't specify anything else to her, nor did I mention that I was constantly on this channel. I kept it as a secret. I felt something telling me that it was wrong to be on this channel. However, I didn't pay attention to this warning.

One evening, I was in my room, wide awake, when Satan dragged me into the dream world. I didn't enter willingly. I found myself in this large room and saw this person playing a grand piano; the music he played intrigued me. Who was this person playing the piano? I didn't imagine any of the scenes. I was taken deep into the spirit world in a moment of time. As I was viewing this scene, I suddenly fell asleep.

Another time, while I was watching one of her videos, my eyes were suddenly opened to the dream world. The scene was about the bride of Christ gathering together in heaven. However, this wasn't from the Lord but from Satan.

I watched a video clip she promoted of a man teaching people how to hear the voice of God. As I clicked on the clip, he said to just listen to the voice inside of your head. This is what I picked up on from this teaching. I got into the shower and meditated on my thoughts; I searched inside my mind for a voice from the Lord. All of a sudden, I heard male demonic voices all yelling inside my mind. I know now it wasn't my own thoughts but spirits. I was completely wrong to look inside my mind. You cannot hear from the Lord like this. The Lord told me one day that none of this man's teachings were from the Lord. You will most likely come across a devil by doing this and not find the Lord's voice this way. This man teaches on the 4 keys of hearing God's voice, which are:

Key one: Recognize God's voice as spontaneous thoughts

God can speak to us in our thoughts, but be aware that most of the time you will be hearing a demonic spirit speaking to you.

Key two: Become still

Key three: Look for a vision as you pray

By doing this key, you enter back into your imagination and this is a very dangerous place to seek after. The demons can appear to you and the visions you're seeing is not from the lord, but from Satan.

Key four: Two way journaling

He writes down the conversation by journaling on a day to day basis with these thoughts, visions etc. Like I had said earlier, most people are responding to a demon and not God. By teaching people to do this, he is allowing the devil to deceive the Christians into believing they are speaking to the Lord. God will allow a person to be deceived if they're seeking after these things. Don't be fooled into believing that God would not allow demons to infiltrate these people because they confess Jesus Christ. I've been infiltrated and I loved the Lord Jesus and God. Satan still infiltrated my heart, mind and emotions. Satan did this because I chose to be involved in the daydream world willingly.

This happened to me before I had a deep and personal relationship with God. Please be aware of such teachings and do not search your mind like I did for the voice of the Lord. These demonic voices stopped and disappeared on me. After hearing the demonic yelling of voices that came from inside my mind, I opened the front door and went outside my house; I looked up at the moon and wondered how beautiful God's creation was, when I heard a subtle whisper inside my mind. A voice just spoke to me, but no one was there. This was an evil spirit which came to me and whispered something inside my mind.

This demon came to me gradually over a two-month period, and it started portraying to me to be our Lord Jesus Christ. He was luring me over to him by pretending to be Jesus. I don't know why to this day I fell for it. He was trying to win me over by communicating with me about being one of his brides. I became brainwashed and started to listen to him.

At this stage, I could feel the presence of demons inside my house. I felt surrounded by torment, and it was putting severe pain throughout my entire body. The more and more I visited Anne's channel, the more deluded I became. I thought that I had found the Lord.

At around this time, I went into our lounge room and saw Satan. He stood opposite me, and I started to resist him like the Bible teaches. I referred to this verse:

"Wherefore take unto you the whole armour of God, that ye may be able to withstand in the evil day, and having done all, to stand." (Ephesians 6.13KJV)

I know now it wasn't Satan himself but a hallucination of him that was portrayed to me. I now believe it wasn't a hallucination, but it was a demon that had appeared. I had no control over what was shown to me. I resisted, and he then disappeared. I was so happy; I thought I won. I quickly decided to praise the Lord by playing a Christian anthem. I was dancing around, praising and singing to God, when all of a sudden, an invisible spirit entered my house. This evil spirit stood in front of me and then quickly grabbed me in reality and danced a waltz with me to this beat. I ended up dancing with it and became overwhelmed by the experience. The spirit then knocked me into the kitchen wall and continued dancing with me. It then entered my body; it spoke through me and said, "I am the queen of heaven," and other crazy and evil stuff. It's strange because this spirit was invisible, but I could still see this demon and feel his presence.

I saw this spirit as an invisible human man, presenting itself as romantic and alluring. This was the way it portrayed itself to me, as it grabbed my hands and gently and forcefully danced this waltz with me. I completely forgot who I was as I danced with evil and was enjoying the experience at the same time. I really regret this now with tears. I really didn't understand what came over me.

One morning, I visited a website that promoted the serpent seed. This person wrote in graphic detail what he believed the serpent did to Eve, and as soon as I started to read this, a spirit entered my body and started giving me a strong sexual desire. I resisted while I sat at the computer, still reading the text. I wasn't sure what was happening. It was trying to give me an orgasm while trying to pervert me towards this doctrine. This Christian man had written a doctrinal error. The author wrote a detailed story of the serpent sleeping with Eve sexually, and the spirit took advantage of me; it wanted me to accept this sexual desire. I didn't have a say in what was happening to me. I just had to resist this; however, I was so overwhelmed by it that I couldn't think straight. I didn't pray or rebuke it in the name of Jesus. I just sat there, completely resisting this supernatural urge. It stunned me that the spirit was able to do this with such force. After I resisted the spirit, it quickly left.

I found a binding prayer on Anne's channel. I said, "I'm going to pray this five times a day because it's not hard to pray." It referred to unidentified flying objects and binding the enemy from all witchcraft and evil curses, things like this. I started to read the prayer and over time began to say it in a very evil way. I spoke out this prayer almost like I was casting a spell, not praying. While I was praying this and being on Anne's channel, I started to see UFO's around. I believe that UFO's and aliens are all part of the devil's kingdom of darkness. They are part of a deception that will take place just before the second return of the Lord Jesus Christ.

I was driving the car to my daughter's school in order to pick her up, and Joshua came with me, when I was unsuspectingly drawn to look up into the sky. As I looked up, I clearly saw two circular reflective discs in a diagonal line. These discs disappeared right in front of my eyes. I then saw them reappear.

I quickly said to Joshua, "Look! There are UFO's outside the car," pointing at them.

He missed it.

The reflective discs appeared another day while I was in the backyard. I was sitting outside on the steps of the trampoline and just looked up and saw them. I saw two reflective unidentified flying objects in a diagonal line. I told Violet to look up, but it was too late, as they were gone. She never saw them.

On another day, I was at home taking photos when I was again drawn outside to the backyard. I had the camera in my hand; at the time, I thought that the Lord took me outside. However, I know now it was a spirit. I took a photo of an image from my camera. I wasn't sure what it was exactly; it could've been a plane. This thing had a round circular shape with a red tail following behind it. I saw it in the distance.

On a different night, I again took the camera outside and asked the Lord if he could show me another unidentified flying object, just like the ones I had seen. I know now that I should have never asked the Lord for this. All of a sudden, as I was looking at the night sky and the stars, I felt this searing pain running through my body. Something hit me from behind, so I turned around to see what it was, and all of a sudden, out of nowhere, this starlike object flashed out of sight in the blink of an eye. It just disappeared. It was another UFO. I went inside and didn't tell anyone what had just happened to me.

I was invited to a wedding with Joshua. I felt sick, and to make it worse, I was attacked by spirits. They were all around me; they made me feel dizzy and almost faint. I could hardly stand up on my feet from all the attacks I received that day. I struggled to get ready. For some reason, I couldn't comprehend that demons were attacking me. We dropped the children off at my in-laws' place, and Joshua and I drove off to the wedding. As we were driving, I noticed a pillar of fire burning from the corner of my eye. This pillar of fire was high in the sky, far away in the distance. I didn't mention this to my husband but just kept on staring at this in amazement. I didn't know what it was, but I knew it was supernatural in appearance. Shortly after we arrived at the wedding, the entertainment commenced. It was a modern hip-hop routine. I was stunned by the evil which surrounded me and felt the presence of evil inside that room. I couldn't take it at all. I had to walk outside of the room. I mostly stayed outside of the room, unable to take the secular music and the atmosphere that came with it. When the wedding reception came to an end, I was keen to get back home.

One mid-afternoon, I decided to take a bath. I was trying to relax and decided to start my imagination up again. Anne said that she would dance with the Lord Jesus in a vision that she had. Yes, dance with Jesus in a vision! This is how a demon can operate. Satan's agenda is to fool everyone, and he can do it in a very drastic way. Unfortunately, Anne will never believe the truth because she is deceived by this demon. All she has to do is ask this spirit if the Lord came in the flesh. While in the bathroom, I started to imagine a scene like I used to in my daydream world. Being completely relaxed in a meditated state, this world instantly opened up again. I let the enemy in and started imagining my character having fun, racing under the sea. While I was in this state, I was suddenly taken to a ship, where I sat next to an image of Jesus and played with the water, sitting next to him. I didn't come up with the ship or the image of Jesus; they just appeared without me thinking about it. This Jesus was a demon that entered my dream world.

I got out of the bathtub, and again a demon affected my heart in the supernatural. I was in so much pain, I cried out in tears. I grabbed the iPad and sat down as I listened to a hymn named "Be Thou My Vision," while I cried my heart out to God. As I was crying, I felt my heart heal supernaturally. I know it was God who healed me, who picked up all the broken pieces and put my heart back together. This was truly the Lord's work; even though I fell away from the truth, in that moment, I put my trust in him, and he healed me.

I instantly felt better, but instead of realising I was being attacked by demons and only turn to the Lord, I went back to this channel and watched another video. I was addicted to this male voice which revealed himself through the messages that she delivered.

As I started to search Anne's videos, I came across one which showed me how to meditate with meditation music. I thought I would do this, and as I listened to her voice, I imagined sitting on a bridge. Suddenly, I saw an image of Jesus walk up to me as I sat on this bridge. We decided to walk off the bridge, and the scene then took me and this Jesus to a beach. I played in the sand and made a sandcastle, placing diamond love hearts on top of the sandcastle. As I was doing this, I was having a conversation with this Jesus figure. I told him, "I am heartbroken and upset." Somehow, I was comforted by this experience. It's strange because I knew not to meditate before I fell away, but I went blind and didn't understand that I was meditating, even though I knew I was. You shouldn't meditate this way. Be careful of any forms of meditation, as we should only meditate on the word of God. The enemy got to me during meditation. This Jesus was again a demon. A messager of Satan.

Also, the demons kept on trying to sexually pervert me towards the Lord Jesus. However, I only saw Jesus Christ as my saviour. I never truly fell for this woman's teachings concerning being one of Jesus' real brides. I continued to question this. I believe that the saints of God are the bride of Christ. When I listened to these messages, for some strange reason, nothing registered within my brain that this was false. Every sound doctrine which I knew of previously began to escape my mind. I had filled it with false messages from a demon. Over time, the false Jesus who surrounded me twisted my mind, which caused me to fall for a few of her doctrines.

I started dreaming in a very perverse way at this time. I had these dreams where I dreamt that I was holding hands with a false Jesus. This Jesus was the same image from the ship and meditation. He showed me that he was giving me baby pink wedding flowers. I also dreamt that I was writing in a journal, and I had the false Jesus sit next to me, like I was in a romantic position with him. He tried to correct my writing by saying, "What are you writing here?" in a gentle manner. I woke up confused by these dreams. This is how the enemy works. They plant these types of dreams to lure you away into sin and deception. Satan can even use other types of dreams to get you to desire another person or put hatred in your heart towards others. Satan tried to do this to me several times throughout my life.

Another day, I was at home when a demon entered me. I felt this strong supernatural desire hit me hard. I was forced to the ground and lay still, resisting the urge to have an orgasm. I didn't understand at the time that I was wrestling with a spirit. The sexual pressure grew more and more, until it finally gave up and left my body. I fought hard against it and never gave up. I didn't want what Satan was offering me. They were forcing me to accept this, but I refused.

I was resting on my bed when I got attacked again. The sexual urge rushed through my private parts, and I started to resist it. This was the third time it had happened, but this time, it was different. The spirit started telling me in a silent way that he was the Lord Jesus and to have this with him. Perversion set in, and I dashed into the shower; I quickly undressed and sat on the ground, as I resisted it with the water running over me. I wanted the feeling to stop. After a few minutes, it left me once again.

One night, I was waiting for Joshua to get ready, as we were all going out for dinner. I decided to get the children into the car; they were ready to go. The moon was perfect that night, and there was a peaceful stillness in the night air. I couldn't understand what it was, but it felt supernatural, and I took note of it. We went out to dinner with my husband's family and then returned home. Joshua headed off to work, and I put the children to sleep and lay down in my bed.

I heard these words reach me: "I am going to stop the great tribulation and rapture you." I was told this by a demon portraying itself as Jesus. He then alarmed me and yelled in a panic, "I am coming now!"

I jumped out of bed and went into the kitchen. Suddenly, the demon spoke again and told a few demons who were masquerading as angels to take me back to my bed. I felt a spirit pull me along until I reached my room. As I climbed into bed, I felt a horde of demons hit me like a ferocious wind and with such force that I thought I was going to die. They put me through such absolute fear that I passed out. It was one of the worst experiences I have ever had. It was meant to kill me, and I believe if it wasn't for the Lord, I would have died out of fear. For some reason, the Lord didn't want me to die that night.

A demon tugged at my body, which pulled me out of my slumber. I arose out of bed and forgot that I had been demonically attacked just hours earlier. I acted as if nothing had happened to me. It was around 4 a.m. when I decided to turn on the computer. I wanted to play a popular Christian song. The lyrics talked about the dawn, and I suddenly had a thought enter my mind: The rapture is going to happen this morning.

Convinced by the lyrics and my own messed-up thoughts, I opened the roman blinds and stepped outside into the backyard. I looked about aimlessly at the darkened morning sky and saw the stars twinkling high above my head. They were all beautiful, and I marvelled at them all.

I walked over to the trampoline and took a seat just above the steps. The darkened sky started to fade away, and the stars began to disappear out of my view. I saw the most perfect morning that day. It was peaceful, there were birds flying by, and I marvelled in awe at the most perfect scene. Dawn was approaching, I thought. Then I heard a voice start to speak to me. It was the false Jesus spirit. We started a two-way conversation again in which it told me I wasn't allowed to go back inside the house, or the Great Tribulation would still occur. I thought I would be the one to help stop all the upcoming disasters that the tribulation would bring, but at this point in my life, my view of the Bible was extremely twisted. Anne's channel had warped my mind with false doctrines and demonic messages.

I ate into every word this spirit told me. He continued, "We will have a honeymoon together in heaven for seven years. We will then come back to Earth to rule together." He was referring to Anne's doctrine regarding each bride having a seven year honeymoon in heaven with Jesus.

I started to cry with all my heart, thinking I didn't want to go without my children. I couldn't imagine missing out on their lives for seven years. Suddenly, from out of nowhere, the sun appeared in the sky. Thinking it was the dawn, I waited in excitement for the rapture to happen. The sun was still in front of my eyes and was not rising. I waited and waited, but nothing happened. I had just experienced a vision from the devil which fooled me completely and left me wondering.

I heard a set of keys jingling together from the backyard. Somebody was opening the front door. It was Joshua. He had just come home from working a long overnight shift. I remembered the spirit's words about not going inside, but I was tired and decided to risk it. I made a cup of coffee for the both of us and started to panic a little as I realised I had just witnessed the sun standing still. I went online and looked up the latest news articles to see if there had been any reports on such a massive event. There was nothing on the news, and no one reported anything on the sun. I became fearful and started longing to escape to get away from it all. We had a holiday booked, and I was relieved that we were going away.

Chapter 7

THE HOLIDAY

Packing our bags was a challenge. The false Jesus was helping me pack our bags. He said, "Just take this many; that's enough clothes for the week." He was actually helping me but also stopping me from packing. At this stage, I was a mess. I lost every sense of soundness that I thought I once had.

It was 1 a.m. the morning that we were leaving to go on holidays. I had finished packing our bags when I heard bird sounds coming from the bathroom. It made me feel like I was trapped inside my mind. I started to touch the white tiles of the bathroom and then began to push at them. I started telling myself, "This reality can't be real." I believed this lie.

I went into our bedroom, confused by all of it, and sat down on the floor, leaning against the wall. A voice suddenly broke through the air. God was calling me (so I thought). He wanted to pull me out of this trapped reality. He told me I was a one-hundred-year-old lady who was dying and had been trapped in my mind for years. This was an evil spirit that started to destroy me.

I sat on the ground, accepting this fact, when my mind suddenly veered over to my children and husband, assuming they weren't real. I tried to die and let go but couldn't. This demon hit me hard with the most diabolical lie I had ever seen, and I had fallen right into its trap. I gave up trying to die and climbed back into bed. The demon made me think that I went crazy.

When I awoke in the morning, I walked out to the front yard and saw the beautiful flowers.

I said, "The flowers are too beautiful; my daydream world wasn't as realistic. The Earth was too detailed; this had to be the real world."

This brought me back to reality. I was not trapped in my mind. Accepting this fact, I started to become extremely fearful and had to leave the demons behind. Around this time, I did and didn't know that I had demons attacking me, for fear and delusion played a large toll on my mind.

As I ran away from the house, scared and relieved, thinking that I could escape the torment and go on holidays, the evil spirit appeared to me again. It was trying to comfort me on the shuttle bus to the airport. He kept repeating these words: "It's okay," and "It'll be okay." A tormenting feeling came over me. I leant on the window, listening to this sound all the way to the airport. As I got to the airport, the false Jesus told me to write a letter to this YouTube channel and try and stop it, because it wasn't from God. "When I get back, I'll stop the channel," I replied.

Even with the spirit telling me the truth, I still couldn't wake up from being completely deluded and blind.

We boarded the plane, and it took off. Everything seemed to go back to normal; however, I was extremely tired and wanted to sleep, but couldn't. Ruby was on my lap, and Violet was in the seat next to me. Joshua fell asleep as soon as he sat down. Just before the plane was due to land, a voice suddenly broke the air, instantly attracting my attention. It was meant to be God. It spoke out quickly, looking for me, and then disappeared, leaving me in absolute fear. The demon made me feel as if I was trapped inside my mind once again. I became nervous, quiet, and still. I began to reconsider my life, pondering that I was indeed trapped inside my mind and not actually living in the real world any longer.

As the plane landed at our destination, it seemed to shake violently. I sat in the seat of the plane, stunned by this, but no one else seemed to be affected by it except me. The non-realistic feeling came over me yet again, making me believe that I was trapped again. I had just eaten into a lie from Satan. It might sound like nothing, but if you heard this and experienced something like this, you would believe the lie also. It was designed in such a way to make me think that I was truly trapped inside my mind. At that moment, I really thought I was; it felt as if I was truly alone in this make-believe world.

I got out of my seat, grabbed our hand luggage, and disembarked the plane. I asked Joshua to let me go to the bathroom at the airport terminal, and Violet followed me there. I saw her at the sink, washing her hands, and the next moment, she disappeared from my vision and then reappeared instantly, right in front of my eyes. I thought I was still trapped, so I didn't panic. I was walking around in a daze with this idea that Satan put inside my head.

We were picked up by a shuttle bus which drove us to the car rental office in order to pick up our hired car. The evil spirit claiming to be God spoke to me again; he told me that I was stuck in a make-believe world that I created, and he wanted to pull me out of it. He also told me that I was the most talented person for making up such a world and that he wanted to use me to create other worlds with him.

"I want to stay until my holiday is over," I replied. "Give me a week."

I really wanted to go to Morton Bay island and walk on the beach with my kids. A beautiful image came to mind: I was walking along the beach and watching the sunset with my kids and husband. It gave me this peace. We then drove off to our hotel, stopping at a local shopping centre on the way. The shopping centre was about ten minutes away from our apartment, and we decided to let our kids play in an indoor playground. I bought a cake and coffee for me and Joshua and sat there as we looked on at the children. We needed to buy groceries for our apartment, and once again I was attacked by demons. Joshua didn't notice anything strange, as I kept it all to myself, trying to protect him and my family from Satan.

We finished shopping, packed our groceries into the car, and drove off. As I stared at the setting sun, a thought came into my mind that I was stopping the sun from setting. I still believed I was trapped inside my world that I created and thought I was able to control the scenes around me. I had a deluded feeling of peace run through my mind at this stage. We arrived at the check-in counter and went upstairs to our apartment on the fourth floor.

We unpacked everything and decided to stay in for the night, feeding the children and putting them to bed. I decided to go and have a bath. As I relaxed in the bathtub, with the water filled to the brim, my children woke up, opened the bathroom door, and walked in. I saw them both at the edge of the bathtub, and then they disappeared out of my view and re-appeared as quickly as they left.

I was shocked and made a fearful noise. Fear gripped me, and a thought entered my mind: My children are demons.

They walked out, and my reality shifted. I thought I went to hell. I saw the old floor tiles of the bathroom almost come alive; it was a haunting scene. I was reminded that Joshua and I died in the car accident we were involved in. We didn't survive it, and Violet went to heaven, but we ended up in hell. I pleaded to this false Jesus to come and rescue me. I heard the false Jesus tell me that he was going to rescue me from this place. He continued to say that Joshua was going to walk inside the bathroom, grab a knife, and kill me in a very horrific way, and then the scene would play all over again. That's when the false Jesus would rescue me. This spirit made it seem that this was to be the routine that was held in hell.

Joshua suddenly entered into the bathroom. I was closing my eyes when he started to call my name, "Danica, Danica," shaking me to get my attention.

My eyes and face were almost under the water; I thought, He's about to kill me! I tried my hardest to bear what was about to take place, submitting to it in fear. He continued to call my name and shook me; I finally opened my eyes and sat up. Joshua was just trying to snap me out of it. He had no knife, and it was all a lie. I now wonder why he came into the bathroom in the first place. It was odd that he did at that exact moment of time. The hell scene disappeared out of my mind, so I got out of the bath and didn't mention a word to him of what had just happened to me. From that point on, he started to realise something wasn't quite right with me.

Joshua went back to bed. However, I was wide awake and couldn't sleep. A demon entered the room, an evil presence that I just couldn't shake off. I felt torment and absolute fear around me. As it approached me, I felt this fear tingle inside my body. Alarmed by it, I sat up all night long in a chair. When it hit the early hours of the morning, a thought came inside my mind. The devil gave me this thought: "I rebuke you in the name of Jesus Christ sharply."

I was truly trying to fight this demon but didn't know how. As I was repeating these words, another thought entered my mind: The demons were trying to force me to blaspheme God. I had to resist this thought and rebuked it immediately. As the sun rose, I felt the torment and fear flee away as this demon left.

Joshua and the children woke up around 7 a.m. I was making breakfast for them when I started to talk to this false Jesus again. I laughed and carried on, forgetting the ordeal I had just experienced. The worst thing happened to me, as the thought of Violet being a demon re-entered my mind. I became annoyed at her with every little gesture she made and started to overly discipline her because of it. My love for her started to turn to anger because of the false reality I saw in her.

I got the ironing board out and started ironing Joshua's shirt. As he put the shirt on, I saw a pentagram marked onto his shirt and quickly tried to make him take it off. When he saw the shirt, he complained and said, "You ruined my shirt." He didn't see the pentagram but only the iron marks. I took it away and tried to hide it because it was satanic, and I wanted to protect him. I was concerned with him wearing this. He then grabbed another shirt from the room and put it on instead.

We had plans to visit an amusement park that day. I was approached by a demon; it came up to me and said, "If you go to this amusement park, your children will die on the rides."

I was afraid of this, so I told Joshua that I was sick and that we couldn't go today. I locked myself in the bathroom with Ruby. Joshua was upset with me and stood at the door, trying to find out what was wrong with me. I convinced him that I was going to rest on the bed with Ruby because I wasn't well.

As I locked myself in the bathroom, I continued hearing many voices, which were all tormenting me. These voices were demon spirits. My husband thought I was just sick and left the apartment upset; he went out to lunch with Violet. The false Jesus told me that he was about to come and rapture me, and when he came, the Earth would burn. I was scared to witness this event, so I stayed in the bathroom for a couple of hours.

As time passed by, I took the risk of leaving the bathroom. I asked God two things. The first thing I said was, "Please shred me." I was in so much agony, I wanted to die. The other thing I asked God was to touch my heart and to feel the pain that I was in. I then called Joshua on the phone and apologised to him about ruining the day. We talked, and he told me he still wanted to go out, and I agreed to this. He arrived back to the apartment, and we left the building with the children.

My children, Joshua, and I rode on a vehicle that allowed you to go sight-seeing. We bought last-minute tickets, and there were four empty chairs waiting for our family. The entire vehicle was booked out for that session. What a weird thing, I thought. Four empty chairs for us. As we took our seats and drove off, the false Jesus started up a conversation with me. During the ride, my reality shifted, and I started to believe the vehicle was full of witches, warlocks, and government spies. I looked at Violet, and the thought of her being a demon child was still fresh in my mind. I became annoyed at her again, and as I saw the host of the tour hovering around Violet, I kept telling her to leave my child alone, thinking the host was trying to pass on witchcraft objects to her. She wanted to give Violet a few stickers or something of the kind, but I thought she was giving her occult objects to perform spells. The way Violet was acting was encouraging my thinking. Satan tried to put hatred in my heart towards her. I could feel it. I found that I lost a lot of love for her due to this experience. However, thanks to the Lord,

I've gained it back and love her even more now. This is what Satan had placed inside my head.

When I left the house to go on holidays, I decided at the last minute to take the Bible in my handbag and leave the binding prayer at home. I made a quick decision not to take the binding prayer, due to the fact that I sensed it wasn't from the Lord.

After the tour, we went into a shopping centre. I saw the sign of a shop change into the word "CERN" right in front of my eyes. All the toys were shown to me to be deceitful. I felt like my eyes were open by the devil, and I was shown this. While walking around, I felt this evil spirit lifting up my skirt in public; I had to keep pulling my skirt back down. I was becoming annoyed and stressed by it, and wanted to return to our apartment.

The reason why Satan showed me the word "CERN" was because of all the YouTube sites that I visited. Many Christians are concerned about what CERN is researching. Some Christians have posted up video clips of how fallen angels are going to re-enter the earth through CERN's technology. They believe that this is the bottomless pit/Abyss. Let me explain what CERN's is researching. I will quote from CERN's official website.

"At CERN, the European Organization for Nuclear Research, physicists and engineers are probing the fundamental structure of the universe. They use the world's largest and most complex scientific instruments to study the basic constituents of matter – the fundamental particles. The particles are made to collide together at close to the speed of light. The process gives the physicists clues about how the particles interact, and provides insights into the fundamental laws of nature. The instruments used at CERN are purpose-built particle accelerators and detectors. Accelerators boost beams of particles to high energies before the beams are made to collide with each other or with stationary targets. Detectors observe and record the results of these collisions."

I believe the Lord is in control of everything and we don't have to fear these things. Put all of your fears into the Lord's hands.

We arrived back at our apartment, and as we opened the door, I saw this middle-aged woman with blonde hair sitting on the hotel chair. In an instant, she vanished into thin air. I panicked as I felt a shock run through my body. I thought this woman was a witch and that Violet was working with her to attack me, being a demon child in my delusion. I believed this woman was a demon that manifested itself to me.

In fear and terror, I quickly searched the website on my iPhone for the binding prayer from Anne's YouTube channel. I should have turned to the Bible or prayed on my knees to the Lord, but because of fear and terror, I didn't. Panicking, I looked it up and let it play. Joshua became annoyed and complained that I was on this channel again. He asked me not to go on it while we were on holidays. I should have listened, but because of all the torment, I had this feeling of constant fear that hit me hard. I couldn't shake it off. My peace was taken away from me.

The fear left me, and another reality shift happened to me. As I was in the kitchen, I thought Satan entered into Joshua. It felt that real. Joshua started to talk to me, so in fear, I began to sing "In the Name of Jesus."

Joshua constantly told me to stop, as he had enough of hearing this song. I took Ruby out of his arms. In fear of him, I told him, "This is not your child, she is my child."

I hurried to the main room and tried to lock the door behind me, but Joshua, who I thought was possessed by the devil, followed me and confronted me.

I continued avoiding him and asking him to leave me alone. As the scene kept changing, I thought now that Joshua was actually Satan; I was married to him, and the place we were staying in was Satan's kingdom in hell. There was an eerie feeling around me, and I felt evil. I thought I was trapped in hell, like it was another world, and that my children were both demons. Satan had altered my reality, and I believed a lie. When this reality shift happened, it was so subtle that you couldn't pick up on what the true perception of reality was. My perception on what appeared real was just slightly altered. This alteration was just enough to make me strongly believe in the lie that Satan was showing me.

I told Joshua to leave and take Violet with him. I quickly went outside onto the balcony, scared out of my mind, and I sat in a chair, waiting for him to pack his belongings and leave the apartment. The false Jesus appeared again and told me he was coming to rescue me from hell. I saw the moonlight appear supernaturally on the balcony, and it shone with a silver light, making me strongly believe the lie. It felt like it was a confirmation, something solid that it was going to happen for sure.

The spirit told me, "You're leaving your husband; what's the worst that could happen?" He then added, "The police and media will arrive; be ready for it."

I sat outside with Ruby on the balcony. Joshua came out because I had Ruby in my arms, not willing to let her go. I yelled at him in fear and started to sing, "In the Name of Jesus." He was concerned with my behaviour and called his family for help. He left the balcony, took Violet with him, and contacted the police.

I continued to sing "In the Name of Jesus" for a few hours straight, not stopping to take a rest. I was in absolute fear over the situation. The words to this song are as follows:

"In the name of Jesus, in the name of Jesus, we have the victory, In the name of Jesus, in the name of Jesus, demons will have to flee."

Three police officers confronted me and covered me. I continued singing, thinking they were demons (again, this perception of reality was shown to me) and if I had stopped singing, I wouldn't be rescued by the Lord. I would be lost in hell forever. I was holding onto my daughter, trying to get us both out of hell, waiting for the Lord to rescue us this time.

The police snatched Ruby out of my hands and wrestled me to the ground. As the ambulance officers gave me an injection to put me to sleep, I got a glimpse of the police officer handing Ruby to my husband, who I still thought was Satan. It killed me inside. I fought back with all my strength but failed. It was a nightmare experience, a moment of time that you just cannot understand. I thought my child was doomed because I let her go. I just went through severe trauma, and it affected me seriously.

I woke up in a local hospital. I forgot that I even had children or a husband. I didn't know who I was exactly. I saw someone guarding me at the hospital. Suddenly, a demon said in a booming male voice, "Repent!" I thought it was God, our Father, so I said "Repent, repent, repent!"

He also told me to say, "CERN, Hadron Collider, fallen angels are going to re-enter the Earth," so I yelled out those words. Everyone in the hospital ward heard me. I was referring to YouTube and all the videos I watched on fallen angels and the Hadron Collider. I was scared to be saying this, but thought I was doing people a favour because I wanted to warn them. It just made me look insane to the doctors and hospital staff.

Since we are on this topic, I want to explain an event that is coming to the Earth which is written in the Bible called "the Day of the Lord." I will tell you an interesting testimony which God did regarding this study. One day, I was sound asleep when I heard an alarm clock sounding. God our Father woke me from my sleep with this sound. It was not my alarm clock, but a supernatural sound that came to me. You see, I had just written the below information regarding the Day of the Lord a few days before and wanted to go back and add it in the book, but I was not sure if I should. However, the Lord decided that he wanted me to add this to my book. As I awoke, he pointed to a spot within my book where he wanted me to insert my information. I immediately got up and added this information to my book at the point where God directed me to. I knew it was the Lord, and this is the information which God wanted me to reveal.

A day is coming when mankind will face one of the most horrific times in history. This day is called the Day of the Lord. God's wrath on humankind will be unleashed due to iniquity and evil done in this world. Like in the days of Noah, the ungodly will be destroyed from the Earth in the time of the Lord's wrath.

Jesus is the only door to salvation, and there is no other way to God but through him. People need to repent and seek God; you are never promised tomorrow.

"And I will punish the world for their evil, and the wicked for their iniquity; and I will cause the arrogancy of the proud to cease, and will lay low the haughtiness of the terrible." (Isaiah 13:11KJV)

"Near is the great day of the LORD, Near and coming very quickly; Listen, the day of the LORD! In it the warrior cries out bitterly.

A day of wrath is that day, A day of trouble and distress, A day of destruction and desolation, A day of darkness and gloom, A day of clouds and thick darkness, A day of trumpet and battle cry Against the fortified cities And the high corner towers. I will bring distress on men So that they will walk like the blind, Because they have sinned against the LORD; And their blood will be poured out like dust And their flesh like dung. Neither their silver nor their gold will be able to deliver them On the day of the LORD'S wrath; And all the earth will be devoured In the fire of His jealousy, For He will make a complete end, Indeed a terrifying one, Of all the inhabitants of the earth." (Zephaniah 1:14–18KJV)

In the Epistle of Barnabas, it talks about how the world is coming to an end, after the Antichrist or Lawless One comes and is destroyed by the Lord Jesus Christ:

> Give heed, children, what this meaneth; *He ended in six days.* He meaneth this, that in six thousand years the Lord shall bring all things to an end; for the day with Him signifyeth a thousand years; and this He himself beareth me witness, saying; *Behold, the day of the Lord shall be as a thousand years.* Therefore, children, in six days, that is in six thousand years, everything shall come to an end. (Barnabas 15:4) (English Translation by J.B. Lightfoot)

> *And He rested on the seventh day.* this He meaneth; when His Son shall come, and shall abolish the time of the Lawless One, and shall judge the ungodly, and shall change the sun and the moon and the stars, then shall he truly rest on the seventh day (Barnabas 15:5)

When the day of the Lord comes, a supernatural army of locusts will rise out from the bottomless pit, along with other supernatural disasters/plagues. I will only discuss the supernatural locust army.

Read Revelation 9 from the Bible to receive more information regarding this study.

Let us start with Abaddon/Apollyon, the destroyer. Who is he exactly?

The destroyer, or Abaddon/Apollyon, is an angel who is locked in the bottomless pit. I believe the bottomless pit is hell. He will be the king of a great army, which is depicted as the locust army. This army is depicted as locusts because they are vast in number and strength, and they devour everything in their path.

"And they had a king over them, which is the angel of the bottomless pit, whose name in the Hebrew tongue is Abaddon, but in the Greek tongue hath his name Apollyon." (Revelation 9:11KJV)

When the day of the Lord arrives, an angel falls from heaven and opens the door to the bottomless pit, releasing this army upon the Earth.

"And the fifth angel sounded, and I saw a star fall from heaven unto the earth: and to him was given the key of the bottomless pit.

And he opened the bottomless pit; and there arose a smoke out of the pit, as the smoke of a great furnace; and the sun and the air were darkened by reason of the smoke of the pit.

And there came out of the smoke locusts upon the earth: and unto them was given power, as the scorpions of the earth have power." (Revelation 9:1–3KJV)

The locust army mentioned are not locusts like some people depicted in pictures, but supernatural beings, whether fallen angels or demonic beings. They are soldiers all ready for battle. Their appearance is described below:

"And the shapes of the locusts were like unto horses prepared unto battle; and on their heads were as it were crowns like gold, and their faces were as the faces of men.

And they had hair as the hair of women, and their teeth were as the teeth of lions.

And they had breastplates, as it were breastplates of iron; and the sound of their wings was as the sound of chariots of many horses running to battle.

And they had tails like unto scorpions, and there were stings in their tails: and their power was to hurt men five months." (Revelation 9:7–10KJV)

The prophet Joel also mentions this locust army in detail in chapter 2.

"Blow ye the trumpet in Zion, and sound an alarm in my holy mountain: let all the inhabitants of the land tremble: for the day of the LORD cometh, for it is nigh at hand;

A day of darkness and of gloominess, a day of clouds and of thick darkness, as the morning spread upon the mountains: a great people and a strong; there hath not been ever the like, neither shall be any more after it, even to the years of many generations.

A fire devoureth before them; and behind them a flame burneth: the land is as the garden of Eden before them, and behind them a desolate wilderness; yea, and nothing shall escape them.

The appearance of them is as the appearance of horses; and as horsemen, so shall they run.

Like the noise of chariots on the tops of mountains shall they leap, like the noise of a flame of fire that devoureth the stubble, as a strong people set in battle array.

Before their face the people shall be much pained: all faces shall gather blackness.

They shall run like mighty men; they shall climb the wall like men of war; and they shall march every one on his ways, and they shall not break their ranks:

Neither shall one thrust another; they shall walk every one in his path: and when they fall upon the sword, they shall not be wounded.

They shall run to and fro in the city; they shall run upon the wall, they shall climb up upon the houses; they shall enter in at the windows like a thief.

The earth shall quake before them; the heavens shall tremble: the sun and the moon shall be dark, and the stars shall withdraw their shining:

And the LORD shall utter his voice before his army (saints): for his camp is very great: for he is strong that executeth his word: for the day of the LORD is great and very terrible; and who can abide it?" (Joel 2:1–11KJV)

They could be fallen angels because Jude mentions that angels are under darkness unto the judgement of the great day:

"And the angels which kept not their first estate, but left their own habitation, he hath reserved in everlasting chains under darkness unto the judgment of the great day." (Jude 1:6KJV)

When will the day of the Lord occur?

According to scripture, no one knows the day or the hour. However, when Jesus returns to the Earth, the day of the Lord arrives with him.

"But of that day and hour knoweth no man, no, not the angels of heaven, but my Father only. But as the days of Noe were, so shall also the coming of the Son of man be. For as in the days that were before the flood they were eating and drinking, marrying and giving in marriage, until the day that Noe entered into the ark, And knew not until the flood came, and took them all away; so shall also the coming of the Son of man be." (Matthew 24:36–39KJV)

"And I beheld when he had opened the sixth seal, and, lo, there was a great earthquake; and the sun became black as sackcloth of hair, and the moon became as blood; And the stars of heaven fell unto the earth, even as a fig tree casteth her untimely figs, when she is shaken of a mighty wind. And the heaven departed as a scroll when it is rolled together; and every mountain and island were moved out of their places. And the kings of the earth, and the great men, and the rich men, and the chief captains, and the mighty men, and every bondman, and every free man, hid themselves in the dens and in the rocks of the mountains; And said to the mountains and rocks, Fall on us, and hide us from the face of him that sitteth on the throne, and from the wrath of the Lamb: For the great day of his wrath is come; and who shall be able to stand?" (Revelation 6:12–17KJV)

I became inspired one day and wrote this poem about the day of the Lord. I thought I would share it with you:

The earth will tremble at the presence of Almighty God.

The stars will fall from the sky.

Humble yourselves and repent!

For the day of the Lord draws nigh.

It's a day of darkness, of trumpet sounds!

The sun will turn black.

The moon will go blood red.

All this has been all written and said

by the prophets of old.

All this has been foretold.

It's a day of terror, torment, and fear.

So repent, all sinners!

For the day of the Lord draws near.

At the hospital, my brain was in severe pain. I felt the weight of my head and thought I was going to die at any moment. I complained to the nurse about my head, and she wanted to lower my bed down, but I yelled out, "Don't!" out of fear of death. My head was all scarred inside, and putting the bed down would have killed me, I thought. The doctors decided to do a CT scan immediately, but as I was about to take the test, the pain was supernaturally healed. The Lord had healed me. I felt his power run inside my head just before they took the scan. I became annoyed that I was healed because I thought I had something to prove to the doctors. I wanted the doctors to see just how bad I was and that I was telling the truth. The Lord, however, knew what he was doing, and from that point on, I had no scarring inside my head. I was completely healed by the Lord. Just before the test was about to commence, I fell asleep, as I believe they must have drugged me at this point. I was knocked out cold.

I had a glimpse of the hospital staff transferring me, as they placed me in an isolation room all by myself. This room was creepy and old, with a mattress on the floor. I was confused and dazed at the time of waking up from the drugs that knocked me out in the first place. I sat up and saw a nurse standing in the doorway. Her eyes were fixed on mine as she was holding up a newspaper, and it shocked me. I don't know why, but I thought Violet died because of how this woman presented herself. She just stood there. "Who was she?" I thought. Was she working for Satan? Or was it something that the mental health nurses do? It felt as if the nurse was taunting me with the newspaper. A male nurse opens the front door to the isolation room and in hatred, with a large amount of force, he throws my bra at me; smacking my body. The nurses had dressed me into a hospital gown, removing all of my clothing. I'm upset, and don't know how to reach to this treatment. My memory suddenly lapsed over, and then the room shifted and with it I see a new reality.

I thought I was in hell for real. An eternally lost feeling came upon me. It made me think I was lost for all eternity, not ever being allowed to leave. I was locked in an asylum, in the depths of hell itself, I thought. I looked around this cell and felt completely lost. A spirit of a woman's face appeared on a plaque which was attached to the wall. It started to change faces. I jumped back away from the wall and freaked out. This spirit convinced me that this was my eternal punishment, being locked in a cell with a spirit to torment me. It sent a searing pain down through my body. I was so afraid and felt tormented. I stood up and began to yell and point at the spirit, trying to rebuke it.

I quickly got on my knees and prayed with all my heart to the Lord, asking him for a second chance and to let me leave this tormenting place. I was really scared by this experience, which had left me without hope. Being lost forever and ever is something I never want to experience again. I gave up praying and then realised that the door was open. I got up and went outside to find a bathroom. I arrived at the bathroom and heard a spirit ask me, "Would you marry Satan? He is Jesus' brother." I said yes without even realising what I just said. It occurred to me later that the demon also wanted me to sell my soul to Satan. I knew that Satan isn't Jesus' brother; this is a lie from the devil.

I saw a nurse, but she didn't speak to me. I walked away from her to discover another room, then walked outside and looked at the walls, unsure of where I was. I saw the light reflecting back off the walls and walked around without a clue. I was lost. My mind was gone; I was devoured by the insanity that had fallen over my mind.

I had been brought to a maximum security mental health facility. I followed the nurse as she silently directed me to this place. No one spoke to me the entire time, making this experience a living nightmare. I was taken in silence to a single bedroom, where I saw another patient who asked me if I was pregnant. I looked down at my stomach, and Satan made me think I was. A thought entered my mind: The closed rooms were sacrificing rooms in which to kill newborn babies. I panicked. I went to another bathroom, thinking I couldn't live in hell any longer, and attempted to drown myself. As I tried, the Lord took the water out from inside my body. I truly didn't want to kill myself but just wanted to leave hell. By killing myself, I would have ended up there.

I returned to my bedroom and kneeled down to pray, but I saw a demonic-looking dwarf in the mirror, staring at me with a weird-looking head and a nasty grin across its face. As I looked in the mirror, the demon just sat beside me; when I turned from the mirror to see the demon, it wasn't there, but it was there in the mirror. I just stared at the mirror until the demon left.

Joshua and the children came to visit me. When I saw them, I recognised them and forgot about the ordeal at the apartment building completely. I didn't see them as demons or Satan anymore, as this left my mind. I was just so happy to see them all and remembered just how much I loved my children.

My in-laws, Tina and Andrew, flew out and came to my family's aid when they heard about my situation. They assisted Joshua in looking after the children and encouraged my own family to visit me. Tina and Andrew visited me every day in hospital, and after three days, they decided to take the children back home with them, while Joshua remained by my side.

September 28, 2015, was the night of the super blood moon. I was looking forward to seeing it, because I missed the blood moons each time they appeared that year and in 2014; due to cloudy nights, I never got to see one. However, I thought I could catch a glimpse of this one while on my holiday, as the weather was forecasted for a clear night. I also heard a few Christians say that maybe the rapture would happen on this date. I started to believe that this was possible and kept an open mind about it.

That night, I went outside into the courtyard and suddenly heard the sounds of horsemen riding by. I believed that they were the horsemen of the Apocalypse. I know that they didn't actually ride by me; however, at the time, it appeared this way. I know now by reading scripture that the riders on the white, red, black, and pale horse are actually already riding throughout the Earth. They are not really the horsemen of the Apocalypse, like everyone thinks they are. They are actually here to kill humankind with hunger, sword, beasts, and death. They are four spirits that have been given power over the 1/3 part of the Earth to kill people with the conditions that war, famine, destruction and death bring to the Earth.

"And I saw, and behold a white horse: and he that sat on him had a bow; and a crown was given unto him: and he went forth conquering, and to conquer. And when he had opened the second seal, I heard the second beast say, Come and see.

And there went out another horse that was red: and power was given to him that sat thereon to take peace from the earth, and that they should kill one another: and there was given unto him a great sword.

And when he had opened the third seal, I heard the third beast say, Come and see. And I beheld, and lo a black horse; and he that sat on him had a pair of balances in his hand.

And I heard a voice in the midst of the four beasts say, A measure of wheat for a penny, and three measures of barley for a penny; and see thou hurt not the oil and the wine.

And when he had opened the fourth seal, I heard the voice of the fourth beast say, Come and see.

And I looked, and behold a pale horse: and his name that sat on him was Death, and Hell followed with him. And power was given unto them over the fourth part of the earth, to kill with sword, and with hunger, and with death, and with the beasts of the earth." (Revelation 6:2–8KJV)

If we look at Death, he is actually an enemy of God. This is the rider on the pale horse that is depicted in the book of Revelation. Death will be the last enemy to be destroyed and put into the lake of fire.

"The last enemy that shall be destroyed is death." (1 Corinthians 15:26KJV)

"And death and hell were cast into the lake of fire. This is the second death." (Revelation 20:14KJV)

Satan was the one who had the power of death:

"Forasmuch then as the children are partakers of flesh and blood, he also himself likewise took part of the same; that through death he might destroy him that had the power of death, that is, the devil." (Hebrews 2:14KJV)

Jesus now has the keys of hell and death:

"I am he that liveth, and was dead; and, behold, I am alive for evermore, Amen; and have the keys of hell and of death." (Revelation 1:18KJV)

The book of Job gives us some clues about the horsemen. I'll give you a few verses, and you decide if it fits:

"Destruction and death say, We have heard the fame thereof with our ears." (Job 28:22KJV)

"In **famine** he shall redeem thee from death: and in **war** from the power of the sword. Thou shalt be hid from the scourge of the tongue: neither shalt thou be afraid of **destruction** when it cometh. At **destruction** and **famine** thou shalt laugh: neither shalt thou be afraid of the beasts of the earth." (Job 5:20–22KJV)

Like in the book of Job, it mentions death, destruction, war and famine. These could be what these four horse riders of the book of Revelation are.

While in the courtyard, I wondered about looking at the stars. At this moment, the false Jesus came and said, "I'm going to rapture you" I fell for it again. I looked up at the moon and saw beams of light rising up towards the moon: another vision from the devil. I thought that the rapture had just happened, and I waited eagerly for it, but it was too late. It then occurred to me that I was left behind in the Great Tribulation. This is when I still believed in a pre-tribulation rapture.

As I wondered the courtyard, a scenario unfolded and Satan and his demons started twisting my reality again. Through my eyes, I saw the hospital staff trying to bring me back inside the mental health facility. I resisted them because I thought if I entered back inside the facility, I would've been sacrificed by the staff. I assumed that all the staff were satanists and working for the devil.

During this time, three hospital workers approached me. They grabbed me and attempted to take me inside the facility. I panicked. It felt so real what Satan did; it really felt as if I was going to be sacrificed. As soon as the hospital workers touched me, I was hit hard again by demons. A whirlwind of terror and fear hit me. My reality shifted dramatically as I was dragged by the demons. Time and space seemed to speed up around me, as I was ripped by demons, mentally and physically. I was left broken and hurt by the hospital staff, for I tried to fight back hard against the demons and the staff. The hospital staff did not realise what had happened to me, and I was in too much pain to respond. They drugged me and left me on the grass, crying my eyes out. As I moved my foot with my eyes still shut, I felt dead body parts lying next to me. The flesh felt solid, and I knew it was a mass grave surrounding me. It was my worst nightmare coming true. I lay there and cried out like a child. I said, "Jesus, I love you!" referring to my Lord and Saviour: not the demon but our Lord Jesus.

As I laid there, I could hear voices of demons and one voice sounded like Satan. In my reality, I heard what I thought was Satan executing the staff (who were meant to be the satanist) because they had failed to sacrifice me. Uneasy sound effects echoed the air.

The next minute, I was placed into my bed by the staff. All battered and bruised by the experience, I started to physically recover supernaturally. It was our God healing me completely; he took away my physical pain. During the night, I heard dramatic voices in the air; I was told I was going to be crucified and killed on a cross. I continuously heard all these uneasy comments and sound effects until I finally crashed out.

The next day, the Lord helped me. I started to see demons around me, so I began singing "In the Name of Jesus." The name Jesus came to me in a vision. As I was singing this song, Jesus' name blocked out the demons that were appearing in front of my eyes.

When Joshua arrived at the hospital, he gave me the Bible that was in my handbag; I had asked him to bring it. I opened the Bible and turned to 1 Chronicles. As I was trying to read the first chapter, an evil spirit came to me. He stood next to me and began to pronounce some of the names to me. He wanted to show me that he could read the Bible well. I knew that it was an evil spirit and not me reading these words. I found it difficult to pronounce these names without someone reading them back to me. He was able to read each name to me without making an error. I stopped interacting with him and walked away from the spirit.

A few days later, I was moved to a less secure area of the mental health facility. I started to recover more once I saw my father and younger brother, Samuel, who travelled the distance to see me. I played soccer with Samuel, and it kind of brought me back. I told them Satan attacked me and tried to convince my family what took place in my life. Samuel didn't believe my story and looked at it as only psychosis.

Aunt Kelly gave me a Christian book during my stay in hospital. However, I didn't have the opportunity to read it myself, as I saw a lady who was depressed and missing her child, so I gave it to her to read. I witnessed to her about our Lord Jesus, and I prayed for her. She was grateful and took the book. She told me she was reading it, and I told her to keep it, knowing it could bring her to the Lord Jesus.

I decided to walk around and headed out to the courtyard. I saw another woman standing on a table in a very unusual yoga position. I just looked at her and wondered. I decided to approach her and said something. Surprisingly, she just hissed at me like a snake. I stepped back, realising she had a spirit inside of her. I saw another lady holding tarot cards and told her that she shouldn't read them. She hated me from that moment on and made others hate me. I was more relaxed at this new facility; I was extremely nice to the nurses and asked them if they wanted prayer.

The entire time I was there, I hadn't realised I was in hospital. I couldn't comprehend it because no one told me where I was. It wasn't pointed out to me, and I was too sick to ask any questions. I had been in a very insane state of mind the entire time I was admitted, and I was just starting to come out of it when they moved me to the other ward. I was finally discharged seven days later, driving back home with my father and Joshua.

Chapter 8

FINALLY HOME

We finally arrived home from our nightmare holiday. The day we drove home happened to be our wedding anniversary; we celebrated nine years of marriage. The years had passed by so fast. I was relieved that we were still married because Satan and the demons had tried to separate us while on holidays. The situation that happened to me severely rocked our relationship.

The next morning, I constantly thought about the masquerade mask I had sitting in the glass cabinet. I wanted to grab a hammer and smash it to pieces. This mask had red feathers with a golden exterior and a golden bead in the middle of its forehead. As I came back to Christ, it felt wrong to have this mask. I knew I had to find a way to get rid of it. Although the mask cost $255, I wanted to destroy it; selling it was not an option.

That morning, while lying down next to Joshua, I asked him if I could get rid of the mask, as it was now haunting me. With a sense of defeat and hesitation, he looked at me and answered, "Yeah, fine."

As soon as he replied, I leapt out of bed, opened the glass cabinet, took out the mask, and ripped it into pieces. Joshua was surprised and upset at me for doing this. I wanted to get rid of any satanic thing I possessed, and this was the one thing that I really wanted to take out of my house.

Our children arrived home later that day, after staying with Tina and Andrew. I was racing around the house, trying to vacuum and tidy up, as I had the nurses coming over and wanted to clean up the house before they arrived. The nursing team were visiting to check up on me. I saw the children's many toys lying on the floor and started to pick them up. Joshua stopped me and said he would organise the toys and put them in their proper place (he wanted the toys arranged correctly). The nursing team arrived while I was vacuuming, which upset me because I didn't finish in time, and the toys were still lying in a great big mess, scattered all over the floor. Embarrassed by the state of the house, I gave up cleaning and started to communicate with the nurses. They stayed only a few minutes and left.

Straight after they left, Joshua and I got into an argument over the toys. I wanted to get rid of some, as there were too many, and just the idea of them got to me. I didn't want to see a single one on the floor. I completely lost the plot and called Sally to pick up myself and the children.

I told her, "I have had enough, and I am leaving Joshua for real."

My sister arrived at our house shortly after I phoned her. As I was packing to leave, a spirit started to speak to me.

He said, "Take the laptop with you to your sister's place so you will be able to complete your testimony."

However, this spirit wasn't from the Lord. I had just started to type my testimony out on the computer. I grabbed the laptop, stuffed it inside one of the bags I had packed for the children and myself, and drove off with Sally to her house. Tossing and unable to get any sleep at Sally's place, I got up and opened the laptop to continue typing up my testimony. The reason why I started to write my experience was to show my family and friends what Satan had done against me. I did not at all contemplate that it would turn into a book.

I tried hard to recall all my lost memories, which took place at home and during our holiday. Over time, these drastic memories returned after looking deeply back into my past. I could remember some of them, but some memories were blocked. I still couldn't recall them completely. After spending several hours on it, I somehow lost the file. It was gone: my whole testimony. I sat there grieved and so frustrated by it all.

The next day didn't get any better. "You are going to hell if you keep listening," a male voice said, which made me tremble. It really frightened me, thinking it was the Lord; however, this was a demon. In fear, I tried hard to stop speaking to the spirit that was lingering around me but failed.

My brother-in-law Jake and sister Sally invited their Baptist pastor and his wife to visit me. The pastor wanted to counsel me and began speaking. He started by offering me prayer and continued to ask if I am saved.

Frustrated by this question, I quickly replied, "Yes, I am."

They made me feel unsure if I truly was. Was I saved? Deep down inside, I was hurt by this question, knowing at the time I was trying hard to come back to God. I had spent every single day reading the Bible and playing hymns until I drove my husband mad. It wasn't until I discovered that YouTube channel that I lost my way from God, and as a result, I was seriously hurt by demons. I was unsure if I was saved now; I really just wanted to serve the Lord with all my heart and thought I was doing his will. I started to explain to them that I had been attacked by Satan, not understanding much about demons and their current involvement in my life at that time. This just left me feeling completely lost and alone.

I began to miss Joshua deeply. I decided to text him, to amend what I had done. I didn't want a divorce, and I wanted my marriage back. Joshua drove over to Sally's place to pick us up. We left Sally's house and drove off to Tina and Andrew's. An uneasy feeling of guilt sat inside my stomach. I shouldn't have taken off like I did. I ended up staying overnight with my in-laws, as Joshua didn't want me home alone with the children. I knew I made a mess of things with him. Unable to still have a good night sleep due to tormenting spirits, I got up the next morning feeling horrible. I had been running without proper sleep for days, but instead of being tired, I had the opposite problem.

That morning, the spirit again began to convince me by saying, "The nurses are coming over again to give you more medication." This was a lie from the demon. You see, I was agitated at the nurses for giving me a stronger dose of medication the night before. I didn't want them to return, as I felt like I lost my independence, which really annoyed me. I was being watched by the nurse while I took the medication. Not wanting to see the nurses again, I asked Joshua if I could go to Sally's house again before they came over. I really thought that the nurses were coming over again. He was tired after a long night at work and did not give me a full answer.

Wanting to leave the house, I said to my husband's family that I was going for a walk. Before I left the house, the spirit beckoned me to run. "Take your bag and run!" I heard the voice tell me. I should not have listened. I was upset at everyone at that stage. However, the spirit tricked me, and I listened to it once again.

I took off to the train station, running the entire way there. I decided to head to my grandmother's place. I wanted to prove to everyone that I was well enough to be alone. I just wanted my independence back. I really upset my husband and his family by running off.

I contacted Sally and spoke to her for a few minutes while waiting for the train to arrive. I told her that I was heading over to our grandmother's place and hung up. My uncle James picked me up from the station once I alighted from the train. I could have walked to my grandmother's house, but Sally had asked Uncle James to pick me up instead. I was surprised to see him standing at the exit gates of the station, waiting for me. I got into my uncle's car, and we drove to my grandmother's house. When we arrived, I felt guilty and became grieved for leaving my husband. I wanted to call him, but my father suddenly turned up at my grandmother's front door. Someone must have told him I was there.

He asked me, "Why didn't you attend church this morning?"

I was not aware that I was to attend his church that morning; I must have agreed with him on the way back from our trip. I didn't even know it was Sunday; I had spent all weekend running away from Joshua.

My cousin's wife Sarah was over also. I asked her if she wanted to go to the shops with me. My father drove us to the shopping centre. We were in a store when I cried out in pain, "I need an ambulance!"

It was supernatural; it hit me hard, and I couldn't move from it. I had chest pain. "What's going on?" I asked, panicked. I tried to reassure myself that this wasn't happening, as I couldn't bear the pain. My father and Sarah took me to the medical centre, where a doctor examined me and cleared me.

I recovered from the attack and felt fine, so we drove back to my grandmother's place. As soon as I arrived at my grandmother's front door, the supernatural chest pain returned. I knew that this feeling which came upon me was not a natural occurrence. Someone was causing me this pain.

"Take me to the hospital!" I cried out.

This time they listened, and I was rushed into the emergency ward, where I was admitted immediately.

I was waiting on the hospital bed; the nurse arrived and handed me some medication for the pain. Sally also turned up at the hospital, joining my father and Sarah.

Thoughts of Joshua again started running through my mind. I wondered what I had done. I left him again. I called him, but Sarah took the phone and began speaking to Joshua instead. I wanted him to know I wanted him back. I made a big mistake by taking off the way I did.

As I sat on the bed, my perception of reality shifted again. I saw Sarah's blue eyes staring back at me and began to see her as a demon. Torment surrounded me, and I felt trapped inside the hospital. However, I quickly took my King James Bible out of my handbag; I found Psalms 23, and Sarah started to read it:

"The LORD is my shepherd; I shall not want.

He maketh me to lie down in green pastures: he leadeth me beside the still waters.

He restoreth my soul: he leadeth me in the paths of righteousness for his name's sake.

Yea, though I walk through the valley of the shadow of death, I will fear no evil: for thou art with me; thy rod and thy staff they comfort me.

Thou preparest a table before me in the presence of mine enemies: thou anointest my head with oil; my cup runneth over.

Surely goodness and mercy shall follow me all the days of my life: and I will dwell in the house of the LORD forever."

During the reality shift, I felt the grip of death run through my body. I thought I was dying. After Sarah read the passage, I noticed the room turning back to normal and the torment leaving me. The grip of death also left me.

Shortly after things had returned to normal, the demon provoked me and said, "Witness for the Lord!" Pondering what I had just heard, I received some encouragement to approach a patient and witnessed to him about Jesus. I realised I did not know how to witness well but did my best with the knowledge I had. As I walked back to the bed, I spotted a male nurse, approached him, and spoke to him about Jesus. He looked at me as if something was wrong with me.

Sarah received a doctor's letter from the nursing staff, and she told me that they wanted me to be transferred to hospital closer to my house. I was still thinking it was for the chest pain. My father, Sally, Sarah, and I left the hospital and headed to my grandmother's place first.

We stopped over at my grandmother's place to grab a few sandwiches; the spirit told me, "Don't go to the hospital." I told my family that I was not going to the hospital and that I felt fine and just wanted to go to sleep.

"No, you have to go," Sarah said. I took her advice, and my father, Sally, Sarah, and a family friend drove me to the hospital.

We arrived at the hospital and walked up to the main entry. Sarah showed the nurse my letter, and she directed us to this secure facility outside the main hospital building. It was a mental health facility. At the time, I thought I was going back to hospital for my chest pain, but the doctors had other plans for me. I never did read what was written in that doctor's letter. However, one day I glanced at the computer screen at my local doctor, to find a letter which stated that I had delusions of God.

I was admitted again, thinking I was in the main hospital. Nobody told me that I had just been admitted into a mental health facility. The nurse directed me to my bed sometime after midnight, so I went to bed and settled in, but I was unable to sleep. "Get up and repent," a demon encouraged me. I began to cry my eyes out as I walked outside my ward. I knelt down on the ground and felt so much regret as my tears flowed down my face.

"You need to stop this," a male nurse warned me. I refused and began to cry harder, unable to hold it all back. Kneeling on the ground, with my eyes closed in fear, I was dragged away by two male nurses; they took me down the corridor and into another facility. This is when things became a little unusual; I do not recall anything after this moment.

I awoke in shock as I found myself in an isolation room: four walls, a glass window, and a solid metal door. The room was creepy and old, and the mattress was on the floor. As I approached the door to the outside of this room, I realised it was not locked. The door swung open, and I saw this bright blue room staring back at me. My whole world was shaken up. I walked outside into the blue room and wondered where I was.

I pondered in absolute shock as I walked around, looking at the faces of strangers. It took me a little while to realise that I was in a mental health facility. Why couldn't someone just speak to me directly and explain that I was going to a mental health facility? I began to get extremely angry. This set me off, and I no longer acted like a civil human being. I demanded to know my rights and asked to be discharged from this place, but they refused and held me against my will for seven weeks.

The nurse took me to my room and showed me my bed. As I sat on my bed, I pondered how to get out of this place. I contacted my family and yelled at everyone for leaving me behind at this facility. Angry and hurt by my family, I started to feel this urge around my mouth. I was able to talk in third person. A spirit entered me, convincing me that he was God, so I began to allow this spirit to speak through me.

I was trying to convince my entire family that God was speaking through me. The spirit which spoke through me told everyone that they were going to hell. Without understanding the demons, I just believed that I was allowing God our Father to speak through me. This is how a lot of people receive false prophecies by spirits speaking through them. Most are very subtle, and you cannot even tell that it is not from the Lord.

Joshua came to visit me. I allowed the spirit to warn him that he was going to die in a car accident. Dismissing these words, he thought I was just talking in third person. He was unable to distinguish the evil spirit that was speaking through my mouth. My family continued telling me this wasn't from the Lord, but I chose to be deceived willingly by an evil spirit. I didn't know the enemy could do such a thing. If someone just pointed out that I had a demon speaking through me, I might have woken up and realised this fact. However, no one did.

A man in his early 20's started a conversation with me, and I began to try to convince him that God was real. I wanted to show this man that God was speaking through me, so I allowed the demonic spirit to take over my mouth. This demon spoke through my mouth, just like a person that channels demons. The only reason I allowed it was because I thought it was the Lord God, and wanted to help this man come to Christ. He looked at me in shock and was unable to understand what was happening. He could see my voice changing. I was truly in the wrong by doing this.

False prophecies: a phrase I want to remove from my life. I wrote several letters in the name of the Lord to my family members and friends, and delivered one to my grandmother's church on one of my day leaves from the mental health facility. The spirit portraying itself as Jesus came to me again. He directed what he wanted me to write down on paper. I was fasting one day when he came; he told me to write some prophecies down as he spoke. Scared I would be caught by the nursing staff, I hid myself away, taking some paper to write these prophecies on. I secretly recorded this spirit's message on this paper.

While in the facility, an old friend named Lisa came to visit. Lisa had just recently come back to Jesus. Sometime after she came back to Jesus, Lisa claimed that a demon had entered her. She went to visit her doctor and told him about the demon. The doctor instantly diagnosed her with schizophrenia. Lisa claimed she was no longer the same person and found it hard to work and to do the things she used to do easily because she became physically sick. Just to be clear: Christians can have demons.

I took on a bold personality whilst in the facility. My personality had changed completely; I was no longer the nice quiet girl who sat in hiding, shaking with fear from public speaking. My nerves had disappeared, and I didn't shake in fear any longer. God had changed me. I stood up one day while in the facility and read a chapter out loud to everyone from the Bible, reading Matthew 24. I felt the true Lord God helping me speak these words to everyone. As I began to read, a fight broke out between a few men, who started throwing chairs around. During this uproar, the true Lord God showed me that evil spirits were intervening, trying to stop these people from hearing the gospel.

A powerful demon came to me during my stay at the facility. It was the same booming voice from the hospital who was claiming to be God. This time, it was going to try and destroy me that much further. This demon started causing me physical pain by putting me on fire with an invisible flame. I felt the fire burning my body, which left me in agony. "Sing 'Amazing Grace,'" the demon said. I began to sing this in fear, trying hard to control the pain. I thought I was doomed. I sat on the couch and just took the pain. I was full of fear and couldn't recognise that it wasn't God doing this to me. I thought I was heading to hell. I was a confused mess at the time.

"Deny me," the same evil spirit spoke out, but I didn't want to deny the Lord. My heart suddenly became supernaturally faint and heavy. This feeling fell over me; it felt as if I was slipping from the Lord and unable to stand as a Christian. I suddenly said, "I'll deny you!" I was shocked at myself, as I had never spoken out against the Lord in my entire life.

He asked me, "Would you serve me, even if you are going to hell?"

"Yes, I would," I replied.

I thought I was done and that I was really going to hell. He gave me thirty years to live, and then he said I would go to hell. I fell deep into depression and was diagnosed with stage one psychosis (schizophrenia) by the doctors at the mental health facilities.

The supernatural chest pain returned. I knocked on the door to the nursing station, and the nurse opened. I tried informing the nurse about my pain and explained that I needed to go to the main building of the hospital for treatment, but all they could do was give me medication. I felt like Satan just wanted to kill me. I was in agony, as I sat in a chair almost dying and unable to receive more medical assistance. I was desperate; no one took me seriously, and no one came to my aid. I ended up lying on the ground in agony until the pain disappeared.

The booming male demon attacked me again, this time hitting me hard across my head by simply yelling at me. My brain felt supernaturally sunk inside my skull, and this insane feeling of death attached itself to me. I strolled around the facility, thinking, this is it … I'm going to pass away. I just could not recover. As I arrived to my room, I crashed on the hospital bed and fell asleep instantly.

The next day, I awoke and realised that I was still alive. I had not passed away. I did not think I would see another day. I started to become very sick physically from being tormented by the demons, and being locked up against my will didn't help me. My mind started to crumble and wither away. I started to feel like my body was going to die from imprisonment.

The torment kept on coming, though. One day, I was in so much torment that I ended up falling to the ground in front of my family. Nearly every time I saw my family, my eyes would become shut supernaturally. I could feel the effects of the supernatural touch on my eyes, and my speech became sluggish. I couldn't physically open my eyes or speak well. My entire family thought I had lost my mind. Satan just wanted to kill me, but instead he ruined my reputation.

I was controlled by the demons at this stage. I would listen to their every word. One day, as I was listening to a demon, I all of a sudden heard these words reach me: "Stop listening," it yelled in absolute power. It was an angelic being, and I knew it was from the Lord. An angel had just spoken to me. I immediately stopped what I was doing and asked myself, "Why am I listening?"

The instant that I asked this, something automatically clicked inside my brain. Immediately, my eyes were opened, and I realised that I was talking to demonic spirits and not God or Jesus. I stopped listening to the demons instantly and realised I was deceived by Satan.

Knowing full well now I was speaking to demons, I decided to ask the spirit, who was portraying itself as our Lord Jesus, whether he was from the Lord, like it states in 1 John 4:1–3:

"Beloved, do not believe every spirit, but test the spirits, whether they are of God; because many false prophets have gone out into the world. Hereby know ye the Spirit of God: Every spirit that confesseth that Jesus Christ is come in the flesh is of God: And every spirit that confesseth not that Jesus Christ is come in the flesh is not of God: and this is that spirit of antichrist, whereof ye have heard that it should come; and even now already is it in the world."

"No, I'm from the enemy," the spirit replied.

It stayed with me a little while longer and then suddenly left. I haven't heard from it since. The spirit which was portraying itself as

God stopped tormenting me, and I was finally awake and no longer asleep.

After seven long weeks, I was finally discharged from the mental health facility after a successful court hearing. In this time period, Joshua and I reconciled our marriage and remained together. I also forgave my family for leaving me in the facility. This place really distressed me a lot. I know nurses are trained to help; I was once a nurse and know how hard this job can be. The only thing I want to say to mental health nurses is please tell these patients what going on with their situation. Don't leave them in the dark, like I was. Not one person told me that I had psychosis or schizophrenia. Not the doctor or the nurses. I had to find out by looking at a piece of paper that my case manager brought out. It really upset me because I really didn't understand why I was locked up and why I was held against my own will for seven weeks. Also, no one could comprehend that I was going through a spiritual battle. Everyone thought I was just mentally sick. Mental health is just one major area that Satan likes to attack people. I had just experienced what it truly felt like.

"For we wrestle not against flesh and blood, but against principalities, against powers, against the rulers of the darkness of this world, against spiritual wickedness in high places." (Ephesians 6:12)

Chapter 9

NIGHTMARES

I arrived home at last and began to recover from the mental anguish of being locked up. I was extremely ill at this stage and could feel a sense of physical sickness through my entire body. I couldn't do anything, but I quickly realised that I hardly had any help and no choice. I pushed myself to my breaking point. I also knew that if I could not cope and look after my children well enough, I could lose custody of them. I wanted to keep my family together, but Satan and the demons continued to make life extremely hard for me.

When I left the hospital, my nightmares became worse; however, with the Lord's help, my mind also became sound. I was not deluded by the demons anymore, and my perception of reality had stopped shifting. Satan could not alter my reality any longer, and even if he did try, I would now recognise it. God was truly back in my life and helping me. I also returned to God completely and stopped watching Anne's YouTube videos.

The demons began to tempt me through severe sexual temptations. This would come over me by the demons internally dwelling inside my body as well as the demons that entered my house. It felt different this time, as it was not the same attack as before, when the demons entered my body and tried to give me an orgasm. This time, they wanted me to willingly seek and desire this feeling. It was an extremely lustful desire that they placed over me; I could hardly say no to this. However, I said no and refused this temptation also. As they tempted me, they would say, "I just want you to lose some weight, sexualise yourself, and have sex with all the demons." After this, a severe sexual desire ran through the lower parts of my body. The demons were trying to lure me away from God and accept this sexual desire they offered me.

As I was falling asleep one night, I suddenly felt a spirit lifting up my hand and feet as well as triggering me to wake me up. I also heard a loud bang in the ceiling to grab my attention. This was the beginning of the spiritual warfare that I was facing every day. My life had just changed severely. I was given a lot of faith and knew I would never be the same.

I started to notice that demons were interacting within my dreams. They would take me to scenes and talk to me while in this dreaming state. The demons used my dreams to communicate with me and torment me most nights. I want to give you a few examples of these types of dreams.

I dreamt that I was in this dark place. It was a creepy night, and I saw the planets in our solar system drift by, with military planes following them. Then in another scene, I heard Satan's voice. He said, "You want to challenge me?" He said this because when I turned to Jesus after I repented, I stupidly proclaimed out of the blue, not thinking, "I want to challenge Satan." This was before the devils attacked me. I awoke, grieved, and put the bed sheet over my head. I truly believe Satan drew me to say these words. I felt unusual the day I said it.

On another night, I dreamt that I was chasing a white spirit and caught it. After I caught this spirit, my head suddenly began to hurt immensely. I thought I was going to die within this dream. In this dreaming state, I called out, "Jesus, I love you," out of fear and shock. My mind returned back to normal instantly; my two-year-old started to cry, waking me out of my dream. As I switched the light on, I had a vision of our Lord Jesus, with a beautiful light surrounding him, and he said, "You will be saved." I knew instantly that it was him. His presence alone told me.

I carried my child back to my room, and we fell asleep. She woke up and vomited on my bed sheets. I became upset, as it was early morning, and I could hardly move. I washed the bed sheets and hung them on the clothes line out back. I was wondering if the sheets would be okay, pondering that it might rain overnight. My mind was full of worries, being unable to organise myself; everything weighed heavily on my mind.

My daughter and I shared my bed that morning. As I went to sleep, a dream came to me, which went something along these lines: As I was hanging bed linens on the clothes line, I saw black, heavy clouds in the air. I took off the bed linen and decided to hang them up inside the spare room. I went looking for the pegs, which led me to the kitchen and dining room. I could see the moon and the black night sky, but inside my house, I could see daylight. I had a glimpse of a baby in a UFO ship flying through the night sky, and then the most horrifically insane feeling began to grip me. I became aware that I was in a dream and tried really hard to call upon Jesus for help. I managed to speak the words "Jesus, we have the victory," within this dream. As I spoke these words, a few demons screeched in fear, and the insane feeling disappeared.

Within another dream, I dreamt I was standing on the top of a waterfall. I saw someone watching a child playing at the edge of this waterfall, when all of a sudden, the conditions changed, and the people all disappeared. I suddenly hung on for dear life, holding onto a part of the waterfall within a cave. I held on with one hand; the other hand was holding onto my husband's expensive camera. As I hung there, the water was flowing rapidly down my body. I also looked like Blade from my daydream world. She was once again present within a dream. "Let go of the camera," a demon said to me. I refused to let go of it, as I did not want to lose it. The demon continued, "It's wet anyway," so I began to pray, and I said in faith, "Jesus! Please keep me in the cave." I heard a voice say "Satan." Then the scene changed, and I fell into a car. A torch light was directed at my face, instantly waking me out of this dream.

What I am about to share with you was not a dream; it happened to me while I was wide awake. I was lying on my bed one night, and my eyes suddenly became open to the daydreaming world. It was like a vision. I saw a hand appear in front of me, and it beckoned me to follow it toward an open door. Curiosity entered my mind, but I decided not to follow the hand. After I said no to the devil, the hand and door disappeared from my vision. The devil attempted to entice me to see what was behind the door. I was intrigued by it and wondered what the devil would have shown me had I have taken the bait.

Early one morning, I heard a voice tell me, "I will deliver you." I felt a presence enter the room. I was asleep, but I was also wide awake at the same time. This was not a dream because I was well aware that I had heard these words loud and clear, in a gentle male voice. There was a pause in which I was given an opportunity to reply to him. "Thank you," was all I could say in return. I had a happy smile across my face, as I knew it was God.

I had been praying to the Lord for over a year, asking him which church was the right one for me to attend. I eagerly wanted to know where I could go that held the truth. One evening, I was praying to the Lord, and he suddenly spoke through me. He directed me not to go to my father's church; instead, I was told to attend the Assemblies of God church. This was the church my grandmother attends. I just knew it was God who spoke these words through me. I know it sounds like when I was deceived by the evil spirits, but this time, I didn't confuse this voice for an evil spirit, so without hesitation, I left the Message Believing church. I believe the reason why I was told to no longer attend my father's church was because they uplift William Branham too much. As well as some of the doctrinal errors found within his messages.

The church my family used to attend closed down, my father found a Message Believers church about twenty minutes away from where I lived. He started to fellowship with this congregation. I decided to attend this church after I repented, knowing full well I did not really believe all the messages taught by William Branham in the first place. I attended this church because of the short distance from our house, and I enjoyed being amongst these people.

I listened to the Lord and left the Message Believers church. I started to attend the Assemblies of God church, as directed by the Lord. I went on a Saturday evening and arrived there just before six o'clock. I said hello to the pastor, feeling extremely awkward because I handed a false prophecy to this church while I was in the mental health facility. I had met the pastor a few times before this visit. For some strange reason, while I was locked up in the mental health facility, I asked him to come and visit me and to pray over me while I was under spiritual attack. However, I did not know him well.

I walked to an empty seat and sat down. The pastor rose and commenced the service. As the musicians began to play a song in the Slavic language, I started to follow the lyrics but found it difficult to sing correctly. As I tried my hardest to sing in that language, I felt God's presence as he corrected my tongue to be able to sing the song. I could barely read the Slavic language, so I knew this was the Lord's doing. He was showing me that the Lord was among his people. I could not believe what I had just witnessed, so I immediately stopped myself from singing, pondering in surprise what I had just experienced.

On another day, I told Grandmother May about this supernatural experience with the Lord. She was not surprised by it; however, what upset me was that she did not believe the Lord had sent me to her church. She believed that this Assemblies of God church taught that there are three Gods, and she was taught to believe in only one, referring to Jesus-only doctrines and Trinitarian beliefs on the Godhead. I heard all of this growing up. She still believed that I was slightly deluded and deceived by Satan, like I was in the mental health facility.

"The Lord did direct me there," I told her. "This is the truth."

I was upset and unable to get it through to her what the Bible really teaches about our Father in heaven, Jesus, and the Holy Spirit. You cannot change a person's mind once it is made up. No matter how hard you try to tell them the truth, only God can change a person, unless they are open-minded towards the truth. Otherwise, they are not willing to change. Most people think what they believe in is really the truth.

I told Grandmother May, "Yes, there is only one God but three who bear record in heaven." At this moment, the Lord Jesus spoke through me and tried to correct her. His presence told me he was upset at her for going against him.

My father found out that I left the Message Believing church. I explained to him that I was directed by the Lord to leave this church during prayer.

He became frustrated at me and told me, "It's not from the Lord."

I tried hard to explain to him that it was, and this was the reason why I left this church. This church had asked me to return to them, but I could not. I had nothing against them; they truly look and act as decent Christians, but it was about the Lord, and he told me to leave them.

Another time, I spoke to my father on the phone, trying to convince him that William Branham's doctrines on the Godhead were incorrect. Branham believed that the Godhead contained one God with three offices or titles: Father, Son, and Holy Spirit. This is incorrect. As I was trying to convince my father, Jesus suddenly spoke through me again. He spoke to my father regarding this subject. I cannot remember what the Lord exactly said to my father. I was more intrigued at the fact that he chose to speak directly through me again. I knew it was the Lord Jesus, as his presence once again told me it was him. I should have paid a bit more attention to his words. However, I knew Jesus was going against this idea of the Godhead that William Branham taught.

I was at my new church one Sunday morning for the ten o'clock service when a little old Slavic woman who had never spoken to me before approached me and said, "The Lord gave me a vision of you, and I went and prayed for you straight away."

I was surprised by this. Her husband told me that he took up a five-day fast for me. I was grateful to the Lord for their willingness to help me, but I just could not understand how he could fast for me. He did not even know me.

One time, I was standing at the bathroom sink when I received these words from the song "Jesus Loves Me": The lyrics were "He will wash away my sins and let his little child come in." I cried because it touched me. Before God gave me these experiences, I was scared. Was I saved? I felt unworthy to enter into his kingdom, and it gave me great hope that I was not perishing.

Another day, the Lord Jesus spoke through me again and said, "You have sickness." At the time, I did not know that I was truly sick, but I thought it was all to do with demonic attacks. I know that unclean spirits can cause sickness in the body, and a good example is this verse from Luke 13:11–13:

"And, behold, there was a woman which had a spirit of infirmity eighteen years, and was bowed together, and could in no wise lift up herself. And when Jesus saw her, he called her to him, and said unto her, Woman, thou art loosed from thine infirmity. And he laid his hands on her: and immediately she was made straight, and glorified God."

During all of this, I have felt demonic sickness from demons. I believe that the demons are the main cause of my sickness.

Chapter 10

RUINED

One day, I was in the bathroom when a few demons started speaking to me. Suddenly, an angel of the Lord spoke out loud to the demons and said, "You have ruined her life."

Knowing it was an angel that spoke, I wondered how the demons had ruined my life. I was not thinking clearly when I pondered this thought. In the past, I was planning to have another child, but when I was locked up in the mental health facility, a demon came to me and suggested not to have another child. I was so ill from the sickness that I actually agreed with the demon. Joshua and I also decided that I should not have another child due to my illness. It saddened me a lot because the spirit put this thought inside my head first.

In my heart, I really wanted a third child. However, I knew I was on the antipsychotics. My body also was extremely ill too. The sickness had almost crippled me. My case manager, who looked after my case, once suggested to me, "You can still have another baby if you would like to have one." She was trying to show me that I was still allowed to have the final decision on what I wanted to do. I couldn't have another one. No-one could see just how physically sick I had gotten.

One afternoon, while I sat inside my car at the front of my daughter's school. I felt the Lord God speaking to me. He had just told me inside my mind and spirit, not to have another child. I was sad, but I knew the Lord was just trying to look after me. He had his own reasons why he didn't want me to fall pregnant once again with a third child.

My husband really wanted a boy, but we had two beautiful daughters. I marvel though, my sister always wanted twins, and the Lord granted her heart's desire and gave her twins. However, I wanted two daughters, and the Lord once again gave me this request. I wanted the first daughter to be beautiful, and she was gorgeous. I wanted my second daughter to have curly hair. At first she was born without any hair on her head. As she got older, she started to get these locks of curls. I knew I had asked for both of these requests. The Lord God had heard my heart's desire and had given them to me.

At home, I was brushing my teeth while facing the bathroom mirror, when all of a sudden; my body became possessed for a few seconds. My face turned scary as I viewed myself. I never thought I could be possessed in this way. However, it never happened again. I was possessed, and I was a Christian. This happened so fast that I did not even have time to call upon Jesus for help. I really believe Christians underestimate what demons are truly capable of doing to them.

As a teenager, I heard a thought enter my mind one horrible night, and it said, "Blaspheme the Holy Spirit."

This was one of the first times I was attacked in this manner. I was in torment over this attack, thinking it was my own mind which was thinking up such things. I never thought about demons at the time, but they were the ones introducing this idea. I immediately turned to the Bible; I looked up scripture and repeated the words, "No, never, never," referring to the blasphemies coming from inside my mind. The scriptures also state that if you blaspheme the Holy Spirit, you will not be forgiven in this life as well as in the next life. This was why I was extremely afraid when these thoughts entered my mind. I cried to God during this attack, and these demons left.

One day in my mid-twenties, these thoughts returned, but this time, I was deep in sin and did not turn to the Lord. Instead, I pumped up the secular music to drown out these thoughts. I also quickly entered into the daydream world to get away from these words. I just wanted to completely forget. I was so afraid to blaspheme the Holy Spirit.

There was a reason why I had developed this fear. Grandmother May had once told me a very scary story about her brother Sam. She said, "Sam had blasphemed the Holy Spirit and the Lord God spoke to one of my family members and said in a prophecy, that he would save all of my brothers and sisters including myself, but not my brother Sam (due to his blasphemes against the Holy Spirit.)" I felt the fear of God come heavily over me, and I was truly afraid at that moment. Satan also knew that I was fearful about blaspheming the Lord. That is why he played on my fears, and sent demons to try and make me blaspheme the Holy Spirit.

The other day, I was sitting at home when I heard a similar voice saying, "Blaspheme the Holy Spirit." It was overwhelming, and it hit me hard; the fear from my teenage years had returned to haunt me. I had to resist with all my heart not to be brainwashed into cursing God.

The unclean spirit repeatedly said after the attack, "You have blasphemed against the Holy Spirit; you are going to hell."

It was tormenting me, and it really felt like it was coming from inside my mind with such thoughts, but it was not my voice. It was a male's voice from a demon, and it was not attached to my own thoughts. I wasn't the one thinking up these words. This is how I could tell it was not coming directly from my own mind.

I visited Grandmother May's house, and we decided to sing a few songs to the Lord. However, my heart was not into singing to the Lord, and I started to become annoyed by it all. I had also been upset by all the attacks I had received. While I was there, I received this song from the Lord, which is translated from the Slavic language: "God, you are love because you save me."

One day, I decided to confront Anne about her channel. I sat down and wrote a message of warning to her. I then saw her transcript of one of her messages and read a small amount. I realised just how far from the truth this woman was. I still do not understand why I ever went onto her channel in the first place. However, reading the Bible again made all false doctrines leave my mind, and I began to conduct an in-depth study on the subject of Satan. I wanted to know the truth from scripture directly on this subject and understand who I was actually dealing with.

I started searching places to see where I could be delivered. I searched websites for an answer and found a Christian healing service. I was hoping to seek deliverance from the Lord by attending this place. While I was in the bathroom, I was singing a song named "Tis So Sweet to Trust in Jesus." When I reached the part where I was to say "trust," I became possessed and said, "Lust." It got me angry. Could a Christian become possessed? Most Christians believe they cannot.

As I went to sleep, I dreamt that I saw an old lady turn into a gross-looking demon right in front of my eyes. While I was viewing this image of her, the most frightening fear hit me. I was trying to get the words out of my mouth to rebuke the demon but could not remember anything but absolute fear. I just could not get a word out until after the attack happened. I woke up and went into the shower. I was getting ready to head off to work when I heard an audible tune reach me. It was an old song that I had not heard since my childhood, called "Something Beautiful":

"Something beautiful,

Something good, all my confusion he understood,

All I had to offer him was brokenness and strife,

But he made something beautiful of my life."

It was amazing that God could give me a song that I had completely forgotten. This was a song I used to sing, and it reminded me of my childhood.

One day, I said, "I wonder what my daydreaming could have been like if I was for Satan." I forgot that we are held accountable to the Lord for every idle word spoken. I went to pray when I was suddenly directed in my prayer again not to listen to the demons and not to go against God. I became concerned and asked God for forgiveness. God corrected me. I started to cry and was scared by my choice of words. It is a hard thing to take when you are corrected by the Lord.

I sat on the couch, my husband started watching a re-run of that episode of that Christian church that the host of the show was mocking. My husband turned to me and made a bad comment regarding how this church acted, when the Lord Jesus started telling me within my spirit that this church was not right and was giving people, like my husband, a very bad impression of Christ and his church. This church was in America. They would go to the streets of

America with signs of hatred toward certain groups. They also hated the nation of Israel, and spoke against them for crucifying our Lord Jesus. They dressed in long dresses and appeared as godly people, but their hearts and minds were far from what Christ wanted his church to become.

In a dream, I saw a row of metal seats. I chose to sit down, and in my hand was my IPod. I automatically had this strong desire to play it and re-enter my daydream world. When this desire entered me, I suddenly started to hear a Christian song come through to me while deep within this dream. Being wide awake in my dream, I decided to toss my IPod away into the lake, which was in front of me. I woke up out of the dream and received these two songs from the Lord: "They Shall Be Showers of Blessing" and 'My Life Is in You, Lord."

I was feeling down for several days with the feeling that I was going to give up and collapse. If it was not for my children, I would have collapsed already. I am in such a bad state right now, and I have been fighting with myself not to collapse or give up. I am constantly calling out to the Lord day and night with tears, asking him for help.

One night, I was lying down on the bed next to Joshua when I was hit hard by a spirit, which swooped down and knocked me to the side of the bed. I was not hurt, but my body shifted. When will all these attacks stop?

Chapter 11

THE TRUTH ABOUT SATAN

Please don't judge me until you read through this chapter. I decided one day to consider who Lucifer was; was he really the same being as Satan? I was reading the book of Job and read how the sons of God, which are angels of God, presented themselves before the Lord, and Satan came among them. Satan came among them? I thought. Something suddenly clicked inside my brain, and for the very first time, it made sense: Satan is evil! Nowhere in the Bible had it ever mentioned that Lucifer and Satan were the same being. The Lord Jesus always addressed the devil as Satan. He never addressed him as Lucifer at all. Look and read for yourselves to see if you can really connect the two together as one being:

"But some of them said, He [Jesus] casteth out devils through Beelzebub the chief of the devils. And others, tempting him, sought of him a sign from heaven. But he, knowing their thoughts, said unto them, Every kingdom divided against itself is brought to desolation;

and a house divided against a house falleth. If Satan also be divided against himself, how shall his kingdom stand?" (Luke 11:15-18KJV)

I knew instantly that the former angel of light known as Lucifer was not the same devil which was taught in the bible, but as this thought entered my mind, I suddenly had a demon hit me hard against my body. It became extremely angry with me as it repeated what I had just thought about Satan, and then it immediately disappeared. I knew the demon could read my thoughts and gestures. Some Christians believe they cannot, but I am telling you out of my own personal experience that they can. The demons knew me well; my past and present.

After the demon attacked me, I thought, did I just come across something? I decided to continue looking into this subject. Most Christians know the story about how Lucifer became Satan. It goes something along these lines: Lucifer was one of God's angels. He rebelled against God by wanting to be like God. He took one-third of the angels into his service. He and the fallen angels were cursed by God and turned into Satan and the demons.

In the book of Isaiah it states:

"How art thou fallen from heaven, O Lucifer, son of the morning! how art thou cut down to the ground, which didst weaken the nations!

For thou hast said in thine heart, I will ascend into heaven, I will exalt my throne above the stars of God: I will sit also upon the mount of the congregation, in the sides of the north:

I will ascend above the heights of the clouds; I will be like the most High.

Yet thou shalt be brought down to hell, to the sides of the pit.

They that see thee shall narrowly look upon thee, and consider thee, saying, Is this the man that made the earth to tremble, that did shake kingdoms;" (Isaiah 14:12-16KJV)

In the book of Ezekiel this story continues:

"Son of man, take up a lamentation upon the king of Tyrus, and say unto him, Thus saith the Lord GOD; Thou sealest up the sum, full of wisdom, and perfect in beauty.

Thou hast been in Eden the garden of God; every precious stone was thy covering, the sardius, topaz, and the diamond, the beryl, the onyx, and the jasper, the sapphire, the emerald, and the carbuncle, and gold: the workmanship of thy tabrets and of thy pipes was prepared in thee in the day that thou wast created.

Thou art the anointed cherub that covereth; and I have set thee so: thou wast upon the holy mountain of God; thou hast walked up and down in the midst of the stones of fire.

Thou wast perfect in thy ways from the day that thou wast created, till iniquity was found in thee.

By the multitude of thy merchandise they have filled the midst of thee with violence, and thou hast sinned: therefore I will cast thee as profane out of the mountain of God: and I will destroy thee, O covering cherub, from the midst of the stones of fire.

Thine heart was lifted up because of thy beauty, thou hast corrupted thy wisdom by reason of thy brightness: I will cast thee to the ground, I will lay thee before kings, that they may behold thee.

Thou hast defiled thy sanctuaries by the multitude of thine iniquities, by the iniquity of thy traffick; therefore will I bring forth a fire from the midst of thee, it shall devour thee, and I will bring thee to ashes upon the earth in the sight of all them that behold thee.

All they that know thee among the people shall be astonished at thee: thou shalt be a terror, and never shalt thou be any more." (Ezekiel 28:12-19KJV)

Demons are darkness, and so is Satan.

The angels that had sinned against the Lord ended up in Hell.

Satan was the one who had cast these angels to the ground. He was the one who ended up decieving them in the end, resulting in these angels being stamped upon by the devil.

The below verse states this about the fallen angels which had fallen:

"And it waxed great, even to the host of heaven; and it cast down some of the host and of the stars to the ground, and stamped upon them." (Daniel 8:10KJV)

The book of Jude states that these angel who had left heaven, are now locked away and will be judged by God on the great day.

"And the angels which kept not their first estate, but left their own habitation, he hath reserved in everlasting chains under darkness unto the judgment of the great day." (Jude 1:6KJV)

I began to contemplate these questions about Lucifer and Satan, so I went straight to the Bible. Satan is the devil, the ancient serpent. So how then is his name Lucifer, who was a covering cherubim, a former angel of light? I also thought this. If the old serpent is the devil, wasn't he always the old serpent, a dragon? If he was an angel to begin with, why then does Satan transform into an angel of light?

"And no marvel; for Satan himself is transformed into an angel of light."(1 Corinthians 11:14KJV)

I know that some satanists can transform from a human being into another creature like a snake. I heard this from a testimony of an ex-satanist. If his people can transform, so why can't Satan transform from a dragon into an angel of light. I believe this is the devil's true form.

"And the great dragon was cast out, that old serpent, called the Devil, and Satan, which deceiveth the whole world: he was cast out into the earth, and his angels were cast out with him." (Revelation 12:9KJV)

"And I saw an angel come down from heaven, having the key of the bottomless pit and a great chain in his hand. And he laid hold on the dragon, that old serpent, which is the Devil, and Satan, and bound him a thousand years, And cast him into the bottomless pit, and shut him up, and set a seal upon him, that he should deceive the nations no more, till the thousand years should be fulfilled: and after that he must be loosed a little season." (Revelation 20:1-3KJV)

In the book of Genesis, we see the serpent tempting Eve, resulting in God cursing the serpent in the garden of Eden. The serpent is Satan himself and not a snake like everyone depicts, especially in children's stories about Adam and Eve and the serpent in the garden of Eden.

"And the LORD God said unto the serpent, Because thou hast done this, thou art cursed above all cattle, and above every beast of the field; upon thy belly shalt thou go, and dust shalt thou eat all the days of thy life:

And I will put enmity between thee and the woman, and between thy seed and her seed; it shall bruise thy head, and thou shalt bruise his heel." (Genesis 3:14-15KJV)

This is the moment God cursed Satan, they were in the garden of Eden and Satan is already depicted as a serpent in this story. Satan is the deceiver and tempter of humanity. In this curse, we can see that the seed of the devil are the tares of this world, the sons of perdition. They are not sexually produced from the devil's seed like in the doctrine of the serpent seed, but spiritually belong to the devil by being the goats, tares and ungodly people of this world who reject the Messiah and the Lord God. The woman is the nation of Israel, the remnant of Israel are now the Messianic jews as well as the Christians of this world who accepted Jesus Christ as their saviour.

"He that shall bruise your head" is Jesus Christ, and the head that is bruised is Satan's head. Satan will only bruise Jesus' heel, which represents the cross, and how Jesus had to die for the sinners. This was the hour of darkness and Satan was the one behind it, when he possessed Judas Iscariot and sold the Lord Jesus for 30 pieces of silver.

According to scripture, God formed the light and created the darkness.

"I form the light, and create darkness: I make peace and create evil: I the Lord do all these things." (Isaiah 45:7KJV)

Think about it: If Lucifer became Satan, then where does evil and darkness come from? God states that he created evil and darkness.

Satan is called the wicked one and the evil one.

"When anyone hears the word of the kingdom and does not understand it, the evil one comes and snatches away what has been sown in his heart." (Matthew 13:19KJV)

Satan has a kingdom/dominion:

"To open their eyes so that they may turn from darkness to light and from the dominion of Satan to God." (Acts 26:18KJV)

Satan is an enemy of God:

"Another parable he put forth to them, saying: The kingdom of heaven is like a man who sowed good seed in his field; but while men slept, his enemy came and sowed tares among the wheat and went his way. But when the grain had sprouted and produced a crop, then the tares also appeared. So the servants of the owner came and said to him, 'Sir, did you not sow good seed in your field? How then does it have tares?' He said to them, 'An enemy has done this.' The servants said to him, 'Do you want us then to go and gather them up?' But he said, 'No, lest while you gather up the tares you also uproot the wheat with them. Let both grow together until the harvest, and at the time of harvest I will say to the reapers, "First gather together the tares and bind them in bundles to burn them, but gather the wheat into my barn." (Matthew 13:24-30KJV)

"Then Jesus sent the multitude away and went into the house. And His disciples came to Him, saying, 'Explain to us the parable of the tares of the field.' He answered and said to them: 'He who sows the good seed is the Son of Man. The field is the world, the good seeds are the sons of the kingdom, but the tares are the sons of the wicked one. The enemy who sowed them is the devil, the harvest is the end of the age, and the reapers are the angels. Therefore as the tares are gathered and burned in the fire, so it will be at the end of this age. The Son of Man will send out His angels, and they will gather out of His kingdom all things that offend, and those who practice lawlessness, and will cast them into the furnace of fire. There will be wailing and gnashing of teeth. Then the righteous will shine forth as the sun in the kingdom of their Father. He who has ears to hear, let him hear!'"

(Matthew 13:36-43KJV)

Satan is a liar and has no truth in him. He was a murderer from the beginning:

"Ye are of your father the devil, and the lusts of your father ye will do. He was a murderer from the beginning, and abode not in the truth, because there is no truth in him. When he speaketh a lie, he speaketh of his own: for he is a liar, and the father of it." (John 8:44KJV)

Satan sinned from the beginning, while Lucifer was perfect from the day he was created until iniquity was found in him:

"He that committeth sin is of the devil; for the devil sinneth from the beginning. For this purpose the Son of God was manifested, that he might destroy the works of the devil." (1 John 3:8KJV)

Like I mentioned before, Satan had the power of death. The word of God came in the flesh and manifested himself as Jesus, so that through death, Jesus might destroy the devil:

"Forasmuch then as the children are partakers of flesh and blood, he [Jesus] also himself likewise took part of the same; that through death he [Jesus] might destroy him that had the power of death, that is, the devil." (Hebrews 2:14KJV)

Jesus has all power in heaven and Earth, over all principalities, powers, rulers, and authority. This also includes the devil. Jesus will put all his enemies under his feet.

"Who is gone into heaven, and is on the right hand of God; angels and authorities and powers being made subject unto him." (1 Peter 3:22KJV)

According to the Bible, Jesus (the word of God) made all things:

"For by him were all things created, that are in heaven, and that are in earth, visible and invisible, whether they be thrones, or dominions, or principalities, or powers: all things were created by him, and for him." (Colossians 1:16KJV)

According to scripture, we are in a spiritual warfare not only against Satan, but against powers, principalities, spiritual wickedness in high places, and the rulers of the darkness of this world.

"For we wrestle not against flesh and blood, but against principalities, against powers, against the rulers of the darkness of this world, against spiritual wickedness in high places." (Ephesians 6:12KJV)

Satan has power:

"And the LORD said unto Satan, Behold, all that he hath is in thy power; only upon himself put not forth thine hand. So Satan went forth from the presence of the LORD." (Job 1:12KJV)

"And the devil said unto him, All this power will I give thee, and the glory of them: for that is delivered unto me; and to whomsoever I will I give it." (Luke 4:6KJV)

These were the questions that came to mind on this subject. It got my brain going, so I started to connect the dots.

The Lord God is called "the Lord of Hosts," because he has these spiritual beings that live in heaven; they do God's will. It's not only angels that live in heaven.

"The LORD hath prepared his throne in the heavens; and his kingdom ruleth over all.

Bless the LORD, ye his angels, that excel in strength, that do his commandments, hearkening unto the voice of his word.

Bless ye the LORD, all ye his hosts; ye ministers of his, that do his pleasure.

Bless the LORD, all his works in all places of his dominion: bless the LORD, O my soul." (Psalm 103: 19-22KJV)

I will give you an example of the hosts of heaven:

"And he said, Hear thou therefore the word of the LORD: I saw the LORD sitting on his throne, and all the host of heaven standing by him on his right hand and on his left.

And the LORD said, Who shall persuade Ahab, that he may go up and fall at Ramothgilead? And one said on this manner, and another said on that manner.

And there came forth a spirit, and stood before the LORD, and said, I will persuade him.

And the LORD said unto him, Wherewith? And he said, I will go forth, and I will be a lying spirit in the mouth of all his prophets. And he said, Thou shalt persuade him, and prevail also: go forth, and do so.

Now therefore, behold, the LORD hath put a lying spirit in the mouth of all these thy prophets, and the LORD hath spoken evil concerning thee." (1 Kings 22:19-23KJV)

As I was studying this, the same demonic voice returned and said, "I'm going to kill you."

After I arrived home and began to write this all up on the laptop, a spirit entered me, giving me a massive headache. He said, "I'm going to kill you, stop writing this."

Did Satan deceive all the Christians with the doctrine of him being an angel of light: Lucifer? What would Satan's real name be, then? It would not be Lucifer. The names Satan and the devil are just titles given to him. They are not his real name. I am comparing scripture, and the Bible should not contradict itself. I truly believe God has opened my eyes to be able to see this clearly. Can you see it?

According to Wikipedia: The translators of the King James Bible version took the word Lucifer from the Latin Vulgate which means "the morning star, the planet Venus", or, as an adjective, "light-bringing." The original Hebrew word means "shining one, light-bearer", and the translation given in the King James text is the Latin name for the planet Venus, "Lucifer."

The name Lucifer itself is not even a real name. Either way, Satan's name is not Lucifer, even if he was the fallen angel mentioned in the book of Isaiah.

I looked into the Dead Sea Scrolls translations and some of the early Christian writings and found that Satan is called by a title of Belial or Beliar; which means without worth. During my research I found a very interesting book called, "Ascension of Isaiah." It amazed me because I read a large amount of truth within its pages about Satan and the coming Antichrist in the last days, and it tied in well with the book of Revelation.

This is an excerpt from the book, Ascension of Isaiah:

"After it is consummated, Beliar the great ruler, the king of this world, will descend, who hath ruled it since it came into being; yea, he will descent from his firmament in the likeness of a man, a lawless king, the slayer of his mother: who himself (even) this king. Will persecute the plant which the Twelve Apostles of the Beloved (The beloved is Jesus Christ) have planted. Of the Twelve one will be delivered into his hands. This ruler in the form of that king will come and there will come and there will come with him all the powers of this world, and they will hearken unto him in all that he desires. And at his word the sun will rise at night and he will make the moon to appear at the sixth hour.

And all that he hath desired he will do in the world: he will do and speak like the Beloved and he will say: "I am God and before me there has been none." And all the people in the world will believe in him. And they will sacrifice to him and they will serve him saying: "This is God and beside him there is no other "And they greater number of those who shall have been associated together in order to receive the Beloved, he will turn aside after him. And there will be the power of his miracles in every city and region. And he will set up his image before him in every city. And he shall bear sway three years and seven months and twenty-seven days.

And many believers and saints having seen Him for whom they were hoping, who was crucified, Jesus the Lord Christ, [after that I, Isaiah, had seen Him who was crucified and ascended] and those also who were believers in Him of these few in those days will be left as His servants, while they flee from desert to desert, awaiting the coming of the Beloved. And after (one thousand) three hundred and thirty-two days the Lord will come with His angels and with the armies of the holy ones from the seventh heaven with the glory of the seventh heaven, and He will drag Beliar into Gehenna (which means Hell) and also his armies.

And He (who is Jesus Christ) will give rest of the godly whom He shall find in the body in this world, [and the sun will be ashamed]: And to all who because of (their) faith in Him have execrated Beliar and his kings. But the saints will come with the Lord with their garments which are (now) stored up on high in the seventh heaven: with the Lord they will come, whose spirits are clothed, they will descend and be present in the world, and He will strengthen those, who have been found in the body, together with the saints, in the garments of the saints, and the Lord will minister to those who have kept watch in this world. And afterwards they will turn themselves upward in their garments, and their body will be left in the world.

Then the voice of the Beloved will in wrath rebuke the things of heaven and the things of earth and the things of earth and the mountains and the hills and the cities and the desert and the forests and the angel of the sun and that of the moon, and all things wherein Beliar manifested himself and acted openly in this world, and there will be [a resurrection and] a judgement in their midst in those days, and the Beloved will cause fire to go forth from Him, and it will consume all the godless, and they will be as though they had not been created."

This king is the Antichrist; Satan will be this king and he will have 10 kings that will rule with him. He is Gog from the land of Magog, and I believe he comes from the Middle East. There is evidence in the Bible from the book of Daniel where he comes out of. It's from the ancient line of the Seleucid kingdom, through the Parthian's and Medes, and this is mentioned in the book of Enoch. Most of the prophets talk about an Assyrian king that will invade Israel in the last days. When you see this occurring then you will see Jesus returning on the day of the Lord to fight against this king, the false prophet and his armies at Armageddon. This king is also the little horn from the book of Daniel.

This king will have power over all nations, they will believe he is a God and worship him as God, setting up his image in every city. The false prophet will make everyone worship this king and receive the mark of his name, which is 666, they will not be able to buy or sell anything, unless they have this mark on their right hand or forehead. Christians or anyone who refuse to worship the image of the beast will be killed. He will kill the saints of God and turn against the nation of Israel. When Jesus returns he fights Belial and his armies, Jesus' will then bring the wrath of God to the earth and will destroy all of the sinners and the ungodly from this world with his wrath. This is how the Lord will rule the nations with a rod of iron.

Continuing my testimony, Joshua and I went to a healing deliverance meeting. A pastor prayed over me. As he was praying, I felt a spirit leave my body, and for a few seconds, I felt slightly delivered. When the pastor prayed over me, he prayed in tongues like my grandmother does, and it sounded familiar. Once he finished praying, he walked away.

As I walked away from the pastor, I heard a voice which sounded like Jesus say to me, "Go and ask the pastor to pray over you again."

It sounded real, and I almost fell for it again. It spoke three times like this, almost convincing me that this was the Lord Jesus talking to me, but I recognised that it was actually a demon. I had to keep reminding myself to test the spirits like the Bible teaches. I still went back to the pastor and asked him to pray over me again. I was so desperate, I needed to get delivered. The realisation hit me hard; I didn't get delivered. I felt a spirit re-enter me.

A lady from the deliverance meeting asked me, "Are you filled with the Holy Spirit?" and I said, "No, I'm not. I'm possessed by an evil spirit which is inside of me."

I know now that I just had unclean spirits dwelling inside and around me; at the time, I didn't understand that I wasn't possessed, even though demons tried to possess me a few times.

At the time, I also didn't know whether I was filled with the Holy Spirit or not. I know the Lord opened my eyes to discernment and gave me some understanding and faith. I'm able to recognise a lot more things now. I believe that I've been given the gift of the Holy Spirit. She tried to show me how to get the infilling of the Holy Spirit, but this scared me, and I left. I'm very hesitant of these things, especially after going through massive amounts of torment. I know you can get a demon which speaks in demonic tongues, and I was scared of getting this. Satan and the demons have hurt me deeply. I believe we should test these spirits. Not every tongue spoken is from the Holy Spirit. You need to test these tongues. You may be cursing the Lord if you have tongues from a demon. Test the spirits to make sure it's from the Lord.

When I was researching places where I could be delivered, I came upon places where they can teach you how to get the baptism or infilling of the Holy Spirit. Please be careful of such things. God gives these gifts; speaking in tongues is not the ultimate sign that you have the Holy Spirit. There are diverse types of gifts that the Lord gives to his children. Speaking in tongues is just one of these gifts. However, this is not the ultimate sign that you have the Holy Spirit.

When I got home from the deliverance meeting, I was upset. I started to call out to God and said, "Lord, am I truly one of your children?" I felt completely lost and without hope. I prayed that the Lord would either heal me or take me to heaven because I couldn't take it anymore. I was in agony because of physical and mental torment and sickness.

As I sat at home, I continued to cry. As I was crying, I felt this heat surrounding me. This was the Holy Spirit; as soon as he was around me, he left. I went to my room and prayed with all my heart with more tears. It left me with hope and gave me comfort, knowing that I was indeed a child of God.

A demon spoke and tempted me to re-enter the daydream world. He continued to tell me that I was truly evil due to my past imaginations.

I refused and decided to lie down on the couch; the spirit said, "Just daydream."

I said, "No, I'll never go back into it."

The spirit sent a tingling sexual temptation through my body and continued to say, "Satan wanted you, Danica!"

I didn't question why he said this but quickly replied, "I rebuke you in the name of Jesus," and it left.

One evening, I said sarcastically, "Why doesn't Satan talk to me directly?" I quickly stopped myself in this thought, for I knew it was evil, but it was too late. Suddenly, a male voice came through to me. I covered my face out of shock, for I knew that this was Satan himself speaking directly to me.

I was grieved, and he said, "You are writing something I don't want anyone to know. I warn you: I will get to you. I will kill you." He spoke in a subtle, smooth tone of voice, almost civil in conversation. It was loud and clear, and I knew I had just heard from the devil himself. He didn't say anything else, just these words.

It was a few minutes to midnight, and I got on my knees and started to pray. As I began to pray, something came over me, and I felt this urge to say, "Please forgive me for talking to demons."

I kept getting this urge until I realised it was from the enemy. Instantly, I tried to stop myself from speaking, but my mouth kept opening up. I kept saying in a male tone of voice, "Danica, I am Satan!"

I tried to rebuke it in the name of Jesus, thinking it was just a demon. It continued to speak through me and said, "You can't rebuke me, Danica. I am Satan."

Confused by this, I climbed into bed. As I sat up in bed, Jesus urgently gave me these words: "I am safe and secure in the rock of all ages, and his banner over me is love."

After receiving these words, I suddenly felt this extremely powerful, tingling presence of an evil being standing directly opposite me. At the time, I couldn't tell if this was a demon. However, it was claiming to be Satan himself. I wasn't able to move from the tormenting presence. I saw an outline of him, but the form was invisible. However, I knew he was standing opposite me. This presence alone put fear and torment through my entire body. My whole body tingled with tormenting pain, and I started to feel faint.

The being said, "I'm not going to kill you tonight, but I want you to stop what you are writing." He continued, "I wanted you for a bride, but the Lord wouldn't allow it."

This being lifted his hand over me, and I felt a very powerful sexual desire, which ran right through the lower parts of my body with intensity that I was almost lured away in a moment of pain and pleasure. I was and wasn't afraid of his presence, for this being gave me mixed signals.

As he was tormenting me, I started to rebuke this being, saying, "I rebuke you in the name of Jesus."

He replied, "You can't rebuke me, Danica. I am Satan."

I was stunned and lay still, unable to breathe, surrounded by an intense feeling of torment. I resisted with all my strength and kept on rebuking, but I wasn't able to get this being to leave me alone. He continued to torment me for a few hours, and then he entered into my body. At first, I thought he left, but a few years later I came to realise that this spirit didn't leave my home, but entered into me instead. However, I couldn't comprehend it at the time. This wasn't Satan, but a demon.

I was extremely messed up by this. However, I thought I would go on the computer and write this all up before I forgot what happened to me. As soon as I got near the computer, I felt this supernatural pressure on my chest, then I heard these words directed to me:

"I warn you … I will kill you."

Scared by this, I decided to leave it alone for the night. I headed back to bed at four thirty in the early morning and fell asleep.

The next day, I decided to write my experience up, but as soon as I went onto the computer, my head suddenly became compressed with physical pain. I was in extreme agony.

This demon spoke and said, "It's going to get worse, not better, for you."

What else could possibly come my way? I thought.

My head still hurts. I kept on crying out to the Lord for deliverance; I asked him again, "Am I your child?"

He responded instantly to me through this song: "God, You Are Love, for You Saved Me" I was in absolute pain, to the point where I was unable to move from all these attacks that I received.

One day, I was walking home from work, when I started wondering if God would tell me something, anything about what was occurring with my situation. I had great hope that he would give me some sort of answer. I was still working at the chiropractic clinic.

As I was awaking from sleep one morning, I said, "You were with the devil! You were a disgrace!"

I kept repeating this until I became aware of what I was saying. This was God telling me what a disgrace I was. I felt the rebuke from God, and it deeply hurt. This truly wasn't the answer I wanted to hear, but God wanted me to be aware that I had been on the enemy's side almost my entire life. I was extremely sad and realised just how evil I was. I had joined Satan without even realising that I did. I had come out of his kingdom, and Satan wasn't impressed at all by it.

Chapter 12

RESIST

One night, I dreamt that I was wrestling with a black dragon. In this dream, the dragon kept trying to destroy me. As I was dreaming, I cried out to Jesus and said, "Jesus, I love you." Once again, Satan wanted to kill me within a dream. As I woke up, the feeling of death disappeared. If it wasn't for God's presence and everything God has done for me until now, I would believe that I was perishing and going to hell.

Another day, I was at church when my mind for some reason wanted to deny the Lord. I quickly grew angry at myself and kneeled down to pray. Suddenly, the Holy Spirit started to correct me. The Holy Spirit spoke through me and said not to go against the Lord. I got home, and my mind again wanted to deny the Lord. I cried with all my heart and prayed again. The Holy Spirit again corrected me and told me not to go against him. I cried with many tears. I was all upset again.

As I was crying, two songs entered my mind. They were "Unto Thee, Oh Lord" and "A Mighty Fortress Is Our God." I went to the computer to play these songs. I also played "Be Thou My Vision." I started to sing along to this song but couldn't remember the lyrics. As I started to sing, the Lord suddenly gave me the lyrics to this song. I sang it correctly, without getting a single word wrong.

I wrote to Anne again regarding her channel. I tried desperately to reach her but was unable to make her see that she was communicating with a demon. She wouldn't even test this spirit. I told her to try and see who was truly speaking to her by asking this false Jesus if the Lord had come in the flesh. Unfortunately, she trusted this Jesus and was unwilling to listen. She wouldn't take my advice and ask this question.

I told her, "Even if this is Jesus himself, ask this question; he will forgive you if you are truly talking to him."

However, this was a demon she was in communication with. The worse thing is that she has thousands of followers, listening to her on a daily basis. One day, the Lord Jesus spoke to me within my spirit while I was communicating with Anne.

He said, "None of her messages are from the Lord, as well as the visions she gets."

I decided to obey the Lord and wrote his words in the comment section on her videos, even to individual people commenting. Even if she doesn't believe, others can see this and consider. We as Christians should fight for the truth, no matter how crazy you look to others. Just fight for what's right.

I was still being attacked by the unclean spirits. I was in torment one day and grew weak. My mouth locked, and I was just about to swear against the Holy Spirit. Suddenly, the Lord performed a miracle and an angel took over my speech supernaturally. I spoke these particular words. I said, "I rebuke you, Satan, in the name of the Lord Jesus."

I was sitting on the couch and felt this incredible amount of torment hit me hard. I sat there, trying to resist. The demons once again wanted me to curse the Holy Spirit. Out of the blue, a male voice spoke to me. It was an angel of light. He gives me these words: "Resist and you'll receive a crown of life."

The spirits I've encountered so far have a lot of character. Some sound demonic, but others don't. They seem to have their own personality. Even the way they speak, you can't believe that it's your mind coming up with such comments. They are not even connected to your own thoughts. Auditory hallucinations are not connected to your mind. They either come from the Lord, from demons, or from Satan, depending on what you get.

This is why a lot of people say, "I have that song stuck in my head." If you receive a song or thought from the devil or demons, rebuke them immediately in the name of Jesus, and the spirit giving you this thought should stop. I've done this a number of times already regarding songs that have entered my mind from the devil. When I notice this, I immediately rebuke it in the name of the Lord.

"They are trying to lure you away from me," God our Father told me one day.

I thought, this could never happen to me because I love the Lord very much.

Soon after I received these words, the worst temptation I ever had happened to me. I was asleep and went into a very realistic dream. I couldn't tell the difference between the dream world and reality for a few minutes. I was overwhelmed by a demon. I felt this demon's hand inside my private parts. As I felt the hand there, I had this unbelievably strong desire to worship Satan. It was 3 a.m. I got up and took a hot bath to stop myself from worshipping him. It was the worse evil desire that I ever had. They could have lured me away with the way I felt. This desire they placed on me was unbearable, to the point where I could have fallen for it. I had to resist this urge and remember that I was a Christian, and that Satan and the demons are darkness, and that we are the children of light.

"Submit yourselves therefore to God. Resist the devil and he will flee from you." (James 4:7KJV)

While sitting in the bath, I received this song from the Lord: "I Serve a Risen Saviour." The song gave me strength to resist Satan. The feeling subsided, and the unclean spirits started to speak to me again. They kept telling me they just wanted me to go to hell.

One horrible night, I was dreaming when all of a sudden my dream shifted. Satan took control of my dream. While in this dream state, I called the Holy Spirit an evil spirit because I was possessed.

I heard Satan's voice within this dream; he said, "You're going to hell."

I replied back to him in disappointment, "I had a feeling I was."

My whole body woke up in extreme anger over this. Satan had put it in my heart to try to blaspheme God. Thinking I was doomed eternally, I sat up in bed, unable to control just how annoyed and frustrated I was about saying these words. I thought I had just blasphemed God. I had hatred within me; I almost cursed God. I sat up in bed, holding it all back, almost unable to control it. However, I didn't curse God, and the anger and hatred towards God left me.

I resisted Satan, and the feeling fled. I can't believe that Satan can control your emotions like this. I was overwhelmed and didn't know what to do. I just had to believe the Lord was saving me. I didn't do this willingly. It was against my will. Satan directed my thoughts to the Holy Spirit, to refer to him as an evil spirit. I'm crying now; I can't believe the devil is able to do such a thing to a Christian.

I thought I was wearing a helmet. My head felt heavy, and I was in constant agony. I finally decided to go to the local medical centre for an answer. I arrived, waited, and was eventually seen by a doctor. She heard my case and sent me to the hospital for a more thorough investigation.

As Joshua and I ended up back at the emergency ward at the hospital, torment started to race through my mind. Unable to cope, I put on my IPod and played Christian instrumental music to soothe my thoughts. I couldn't take it anymore. The torment wasn't just mental; it was also physical. I was pushed to my breaking point, with high levels of stress for over six months. That was how long I had been resisting Satan with evil thoughts against the Holy Spirit. I cried nearly every night for deliverance, unable to bear the tormenting pain that inflicted me. I had great hope that the Lord would answer my prayers one day.

I was finally admitted and seen by the doctors. They did a CT scan to check my brain, and the results came back; it was the same as my CT scans from our holiday: all clear. When they told me that I was clear, my compressions inside my brain increased, and my physical and mental torment grew worse. I believe that demons were causing me these compressions.

When we left the hospital, I was in more agony, physically as well as mentally, than when I arrived. What the doctors had failed to recognise was that the painkiller medication initially given to me, when I had been admitted into the hospital, made my head pain worse. It had caused my physical and mental pain to increase. I became very sensitive to powerful painkillers and wasn't able to take them anymore due to my head compressions and pain.

However, there was nothing else they could do for me. The doctors couldn't recognise that I was in a very bad state. I ended up leaving and went to Tina and Andrew's to pick up the children. In tears, I turned to the Lord. I couldn't sit down. I was completely agitated, to the point where I wanted to pull my hair out. I paced up and down, unable to find rest.

As I kneeled to pray, I called out to the Lord and asked him to help me for my children's sake. I didn't want to lose custody of them due to my sickness. Instantly, he settled me, taking away the physical and mental torment during prayer. I was so relieved and quickly turned to my brother-in-law, Daniel, and told him that the Lord just healed me from torment. He didn't know what to say back to me. He didn't understand what I was really going through. However, this started my road to recovery.

Chapter 13

UNDISCIPLINED

My children and I were all cuddled up together in my bed. We just sang a song to the Lord, and then "I will deliver you" came through my mouth. This was the second time I was told I'd be delivered. Just before I got these words, I was in prayer, and "I love you" came through my mouth. This was the Lord God telling me that he loved me and that he'd deliver me.

While I was lying in bed, I began to supernaturally hear Christians singing a song of praise to God. As soon as I started to listen to them, Satan intervened by placing an awful sound to block the incoming music. I was annoyed; I really wanted to hear what the Lord was showing me. I felt annoyed when Satan blocked the music.

Violet attends a Christian school. She had a school performance one evening, and it was a major production. We went to the school and were directed to our seats. The students were getting ready to play their instruments. All the parents were seated, and we waited for the curtains to open. All I knew about the performance was that my child was to sing a song with her class on stage.

When they opened, the theme was Broadway musical; I was in shock. This was a Christian school. I was upset as I sat there, watching my child perform to the music. I was grieved and thought, I wonder if the Lord can make me sick so I can leave?

I took it back straight away, regretting what I just said, but I got instantly sick and felt a pain in my abdomen. I also felt the Lord's presence; he told me to leave my seat and go outside. The Lord wasn't happy at all with the situation. As the Lord was directing me to leave, a Christian student started to perform a song from a popular broadway musical called, "Wicked." I quickly got up and went outside, walking out in pain. I had offended Joshua by leaving, but I obeyed the Lord and left my seat. I wonder why a lot of Christians are involved heavily with the world like this; the Lord doesn't like it.

The truth is, Satan is a roaring lion and wants to devour everyone. He uses tools like books, movies, music and entertainment to draw people away from the Lord. Some of these popular children's books teach our children to love wizardry, sorcery and evil. Through these types of books, children learn about the occult. The worst thing is Christian parents are allowing their children to read them. As a result, Satan is given the legal right to enter into their lives, along with demons.

One time during book week, a teacher at Violet's school picked a student to win best dressed, out of his school grade. These students all came dressed as their favourite characters from their favourite books. This student that won best dress, was dressed as a young wizard. I was so angry. I watched how Christian parents clapped their hands together and supported this abomination.

My daughter Violet, had also confronted a peer at her school regarding Harry Potter. This peer had told her that he wanted to dress up as Harry Potter for book week. She replied back to him and said, "God doesn't like Harry Potter." He replied back to Violet and had said that he didn't care because he thought that the movie was a great film. Christians, please wake up! God hates anything to do with sorcery, even if it's only meant to be fictional. It always refers to the occult and Satan is the one behind the occult. You can't serve Satan and Jesus at the same time. You need to choose who you want to serve. We as Christians need to stay away from such things and try to live a righteous life.

However, I'm still learning to live a righteous life. I want to confess a few things about my attitude towards unclean spirits. The spirits speak to me most of the time, and I'm sometimes tempted by them. They try to lure me into a conversation. Even though most times, I refuse to speak back to them, I end up listening and smile stupidly about what the spirits have to say. I'm getting better; at least I'm no longer grinning in awe about hearing a spirit. I am now grieved by them. I truly want it to all stop. I pray to the Lord that he can deliver me from them. They just won't leave.

One day, while praying to the Lord, he told me, "Do a three-day fast."

Three days? I cringed inside, knowing full well how hard it would be for me to achieve this. However, I was determined to do this for the Lord. I started but crumbled again and again, until I gave up fasting completely. I just can't do it, I told myself in disappointment. I love the Lord, but I just can't get through the fast. I kept failing. I even vowed to the Lord that I would do this for him. I know, don't vow unless you really mean it. God hates it when you go back on your word. At the time of the vow, I really wanted to do this for God, but my body wasn't able to fast that long.

After I failed this fast, I heard these words come to me: "I will not deliver you." I thought it was the Lord at first, but it happened so fast that to this day, I'm not sure if it was God who spoke or a demon. I became sad and was unsure if I would get delivered. I really lost hope that God would deliver me from the demons.

After this, my family and I went to the shopping centre. Joshua and I sat down and let the children play in the indoor playground. As I sat down, a spirit began to communicate with me. As I was listening to the demon, I accidently said something that I knew wasn't pleasing to the Lord. As soon as these words entered my mind (it had something to do with the Holy Spirit), I felt this presence of wrath come upon me. I sat there on the seat, stunned, unable to speak, for I felt doomed. After the initial shock, I started to cry in public. It felt like God was warning me.

We arrived home, and tears were still coming down my face. Why did I say this? I was so sad, and depression started to set in. My mouth suddenly opened up, and a male voice spoke through me and said, "I am saved."

I raced off to church, against Joshua's wishes. I just had to leave. As I sat in the church, I felt God's presence helping me sing a hymn again. I cried all through the service and then went home, still feeling uneasy.

That night, I felt the urge to go and pray. I got up and started praying, when out of nowhere, a powerful male voice spoke directly through me. He said, "You will never be saved."

I trembled in panic and started to cry uncontrollably.

The powerful voice that spoke these words took over my mouth; it repeated forcefully, "You will never be saved."

An eternally lost feeling came over me again. As I continued to cry, I heard another male spirit say, "Please believe that you are saved. Don't believe a lie."

It was too late; the damage was done. I was in fear of being lost. My whole body trembled at the thought of being lost forever. I cried with all my heart, grieved at the thought. As I lay on the bed, I received this song: "When We All Get to Heaven." It gave me comfort, but I was still in tears from such an attack. It brought fear to my soul and grieved me to the core.

The next morning, I sat on the kitchen chair and said to the Lord out loud, "I am not right." I continued, "Why did I have to go through all of this?"

Suddenly, I felt the Lord's presence come upon me. He spoke through me and said, "I will save your soul."

I quickly got on my knees and cried out with thanks to our God. I was saved. I couldn't believe it. After everything I'd done against God, he still saved me by his grace and mercy.

A few days later, I began to feel the torment again, as wicked floating thoughts started to come into my mind against the Holy Spirit. I ended up pacing up and down the corridor in distress. The enemy was once again putting evil thoughts inside my mind, and I had to resist it. As I was pacing, I suddenly felt this very powerful spirit enter me. It tried hard to possess me.

I straight away panicked and said, "I rebuke you in the name of Jesus."

The spirit pulled out straight away and left me. It was amazing to see how spirits leave in the name of Jesus. His name is powerful.

The Lord started to hold me together. The evil thoughts that Satan and the demons were giving me stopped. My mind was clear. I could feel the Lord grabbing each thought that entered my mind and taking them away supernaturally. My stress levels also decreased. I still longed for deliverance from the demons, as well as healing of the physical pain that affected my body. The demons, however, still wanted me to interact with them, whether in a dream or while I was awake. They kept on trying to lure me over to Satan.

Over the next two days, I was lured away again. The spirits continuously talked to me all day long, for two days straight. My heart started to become drawn away from the Lord due to the constant interaction I received from these beings. What's wrong with me? I thought. The feeling of disappointment sunk deep inside my mind. I was a disappointment to the Lord, and I knew I was sinning. I was unable to bring myself to face the Lord, out of fear of being rebuked by him.

That night, I quickly rushed through my prayers and hopped straight into bed. I just could not face him. As I went into a deep sleep, the Lord spoke to me and said, "I don't want to put you into the lake of fire. I love you." He spoke to me as if I was one of his little children.

His love lingered inside my heart, and the most incredible, comforting feeling surrounded me. I woke up out of sleep and felt loved by the Lord. I quickly felt bad and repented what I'd done for the last two days. The demons just wanted to lure me away from God.

The love of the Father is incredible, and it touched me deeply. "Loved by God," I pondered. How incredible is this? As I started to sing "Amazing Grace," I felt the Lord's presence with me through song, and I just knew he loved me as his child.

On another day, I was considering the covenant that the Lord gave me, as well as the prophecy that the Lord gave to my grandfather about saving us. The Lord spoke to me in surprise and said that I could still go to hell. He was just informing me that it was still possible for me to end up there if I chose to go against him. I took note as he advised me of this. He wasn't trying to scare me, but this is a warning to all: Christians can go to hell. Some Christians believe in the doctrine of "once saved, always saved." This is a lie. Be very careful of such teachings.

"Not everyone who says to me, 'Lord, Lord,' will enter into the Kingdom of Heaven; but he who does the will of my Father who is in heaven." (Matthew 7:21KJV)

Chapter 14

DELIVERANCE

There is a book I really recommend everyone to read: He Came to Set the Captives Free, by Rebecca Brown MD. It's a very interesting book. I believe the testimony and agree with nearly everything that Rebecca wrote. I see her as a genuine Christian who went through a lot of things in her life and is truly hearing from the Lord. The book is about a doctor who helped a woman named Elaine come out of Satanism and dedicate her life to Jesus. Elaine was a witch in Satan's kingdom. When she left Satanism, the demons turned against her and attacked her. I won't give too much away regarding her story. Dr Brown has written a few other books. Prepare for War and Becoming a Vessel of Honor are another two good books to read.

I searched the Internet for another deliverance service and found a church that was hosting one. The man they invited was a healing evangelist, his name was John Mellor. He worked as a missionary pastor with the Aboriginal tribal people. He saw how the tribal witch doctors had power, so he cried out to the Lord with prayer and fasting until the Lord started to work with him. Healing started to take place among the people, and miracles happened. He is now working full time for the Lord, travelling in Australia and also going overseas to set people free from various sicknesses. It sounded promising, and I wondered if God would deliver me if I went to it.

His arrival to my city was set for October 30, 2016. I wanted to meet this man and see if God would finally set me free. I asked my father and Lisa to come with me, but she wasn't convinced that he was working for the Lord and told me not to go to see this man, but I believe the Lord can work through people. Also, his testimony sounded genuine.

The three-day fast still lingered inside my mind. I had to do another fast before the healing service. I just had to do it for the Lord. Even if he didn't deliver me this time, I said to myself, I wouldn't get upset. God has his reasons why some people get delivered and others don't.

The evil spirits started to grieve me again against the Holy Spirit. I was so tired of it now and begged the Lord not to let me go. He was still holding my own thoughts in place. I was so scared to blaspheme and didn't want to return to the torment I went through with the demons. I was drained to the point that I wanted the Lord to take me away from this world. I was afraid I'd blaspheme against him and not enter into the kingdom of heaven. He gave me a quick no in my spirit, and I knew I wasn't going to die anytime soon.

"I want to live," I told the Lord, but I couldn't live in torment. I was recovering from the attacks, but somehow Satan was determined to get me into hell by sinning greatly against God. The Lord, however, wasn't allowing him to completely destroy me. The Lord told me one time during prayer that "I have forgiven you, and I will have mercy on you."

I began the fast but failed again. I just couldn't do it. I was unable to fast for the required length of time. I stopped and wondered if I would ever achieve a long fast again.

On a separate day, my heart became wicked again. I spoke some evil words out loud, and this time, the Lord spoke powerfully through me; he said, "I will save your soul, but if you continue the way you are going, I will not."

I was shocked. I was rebuked with a stern warning and was afraid for my soul. This old me had to go; I cannot even write down what I said. It was something I never want to repeat again. It was enough for the Lord to speak directly through me with this warning.

I spoke in faith and told Satan a few things about never going back to him and never again falling for his traps. I was upset and felt my whole life was a big mess because of what Satan had done to me as a young child, by luring into this dark, demonic dream world. When I entered into this world, I completely left the Lord behind. However, while I daydreamed, I always wondered why my fantasy world wasn't even darker. I always thought someone was watching me. Now I know it was the Lord. I grieved him for twenty-two years through my imagination.

I was again tormented by my own thoughts against the Holy Spirit. I didn't get hardly any sleep. I stayed up and prayed for over three hours straight. At the end of my prayer, the Lord's presence came around me. I stopped praying and asked God if he would deliver me tomorrow at the service, and he said no in my spirit. I accepted this; however, I still wanted to go to the healing service, just in case God surprised me.

I was in physical pain; my hands felt a tingling, swelling sensation, while my head, back, and neck had compressed pain. I also asked him a few other questions; his presence was still around me. I was extremely happy because the Lord was speaking to me directly through my spirit. I also asked him if he would send someone to heal me, and he again said no.

I was pondering if I should see a neurologist. At the time I wanted to find the exact cause of my compressions inside of my brain. I knew that it was caused by a supernatural side through the involvement of demons, but I also knew that there might have been a physical side to the whole thing too. I was in agony. However, the Lord sent me a no into my spirit and I knew he didn't want me to see a specialist anytime soon regarding my health. He was just trying to look out for me. Again, the Lord God had his own reasons why he didn't want me to go see one. I knew I needed more antipsychotics. I had asked my local doctor to increase my medication, but my doctor didn't want too increase the amount of medication that I was taking.

I arrived at my father's place shortly before eight o'clock. I was tired due to lack of sleep, and he offered to make me a coffee. I told him I had one earlier. I patiently waited for him to leave for the church service. We drove for about forty minutes to the church hosting the healing service. We went upstairs and took our seats. The service began with singing and praise to our Lord, and then a pastor introduced the guest healing evangelist. He started to call out people's conditions, and they went out to the front for direct prayer. Most of them claimed some type of healing, and I went up and told him I had compression in my neck, head, and back, as well as schizophrenia. He put his hand on my neck, and I felt the compression go away instantly; my hands stopped the tingling sensation also. When he put his hand on my neck, it felt like Jesus had put his hand on me through John Mellor. It was such a warm and pleasant feeling that I felt that day. I still could hear the demons speaking to me, for I was not delivered from them. The Lord did say within my spirit that I wouldn't get delivered that day.

As I walked back to my seat, the physical pain got worse. I wondered if I truly got healed in the first place; as I pondered this, I again felt the Lord heal the pain in these areas completely. The service ended, and I walked silently down to the car, thinking, did I really just get healed?

I arrived home and told Joshua, "God healed me physically from the pain."

His response was, "Whatever makes you feel better."

What an odd response from my husband. I quickly realised that he didn't understand what the healing power of God can do in a person's life. However, the Lord was right. He said I would not be delivered today. I decided to lay down, and for the first time in a long time, I felt at ease.

Shortly after I was healed from the physical pain, the demons began to put pain back inside my body. They didn't make it easy for me. They brought back the torment. In tears, I cried out to God with all my heart to help me. I couldn't go through anymore torment; I had enough. God's presence came into the room. I quickly asked the Lord if he could send an angel to protect me from the demons. The Lord agreed and told me within my spirit that he would. As soon as he agreed, I instantly felt at peace and the torment ceased straight away. He quickly answered my prayer, and I was very relieved that he did.

I was praying to God, when his presence once again entered into the room. I said out loud to the Lord, "I haven't heard from Jesus for a long time."

I continued to ponder; I wondered if I should ask God for a word through one of his prophetess that I knew of since my childhood.

However, he read my mind and gently asked me not to. I didn't know why he didn't want me to ask him this question. However, I obeyed his request and didn't ask the Lord. Somehow, I drifted off to sleep. I found myself within a dream, when suddenly I was awakened by a gentle touch from our Lord Jesus Christ. I saw him in the spirit. I knew it was the Lord Jesus because his presence told me it was him. The Lord Jesus must have heard what I had said earlier to our heavenly Father. It was an incredible experience and an honour to see the Lord Jesus this way. I'm in awe of our Lord.

I finally started to exercise, which I found amazing because I thought I would never recover from the sickness. A lot had to do with the Lord helping me, as well as the antipsychotic medication I was taking. The Lord was giving me some peace and the ability to cope again. I also needed to get fit again. I used to be pretty fit and weighed in around sixty kilograms before having my second child. I wanted to return back to my normal self in that perspective but found it hard to. The demons were still around me. They kept on telling me how much they wanted me to lose weight, even requesting to be my personal trainer or possess me to help me lose the weight. They wanted me to willingly surrender my will to them and let them take over me. I also refused this. I didn't want to be possessed. As I was in the middle of exercising, a demon entered into me. He started to help me perform better. I didn't feel possessed, but I knew it was in me. My performance level increased to a much higher level of fitness. I stopped when I noticed this and rebuked the demon. He sent a sexual temptation through my body and then left.

Chapter 15

THE DEVIL

"You are welcome to come back anytime," an invitation was offered to me. The voice that spoke was smooth and subtle, almost fooling me into thinking that the devil himself had spoken directly to me. It is hard to distinguish when demons portray themselves as the devil. You can easily believe that the devil himself had spoken directly to you. However, this being was telling me that he wanted me to return back to the world of daydreaming. I'll never return to that world willingly; I'll never watch another demonic-inspired film or series or read another novel that isn't Christian. You also have to be careful with some Christian books, for not everyone who claims to be a Christian is truly one.

I want to warn anyone else who is imagining like I did to think twice before doing so. For you are for Satan and doing his will and not God's will. Any maladaptive daydreamers out there, please consider your ways and do what I did and shut down your worlds. You could end up in hell for it. To all parents, watch your children and teenagers; if they are spending countless hours in a stationary state, listening to music, whether Christian or secular music, then they might be in the world of daydreaming. I know it sounds like nothing, but I'm telling you out of my own personal experience, while within this world, Satan will take advantage of your children's imaginations. He did it to me, and he will do it to your children.

I started to write poetry to get my own thoughts off cursing God. I find if I get my mind focussed on something else, it's easier to cope. You see, I have a problem now. I'm constantly afraid that I'm going to blaspheme the Holy Spirit. I'm in fear over it. I keep asking God to help me through the aftermath of the torment. God is my counsellor. He stops me in my tracks from speaking against him. As I was writing this poem, the Lord suddenly gave me a few words to add. The words the Lord gave me are highlighted in bold. I thought I would share this with you:

The wide and the narrow:

Two roads you can take.

Make up your minds

before it's too late.

The wide is the road that leads to hell.

Unwilling to believe,

unwilling to dwell,

to dwell in our Lord

who died on the cross.

Those who believe in him

will never be lost.

Christ Jesus,

our risen King,

is the ruler of all,

in victory through death.

So we are all called

out of darkness into his marvellous light

that we might find the narrow road

and leave this sinful world behind.

I know Christians have mixed views when they talk about the topic of hell. Most Christians believe that hell exists, but a few believe in annihilation, which is not taught in the Bible. I recommend a book called 23 Minutes in Hell. It is written by Bill Wiese. He is a Christian brother who was sent to hell by the Lord to bring back a message to the world: that hell is a real place and that Jesus doesn't want anyone to go there.

A while back, I was reading a Christian book (by Rebecca Brown M.D) regarding a woman who was one of Satan's brides. In this book, I read how Satan's bride was involved with the devil in a sexual way. Instantly, I had perversion enter my body. I had to put the book down and didn't read it for a few weeks. One day, I asked the Lord if he wanted me to continue reading this book, and he told me yes within my spirit. I obeyed and continued reading.

I had to ask the Lord this question because this is what he rebuked me for that day I spoke evil. I know I said I won't repeat what I said to anyone, but I think I need to write it down because it shows you my heart at the time and why the Lord rebuked me so much. Please try to forgive me for saying this. I really didn't want to add this in my book. I said, referring to the devil and his bride, "At least she got to experience this."

God rebuked me as soon as these words came out of my mouth. I did ask him if he was God, and he said yes back to me. I just knew it was the Lord. You can't confuse it when you get rebuked like this from God. However, I also noticed that Satan drew me to say these words. The way he drew me was subtle, and I knew it wasn't just me saying it. I felt possessed for a moment. This was the same feeling I felt when I said I wanted to challenge Satan. However, I was afraid to continue reading this book after getting rebuked by God. For some reason, the Lord wanted me to read the rest of it.

One evening, I happened to be sitting at the computer, when suddenly a tormenting tingling presence surrounded me. The skin on my face tightened. Satan was again portrayed to me. He spoke and said, "I wanted you to be my bride." The evil being continued, "I want you to have sex with me."

This being once again put a rush of sexual pleasure throughout my body. I flatly refused his offer, and he quickly left. This temptation probably had a lot to do with the comment I made. Satan is a tempter and a master at that, but was this being truly him? I still believe this was a demon masking itself as Satan.

I decided to go to sleep and found myself within a dream. I dreamt I was on this dark path when Satan suddenly stood in front of me. I believe this was also a demon masking itself as Satan. He started to talk to me and introduced the topic of sex. I quickly told him that it was boring and I wanted what the Lord was offering me. I continued to tell him, "I didn't want to miss out on eternity with the Lord Jesus."

When I said these words, this incredible, overwhelming feeling of love entered my body. It was the Lord Jesus who was giving me this incredible feeling. I was filled with such peace. After this conversation, Satan disappeared. The scene changed, and I found myself in the arms of a demon high in the air. He threatened to drop me to the ground; out of fear, I quickly told him not to drop me. I woke up out of sleep and instantly heard a demon tell me, "Satan doesn't want his kingdom to end. The Lord's going to put a stop to it."

Just after this demon spoke, the Lord quickly sent me a song. The song was "Take My Hand, Lord Jesus." I drifted back to sleep and instantly fell back into the dream world. The Lord decided to do something to block me from dreaming. He gave me Christian songs throughout the night. They were loud and clear like a recording. The last song he gave me was "I'm So Glad Jesus Set Me Free." When I awoke out of sleep, I was in such a happy mood. Peace and love lingered inside my heart once again.

I was in a state of sleep and started to dream again. I was talking within this dream about something; I can't remember what I said exactly, but I heard the loudest bang in the ceiling. It was the Lord, and he told me no within my spirit. He was grieved with me. He wanted me to wake up from sleep due to the way I was speaking. I arose straight away and left the dream behind.

On a different night, I went to bed around two o'clock and quickly drifted into a dream. I suddenly found myself standing before an evil creature. He appeared in the human form, but he was not pleasant to look at. I also was naked before him. This creature, who called himself the Father, licked my body in a horrific way and placed me on a bed. He silently informed me that his son was going to have sex with me. While in this dream, I felt this supernatural sexual desire rising throughout my body. The demons once again were placing this sexual sensation inside of me. Suddenly, I woke up in a frantic mess.

A demon came to me and masked itself as Satan. He said, "I gave you this dream." He continued, "You referred to the Father." He was referring to our heavenly Father.

I answered back and said, "I did not!"

This demon then said, "The tingling sexual desire will take several minutes to stop."

I could still feel this sexual desire rising inside of me. During the conversation, the Lord gave me a song. I had to apologise to him for being in such an awful dream. I really didn't want to go to sleep anymore. I always ended up conversing with demon within my dreams. This demon left, and another started to speak to me.

He said, "If you continue the dream, then we know you want this."

I was grieved and distressed; I was almost lured away by sex because of the sexual desire that was placed inside my body. I decided to get out of bed and stay awake. In the past, I've had dreams where I've tasted sweet and sour lollies and other types of food from demons within a dream. These tastes would linger on my tongue. I really didn't understand why the enemy did this.

The next day, I decided to call Grandmother May. As I was on the phone to her, she all of a sudden mentioned this prophetess the Lord God Almighty told me not to seek a prophecy from. My grandmother wanted to speak to this prophetess regarding me, to see if the Lord would send her a word. I told her that the Lord didn't want me to ask him for a word through her. I did, however, want to know what was happening with my situation; deep down, I wanted something more solid from the Lord, and she had a good reputation. My grandmother, however, still wanted to ask this woman for a word. I told her don't worry, trying to be obedient to the Lord, since he told me not to ask her.

As I finished up at work, my health suddenly declined. I felt like death again. I walked to the train station from the clinic, carrying myself in this state. I felt like falling down onto the ground. As I was waiting to catch the train home, I felt the illness throughout my body. I knew demons were once again giving me physical pain. My head all of a sudden got compressed with pain, and I once again cried out to the Lord for help. As I stood at the station, waiting for the train to arrive, I started to hum a tune quietly to myself, but then the Lord changed the tune. "Day by day, with each new passing moment," came out of my mouth instead.

The feeling of death subsided, and I felt slightly better, but not completely set free from the physical pain. I ask the Lord, "Please take me home." I just couldn't handle any more pain. I was stuck in the middle of a spiritual battle. I started thinking about my children. Will I die from this? I thought.

I wanted to see my children grow up, but at the same time, I wanted to depart to the Lord. This sickness was truly killing me inside.

I'm not going back to hospital, I thought. I didn't think they could do anything else for my situation. They probably wouldn't be able to detect a thing, anyway. Tired from all the pain, I decide to do the usual evening routine and took a hot relaxing bath. I wanted to see just how bad my situation would progress first.

After I fell asleep that night, I dreamt I was in my old high school. My old English teacher handed me a book. It was supernatural themed and had a demon on the front cover. I got mad and told him I didn't want to read it and stood up for the Lord, when all of a sudden, I heard my phone ringing. It was my husband, waking me up for work. I had just slept in and quickly had a shower and got dressed, trying to make up lost time. I got my children in the car and headed to my in-laws' place to drop them off. I felt incredible. Yesterday, I felt like death. Today, I had fully recovered and was joyful and glad. I started to write a poem on the train:

You died on the cross for sinners like me,

a death as cruel as this.

In agony, you hung on that tree,

ridiculed and mocked by your people.

They put you to shame.

They saw your good deeds.

You healed the sick and the lame.

The ground shook, and the rocks rent.

The veil was torn in two.

Christ Jesus had just died

for sinners just like you.

What did you do wrong, my King?

You're a lamb without spot.

But they cast lots for your cloak and pierced your side

as they cruelly watched you die.

Three days did you lie in a tomb,

but death couldn't hold you.

In victory you rose and conquered the grave,

that by you many would come to be saved.

I was happy at work until I heard this: "I am the devil … devil! Yes, Danica. I am the devil." He kept saying these words as he reinforced me that he was indeed the devil.

I kept telling him, "I don't believe that you are. You're a demon."

He got angry at me; he grabbed my body internally and squeezed me and said again, "I am the devil." He continued to speak to me and told me, "I want to kill you." He again reinforced it and said once again, "Yes, I really am the devil."

He sent a sexual temptation through my body and then told me he wanted me to go to hell. He left me, and my day declined; suddenly, I was again resisting these incoming thoughts. I spent the rest of the day resisting thoughts about Satan (I didn't want to serve him). I was all over the place again and couldn't wait for the day to be over with. I went home and typed up everything, as I cried out to the Lord. He once again settled me. I told him I didn't want to leave him for Satan.

When my daughter Violet was about two years old. A woman named Melissa started working for the chiropractic company that I was working at. I had not returned back to the Lord yet. Melissa was a chiropractor that practised Reiki.

According to Wikipedia: Reiki is a form of alternative medicine called energy healing. Reiki practitioners use a technique called palm healing or hands-on healing through which a "universal energy" is said to be transferred through the palms of the practitioner to the patient in order to encourage emotional or physical healing.

At the time, I wasn't really aware of how demons operated. I decided to take Violet to see her for a treatment. I saw how she waved her hands around and took a tissue and performed some type of ritual over my child. As I was watching this, something clicked inside of my brain. I started to realize that what she was actually doing was witchcraft. I knew instantly that demons and Satan were involved in this practise. Even though I was heavily involved with Satan within the dream world, I was so angry at Melissa and deep down I knew I had made a grave mistake by taking Violet to see her. It was not a normal chiropractic treatment she performed on Violet, but witchcraft. However, Melissa did eventually leave the company and moved to Perth to live there.

Another time, I walked down to the train station as I was heading home from work, when an asian woman walked passed me. I got a glimpse of something strange. I saw how she stretched out her hand and performed some type of meditation practise with her fingers. The Lord allowed me to see that a demon had entered into her and was giving her a sensation of peace through-out her body. She was in a state of bliss, like I had been when I laid on the couch that day. Satan was the one giving her this feeling.

Feeling low on another day, I decide to call Grandmother May. I asked her if she got a word from the Lord from this prophetess. She said, "Yes, she got these chapters from Isaiah: 42, 43, and 44. The Lord spoke to her and gave her these chapters."

I read these chapters, and God talks about how he is God and there is no other. He also said how he has blotted out my sin like a thick cloud and how he was going to start a new thing. It reads not to be afraid, that the Lord was with me, that he wasn't going to cast me aside. These chapters really touched me a lot, and I could hear God's voice speaking through these chapters to me, as if he was directly talking to me. I still didn't understand why he didn't want me to ask the prophetess for a word. However, God heard the desires of my heart and gave me something to comfort me. I was very happy when I received these chapters.

I also received a prophetic dream from the Lord God. In this dream, I heard a voice and saw my brother Paul as a young child. Paul had lego's inside of his hand, as well as a piece of string. The Lord said to me, "Paul I gave bricks to build when he was younger, but he didn't know what to do with them." The Lord referred to myself and said to me, "I want you to teach them how to build bricks." As the Lord spoke those words, he showed me Paul and my sister Sally within the dream. The Lord was trying to make some type of point to me by showing me Paul and Sally. I have my own theories, but this is prophecy and the Lord hasn't given me the complete interpretation of the dream. As he showed me Paul and Sally. I heard a voice that sounded like my grandmother May. The voice said, "Revelations! You need to write it down."

The reason why the Lord had told me this because I once had gotten a word from the Lord God, and I roughly wrote the Lord's words on a piece of scrap paper (not taking much notice of it at the time). At the time I wasn't planning on writing a book. I thought I would remember the words. However, I lost the piece of paper, and due to my memory loss I also lost half of the words that the Lord had spoken to me that day. I was so upset. I now put everything on the Icloud for safe keeping.

Joshua bought us tickets to go to the circus. We got ready to go with our two children. We arrived just before 6 p.m. and took our seats. The music started up, and I got frustrated. I forgot that the circus played secular music. I truly wanted to leave before it started. The secular music really affected me now. I just couldn't handle it at all. The demons started to talk to me, and I started rebuking them. However, they kept on saying, "You can't rebuke us. You're willing to come into Satan's den." They really didn't leave. They continued to speak to me.

The circus started, and I decided to walk out almost halfway through the show. I took a long walk around the grounds and decided to go back inside to get the car keys and my mobile phone and then sit in the car. Joshua became upset, and I ended up staying at the show. As I took my seat, the demons started to talk to me again. I suddenly felt this very powerful presence next to me. It truly felt like Satan was sitting right next to me. He was in an invisible human form, but I could see him. This was a demon and not Satan himself.

He started to talk to me. However, I just kept on resisting him. He stopped speaking to me. The expression across his face said it all. He was extremely annoyed at me. He had this look of silent anger on his face. He told me he was the devil. I kept on proclaiming to him that I wanted to serve my Lord Jesus. I didn't want to serve the devil. After that, he vanished into thin air. Suddenly, I felt this urge inside my mind. The urge was pulling me to worship Satan again. I resisted with all my strength while I was sitting in my seat. I kept on saying, "I serve the living God, and Jesus is my King."

As I was proclaiming these words, I felt God pulling me out of this loop. I was a mess and extremely tired. The circus ended, and we went out for dinner. I was sitting down when a spirit re-entered into me, and the urge returned. I again resisted this supernatural mental anguish. I finally came to a point where I was able to stop myself and just proclaim that Jesus is my King. It was a spiritual battle beyond understanding. I can't explain how a simple floating thought could make you almost insane. This was what they were doing to me.

I arrived home and quickly rushed to my knees. As I was praying, my mouth suddenly opened up. I thought I had gotten a word from God. (It was hard to recognise whether this word was the Lord or not). I stopped my mouth and asked this spirit who he was.

He responded to me and said he was God. I continued to ask him who he was.

He then said, "I am Satan." He talked through me and said, "I am the devil." He continued, "I am going to kill you." I again realised that this wasn't Satan himself, but a demon.

This was a powerful voice which spoke clearly and loudly through me. I kept on interrupting him while he spoke. He informed me that he could speak through anyone he chose. I was drained by all the attacks; I couldn't care anymore. I believe that I have a shield of faith and the Lord on my side. After he spoke through me, the Lord sent me a song. It was "Onward, Christian Soldiers." I could hear this inside my mind like a recording.

My friend Lisa called me one day and said that she was having suicidal thoughts. I told her that she would probably go to hell if she killed herself. I told her to cry out to the Lord and to seek him with prayer and fasting. The Lord had come to my aid many times before. After our conversation, I decided to fast for her. I didn't do a good job though. As soon as I decided to take up a fast, the Lord instantly gave me three songs in a row, almost telling me to do this for her. Lisa called me back, and I told her to ask the church to take up a fast. She replied that the church didn't believe that true born-again Christians could have a demon inside of them.

I told her, "Yes, they can; both of us are going through this."

Eventually, our church fasted for the two of us. They arranged people to fast for us throughout the week.

As I was fasting for my friend, demons started to compress my entire body. They wanted me to stop fasting for her. I decided to push on instead, wrestling with the spirits around me. My body suddenly became heavy, with pressure which went through my head and chest. I felt this presence, and again I heard a voice speaking to me.

He said, "I am the Devil."

I again said, "You're a demon."

He again repeated that he was indeed the devil. He started to communicate to me and said, "I'm going to kill you in an occult ritual. You'll see what I have installed."

Out of nowhere, my thoughts were drawn to praise the devil. God's wrath suddenly fell over me. God quickly stopped me from worshipping Satan. I resisted and quickly proclaimed that I would kneel only to Jesus.

He said, "I want you to stop fasting. I want your friend to die as badly as I want you dead."

However, I refused. This demon was very close to me physically, for his presence was almost touching my body. After he spoke, he suddenly disappeared.

On another night, I was on the surface of sleep when I started to come up with an evil storyline within a dream. As I was inside the dream, two spirits approached me and wanted me to stop the dream. I asked them while still in this dreaming state whether they were from the Lord. They replied back to me and said, "Yes."

This happened a number of times where I thought the Lord stopped me this way by sending a spirit that was working for him. As I went for a shower, one of these spirits started to talk to me; he spoke about my daydream world and said, "Yes, Satan was the one controlling this world." He continued, "It was the first time you took control of your own life, when you repented. You fell away, though. Satan is luring you again in this dream world."

I asked him if the Lord came in the flesh; he said, "Yes, and I'm working for the Lord Jesus," and then they disappeared.

I started asking the Lord to close the doorway to the spirit world. I didn't want this in my life anymore. What did I get involved in? This was how blind I was: I had willingly entered the dream world for almost twenty-two years through my imagination, and now I was dreaming almost every single night and being taunted by demons.

I was again asleep when suddenly; an evil presence grabbed my arm in reality, waking me up. It tried hard to frighten me with fear. It was meant to be Satan himself, but I knew instantly after the attack that this was a demon.

I yelled at him, "I worship Jesus," and then added, "You're weak! Your kingdom has crumbled. Jesus has destroyed it."

I wasn't scared at all. I fought hard against this demon until it let me go and stepped back in a distance.

He began to speak to me and said, "You're not even afraid, are you?"

The Lord tells us in his word that perfect love casts out fear. This was how I felt now. However, I also knew demons can put you through absolute fear. When I was in the mental health facility, I was suddenly woken by a feeling of pure fear. I was lying still on my bed when I felt this feeling surrounding me. It was chilling and went straight through me. I quickly got up and prayed to the Lord on my knees until this feeling fled.

Over time, I noticed that the Lord was delivering me from the unclean spirits. The compressed pain in my head was healed. No more compression, I thought, until yesterday. I was on the computer, typing away, trying to complete the Antichrist study in chapter 16, when I had a demon enter into me again, and my compression returned. I was all upset again. I thought I had fully recovered. I asked the Lord if he could once again take out these demons that were causing this particular pain. I was crying again to the Lord, unable to bear the pain inside my head.

I'm back to square one, I thought. The next morning, when I awoke, my head was clear again. The demons that were causing the compression were cast out. I noticed that demons would leave my body and then return to talk to me on occasion and cause me pain. One time, a powerful demon returned to grieve me. He entered into me and then spoke to me at the same time he was giving me physical pain. He didn't stay long and then left my body. He didn't possess me but just oppressed me with pain.

Satan had just set up a scene within a dream. I was sound asleep during all of this. This reminded me of my dream world; after this,

I knew Satan had controlled me for twenty-two years. The dream went something along these lines: It looks like sunset; the orange and brownish surroundings of an unknown world stood out to me. Blade happened to appear within this dream. She was standing in a fighting pose, having a large sword in her left hand. Her long red hair flowed down her back. She was wearing tight black leather clothes, which covered her entire body, with a military look plastered across her face. As she was in this position, a young man was facing her in battle. As I was viewing this, King Tayten suddenly entered the scene. I wasn't controlling him within this dream. He walked slowly around the two and started to talk to the young man, pointing out to him how Blade was messing around, knowing full well she would win this battle. The young man was unaware that she was an excellent fighter out to destroy him. King Tayten introduced the idea to him.

He spoke to the young man and said, "She is slowly luring you over to her by allowing you to win."

My question was, who is King Tayten, actually? I always thought that I controlled the characters within my dream world. After this dream, it was evident that I wasn't alone inside my dream world. The characters came alive while you dreamed. You literally felt like you were having a conversation with them. Their gestures and movements within this state were so realistic. It felt like you were inside another world. It was extremely addictive; that's why I used to enter into it. It was like a rollercoaster ride: an adrenaline rush of excitement that gave me constant entertainment.

In this dream, King Tayten's personality was controlling, demanding, and firm towards Blade and this young man. He also wanted the young man to know Blade's plans.

King Tayten suddenly turned to this man and said, "If you run, I will throw a knife in your back."

The young man stood there looking at Blade in a confused, fearful state. Blade allowed the young man to cut her with the sword that was in his own hand; she acted like she was innocent and couldn't fight back. Suddenly, King Tayten started to walk away, and the dream ended.

One a separate day, I was lying in bed when a male voice entered my mind. He said, "Why do you hate me so much after I spent twenty-two years with you?" At the time, it sounded like Satan just spoke to me, but I refused to accept this because I had been confronting demons that were portraying to be the devil throughout the year. I didn't answer his question because the Lord blocked our conversation by sending me a Christian song.

My family and I decided to make a day out at the local markets. We arrived and started to walk around the place, looking at what people were selling. The last time I was here, I had a few demons compress my body with pain. I also noticed the fortune tellers around the place; I wanted to talk to one regarding Jesus. Fortune tellers deal with familiar spirits; they get their powers from the devil. It is an abomination if you seek after them. Although I wanted to do this, I got scared to approach them and backed off. I didn't want to make a scene. As I continued walking around the market, the Lord suddenly pulled me over towards a woman I just walked past. She was a fortune teller.

Stunned by what had happened, I quickly blurted out to her, "Come to Jesus because he's coming back soon."

The woman responded to my comment by saying that she was religious. As I spoke to her, my entire body started to become extremely nervous. It was the same type of nerves I felt as a child. I quickly realised that the demons were causing me to shake uncontrollably to keep me from talking to this woman about Jesus. It wasn't my anxiety or fear; I wasn't afraid to speak to her. I stopped talking and walked away from her, and my nerves disappeared.

As I went to sleep, I slipped into another dream state, but this time it was different. I was in a scene looking through my iPad when the images on the device turned to images of Satan. All of a sudden, I had this solid invisible form approach me within this dream. This being felt solid as a rock. I was on my bed when he approached me. I felt his form as he wrestled with me to have sex. I didn't win the fight, and he ended up sleeping with me within the dream. As he slept with me, he manifested into a man (I saw him on top of me but didn't witness anything else, neither did I feel anything sexual take place).

While in this state, this thought came to me: Satan had just possessed a body and was sleeping with me. However, on waking, I knew this wasn't Satan but a demon. I was upset and horrified at what just happened. I said, "Lord, please forgive me; this is not what I wanted." The Lord straight away sent two songs to comfort me. The songs were "Soon and Very Soon We Are Going to See the King" and "Since Jesus Came into My Heart."

I had to take an extra dose of my medication, for my head pain was returning. However, it wasn't the same compressed pain that the demons had given me. This felt more natural. As I took the medication, I instantly received these words from a hymn. A spirit sung these words to me clearly. He sang, "All because you do not carry everything to God in prayer." I had to confess: I didn't pray at all that day, and I hadn't been praying much for months. God was telling me in a way that this was why I needed an extra dose of medication. Ever since the Lord started pulling me out of torment,

I occasionally cried out to him. I speak to him every day and praise him for everything. After receiving those words, I straight away went to my knees and turned to the Lord and asked him to heal me and deliver me from the demons.

One busy morning, I was racing around, trying hard to get my child ready for school, when the Lord God reminded me to take her homework with me. I completely forgot about it. I was still struggling with my bad memory. When I forget, I completely forget things. My body was healing slowly. I was happy again and feeling joyful. However, I was still not delivered from the demons. One night, I was lying on the bed, trying to fall asleep, when I felt this demon try to enter into me, but he was denied access to me. It felt like he bounced right off me.

On a separate day I heard, "This is the first time I spoken to you," a male voice said to me as I was heading off to hang up the washing. "I'm the Lord your God."

I replied to him, "Did the Lord come in the flesh?"

He said, "I am the Lord."

I again asked him, "Did the Lord come in the flesh?"

He repeated to me that he was the Lord.

I again asked him, "Did the Lord come in the flesh?"

He went silent and eventually revealed that he was not the Lord.

I asked him, "Why did you not answer me straight away when I asked you if the Lord came in the flesh?"

The demon replied, "I didn't want to," and left.

One another day, I heard these words, "If you want, I'll get someone to pick you up," a demon said to me. This reminded me of a Christian testimony I once came across of a man who couldn't decide who to follow: Jesus or the devil. A demon spoke to this man and convinced him to serve Satan. He somehow ended up on this bus specifically full of people all wanting to serve the devil. They were all heading down the same road to worship Satan. While on board the bus, the Holy Spirit spoke to this man, strongly telling him to get off the bus. He hesitated at first but eventually got off. He ended up surrendering his life to Jesus.

I've read a lot of Christian testimonies. I want to share an incident with you regarding a Christian woman who claimed that she had communication with the devil. The story happened a few years ago. This woman received a text on her phone, demanding her to do something inappropriate. She thought it was strange because it was coming from the phone of one of her close friends. Her friend was also a Christian, and what she was asking was a random thing (she never did state what was demanded from her). She texted back and asked who it was. She was not convinced that it was her friend.

The text came back: "Satan," and he demanded her to do that particular thing that he asked of her.

She texted him back and said, "No! I believe in Jesus Christ."

The reply came back, "The Bible is a fairy tale, and I hate Jesus Christ."

She replied back and texted "No, the Bible is the Word of God, and Jesus Christ is Lord."

After sending this text, she never received a reply. She asked her friend about this; her friend said that she was at the movies with her phone off. It was in her purse the whole time. Her friend looked at her phone and found that no messages were sent to her friend at that time. This woman's conclusion was that Satan had spoken to her directly through text.

On a separate night, I was deep inside a dream when I found myself in this elaborate castle. I was on the upper level when I approached the balcony and looked down to the ground. I saw hundreds of people dressed in blue linen, with a cape flowing down their backs. I concluded that they were Satanists (I know now after waking that they weren't actually Satanists). A demon entered my dream and told me, "This is your last chance to witness to them about Jesus."

I started to shout out to the crowd of people that Jesus can save you. It really felt like I was actually talking to a real crowd. A lady came behind me (this was a demon), and I turned around and grabbed her arm.

I started to yell at her with intensity. I yelled, "You will never die for Satan. I would die for Jesus!" Straight after proclaiming these words, I came out of the dream.

Another time, I drifted off into a dream and found myself talking to a demon. I ended up saying something that wasn't pleasing to the Lord, so fear gripped me, and I had to apologise to the Lord while in this dreaming state. As I was dreaming, I asked the Lord if he could send me a song to know that I was still saved. Still within the dream, I asked a demon if the Lord came in the flesh. Instead of receiving an answer to my question, I heard a demon yell out to me, "I wanted you for a bride." Straight after these words were spoken, I felt myself slowly drift back into consciousness. As I returned and opened my eyes, I realised that this dream was so deep that the Lord blocked most of it. When I woke up, I instantly received a song from the Lord. He was confirming that I was indeed still saved.

My heart was being drawn towards the devil. I was constantly resisting the desire that they placed inside my heart. I was frustrated and annoyed again. I got on my knees to pray and asked the Lord to teach me to pray. As I started my prayer, the Lord took over and directed me.

I ended up saying, "I pray that I'm found worthy to escape from all the things that come on the Earth and stand before the son of man."

During prayer, the Lord also directed me to say that my heart wasn't quite right and to pray for this. I cried, for these words went straight through me. I knew that Satan had been trying to lure me over to him for almost two years now. I got up and headed out the door to pick up Violet from primary school. I got into the car and put on a CD and started to sing along. The Lord once again took over my voice, and I sang the song in Hebrew. I knew that I hit rock bottom, but the only way to go from there was up. I had faith in God and believed he was truly with me and would help me through this ordeal that had come upon me. As I got out of the car, I started to recall all the major sins that I'd done against God, and it added up. I couldn't believe how many evil things I had done against him. As I went through the list, I asked the Lord to forgive me for each one. I knew he already forgave me for all of my sins, but I still wanted to ask him for forgiveness. I believe that I've closed every doorway and repented, but I still have demons. My dreams weren't getting any better also. Only God can tell if the Lord will truly heal me from schizophrenia.

I want to explain that I don't like Satan. He tried to destroy my marriage, and tried to ruin my life. One time, I sinned greatly against God; still being in the world, I decided to stop this particular sin and proclaimed out loud, "I don't want Satan to take me down a darker road." I stopped that sin and repented from it and never looked back again. Shortly after I stopped this great sin, God decided he would also pull me out of the world itself, as well as the daydreaming world that I was involved in, so I could come to serve him completely. He helped me come back to him with all my heart, mind, soul, and strength. I'm now extremely glad he did, because I truly love the Lord.

There is a spiritual world, and if you believe in the Lord God, then you must believe in his word, which states that devils do exist. Being tormented the way I did left me in absolute pain, to the point where I sometimes wanted to die. When I did call to God in faith, he answered me, and he will answer you if you seek him with all your heart, mind, soul, and strength. I know that this is a controversial book; when I decided to write this book, I didn't know how it would turn out. I just wanted to share what I truly believe is the truth.

God knows that I have written this book, and while I wrote it, he showed me a vision of what he wanted me to take out of it. I tossed on what he showed me, for I knew it was the Lord who gave me this vision. God was with me while I was writing this book, and I truly hope you believe my testimony.

Chapter 16

THE ANTICHRIST

Before I go into this study chapter. I just want to say, when I first started writing down this information, discovering what was truly written within scripture regarding the Antichrist. A supernatural peace fell over me by the Lord. He was telling me inside of my heart that the below information was good enough to allow others to hear it.

The Antichrist! A title that is well known in Christianity, but who exactly is this man, and where will he come from? The Bible is clear that there are many antichrists. These antichrists have come throughout our history and will continue to rise up. From the time of Nero onwards, Christians have suffered greatly under these antichrists. However, the final Antichrist, known as the son of perdition or the man of sin, is what I'll try to address to you in this chapter of my book.

"Little children, it is the last time: and as ye have heard that antichrist shall come, even now are there many antichrists; whereby we know that it is the last time." (1 John 2:18 KJV)

Most people look at Rome, America, and even Israel when they refer to the Antichrist. However, when I started looking into this subject, it was the Middle East that caught my attention.

According to Daniel chapter 8, the Antichrist comes out of one of Alexander the Great's four generals' kingdoms. After the death of Alexander the Great, his four generals, known as the Diadochi (successors), finally divided the empire into four divisions. These four generals were:

- Ptolemy: ruled over Egypt, Peterea, Palestine, and Arabia
- Seleucus (Seleucid Empire): ruled over Babylon, assisting Ptolemy until he was forced out by Antigonus, who ruled over Babylon, Syria, and central Asia
- Lysimachus: ruled over Bythinia and Thrace
- Cassander: ruled over Greece and Macedonia

Let's look at scripture to support this claim.

"Therefore the he goat waxed very great: and when he was strong, the great horn was broken; and for it came up four notable ones toward the four winds of heaven. And out of one of them came forth a little horn, which waxed exceeding great, toward the south, and toward the east, and toward the pleasant land." (Daniel 8:8–9 KJV)

Who is the goat, the great horn, the four notable ones?

- The goat and the great horn is Alexander the Great, who is the first king.

- The four notable ones are the four generals of Alexander the Great.

"And the rough goat is the king of Grecia: and the great horn that is between his eyes is the first king [Alexander the Great]. Now that being broken [Alexander the Great dies], whereas four stood up for it [these are the four generals of Alexander the Great mentioned above] four kingdoms shall stand up out of the nation, but not in his power." (Daniel 8:21KJV)

Out of one of those (ancient lines) four kingdoms of Alexander the Great's four generals, will come the Antichrist, also known as the little horn.

"And out of one of them came forth a little horn, which waxed exceeding great, toward the south, and toward the east, and toward the pleasant land." (Daniel 8:9KJV)

"And in the latter time of their kingdom [the four generals of Alexander the Great], when the transgressors are come to the full, a king of fierce countenance, and understanding dark sentences, shall stand up." (Daniel 8:23KJV)

This king called the little horn is the Antichrist. How do we find out which of these four generals' kingdoms will be the one that the Antichrist comes out of?

The Bible calls the Antichrist "Gog" and says he comes out of the land of Magog:

"Son of man, set thy face against Gog, the land of Magog, the chief prince of Meshech and Tubal, and prophesy against him, And say, Thus saith the Lord GOD; Behold, I am against thee, O Gog, the chief prince of Meshech and Tuba." (Ezekiel 38:2–3KJV)

Most Christians believe that Magog is Russia, but after some research, I found that Meshech, Tubal, and the land of Magog were once located in the northern parts of the Middle East. Iraq, Syria, and Turkey are all located in the north of the Middle East. It seems fit to say that the Antichrist will rise out of the north of the Middle East, which would be the Seleucid Empire.

"Therefore, thou son of man, prophesy against Gog, and say, Thus saith the Lord GOD; Behold, I am against thee, O Gog, the chief prince of Meshech and Tubal: And I will turn thee back, and leave but the sixth part of thee, and will cause thee to come up from the north parts, and will bring thee upon the mountains of Israel." (Ezekiel 38:1–2KJV)

According to the Bible, the Antichrist or Gog will invade Israel with the help of the following countries:

- Persia (Iran)
- Ethiopia
- Libya

The Bible also mentions names like

- Gomer and all his bands
- the house of Togarmah of the north quarters and all his bands

In the war scroll, a man by the name of Kittim of Asshur is mentioned. This Kittim of Asshur is the coming antichrist. He will invade Israel with an army. Jesus will destroy this king along with his armies when he returns to the Earth on the day of the lord.

Keeping with scripture, the land of Magog has to be located in one of Alexander the Great's four generals' kingdoms. Rome is not part of these four kingdoms; neither is Russia.

I really can't say where Gomer and the house of Togarmah are located in today's countries. This is my own theory, but I believe that they are in the Middle East. Some maps show that Gomer, Magog, Meshech, Tubal, and Togarmah are located in Turkey.

Will the Antichrist invade Israel? Yes, he will. Let's look at a few scripture verses to support this:

"And out of one of them came forth a little horn, which waxed exceeding great, toward the south, and toward the east, and toward the pleasant land." (Daniel 8:9KJV)

The pleasant land is Israel's land. As you can see from the above verse.

The Antichrist will take an army to Israel, surround Jerusalem, and take it captive.

"And when ye shall see Jerusalem compassed with armies, then know that the desolation thereof is nigh." (Luke 21:20KJV)

Our Lord Jesus warns us in Matthew 24, Luke 21, and Mark 13 about the end times. Please read these chapters to receive a better understanding of what I'm trying to show you.

When the Antichrist enters into Israel with his army, he does the following things:

- They pollute the temple.
- He stops the daily sacrifices and oblations in the temple.
- They set up the abomination that maketh desolate.

"And arms shall stand on his part, and they shall pollute the sanctuary of strength, and shall take away the daily sacrifice, and they shall place the abomination that maketh desolate." (Daniel 11:31KJV)

"And he shall confirm the covenant with many for one week: and in the midst of the week he shall cause the sacrifice and the oblation to cease, and for the overspreading of abominations he shall make it desolate, even until the consummation, and that determined shall be poured upon the desolate." (Daniel 9:27KJV)

"When ye therefore shall see the abomination of desolation, spoken of by Daniel the prophet, stand in the holy place (whoso readeth, let him understand)." (Matthew 24:15KJV)

The Antichrist will claim to be God and exalt himself above every God. He will sit in the third temple, showing himself that he is God.

"Let no man deceive you by any means: for that day shall not come, except there come a falling away first, and that man of sin be revealed, the son of perdition; Who opposeth and exalteth himself above all that is called God, or that is worshipped; so that he as God sitteth in the temple of God, shewing himself that he is God." (2 Thessalonians 2:3–4KJV)

In the book of Daniel we are given a time period of 1,290 days. The 1,290 days equals approximately 3.5 years.

"And from the time that the daily sacrifice shall be taken away, and the abomination that maketh desolate set up, there shall be a thousand two hundred and ninety days." (Daniel 12:11KJV)

What happens in this 3.5-year time frame after the abomination that maketh desolation is set up? According to the Bible, it is when the Great Tribulation will occur.

"When ye therefore shall see the abomination of desolation, spoken of by Daniel the prophet, stand in the holy place (whoso readeth, let him understand:)

Then let them which be in Judaea flee into the mountains:

Let him which is on the housetop not come down to take any thing out of his house:

Neither let him which is in the field return back to take his clothes.

And woe unto them that are with child, and to them that give suck in those days!

But pray ye that your flight be not in the winter, neither on the sabbath day:

For then shall be great tribulation, such as was not since the beginning of the world to this time, no, nor ever shall be." (Matthew 24:15–21KJV)

"And he [the Antichrist] shall speak great words against the most High, and shall wear out the saints [Christians/Messianic Jews] of the most High [our Father in heaven], and think to change times and laws: and they [saints] shall be given into his [the Antichrist's] hand until a time and times and the dividing of time [3.5 years]." (Daniel 7:25KJV)

The Antichrist will be given power over all nations and nationalities of the world.

"And it was given unto him [the Antichrist] to make war with the saints, and to overcome them: and power was given him over all kindreds, and tongues, and nations." (Revelation 13:7KJV)

Most people believe in a pre-tribulation rapture, but according to God's word, the rapture happens when the Lord returns; this is the day of the Lord. Jesus will come after the Great Tribulation occurs.

Look at these verses:

"Let no man deceive you by any means: for that day shall not come, except there come a falling away first, and that man of sin be revealed, the son of perdition." (2 Thessalonians 2:3KJV)

"Immediately after the tribulation of those days shall the sun be darkened, and the moon shall not give her light, and the stars shall fall from heaven, and the powers of the heavens shall be shaken: And then shall appear the sign of the Son of man in heaven: and then shall all the tribes of the earth mourn, and they shall see the Son of man coming in the clouds of heaven with power and great glory. And he shall send his angels with a great sound of a trumpet, and they shall gather together his elect from the four winds, from one end of heaven to the other." (Matthew 24:29–31KJV)

"But in those days, after that tribulation, the sun shall be darkened, and the moon shall not give her light, And the stars of heaven shall fall, and the powers that are in heaven shall be shaken. And then shall they see the Son of man coming in the clouds with great power and glory. And then shall he send his angels, and shall gather together his elect from the four winds, from the uttermost part of the earth to the uttermost part of heaven." (Mark 13:24–27KJV)

Looking at the Beast of Revelation 17:

"The beast that thou sawest was, and is not; and shall ascend out of the bottomless pit, and go into perdition: and they that dwell on the earth shall wonder, whose names were not written in the book of life from the foundation of the world, when they behold the beast that was, and is not, and yet is." (Revelation 17:8KJV)

Most Christians believe that Satan will enter into the Antichrist just like he did with Judas Iscariot. In the book Ascension of Isaiah - Satan is this lawless king and man.

"Beliar the great ruler, the king of this world, will descend, who hath ruled it since it came into being; yea, he will descent from his firmament in the likeness of a man, a lawless king, the slayer of his mother: who himself (even) this king." Ascensions of Isaiah

"Then entered Satan into Judas surnamed Iscariot, being of the number of the twelve." (Luke 22:3KJV)

"And the beast which I saw was like unto a leopard, and his feet were as the feet of a bear, and his mouth as the mouth of a lion: and the dragon gave him his power, and his seat, and great authority." (Revelation 13:2KJV)

"And they worshipped the dragon which gave power unto the beast: and they worshipped the beast, saying, Who is like unto the beast? who is able to make war with him?" (Revelation 13:4KJV)

Let me explain the Beast to you. I believe there are three parts to the Beast.

The Beast will be and is the:

- Fourth kingdom: This could be the Ottoman Empire that was divided, like in the book of Daniel it mentions a statue showing the different kingdoms that have reign on the Earth.
- Gold was Babylon

- Silver was Medo Persia
- Brass was Grecia
- Iron was the fourth Kingdom, most christians believe that it is Rome. However, It could be the Ottoman Empire because we have the iron and the clay mixed together, which are on the feet and toes of the statue. Each foot on the statue has 5 toes, which equals 10 toes. I believe these 10 toes represent the 10 kings that will rule with the Antichrist. This iron and clay rule is when the Antichrist rules over the whole earth. We also see a stone smashing at the base of the statue were the toes are located, the stone is Jesus Christ and it is smashing the Antichrist's kingdom. This stone grows into a mountain and covers the whole Earth, this is when Jesus returns and rules the whole earth with a rod of iron (the rod of iron represents the wrath of God upon the Earth). He will defeat the Antichrist. Jesus destroys all the kingdoms of the world and establishes his kingdom.

"Thou, O king, sawest, and behold a great image. This great image, whose brightness was excellent, stood before thee; and the form thereof was terrible.

This image's head was of fine gold, his breast and his arms of silver, his belly and his thighs of brass,

His legs of iron, his feet part of iron and part of clay.

Thou sawest till that a stone was cut out without hands, which smote the image upon his feet that were of iron and clay, and brake them to pieces.

Then was the iron, the clay, the brass, the silver, and the gold, broken to pieces together, and became like the chaff of the summer threshingfloors; and the wind carried them away, that no place was found for them: and the stone that smote the image became a great mountain, and filled the whole earth." (Daniel 2:31-35KJV)

The other two parts of the Beast of Revelation are:

- A king : This is the man of lawlessness
- A spiritual being: This is the beast of the bottomless pit, who is Satan himself.

In the books of Daniel and Revelation, the Beast is revealed to us:

"After this I saw in the night visions, and behold a fourth beast, dreadful and terrible, and strong exceedingly; and it had great iron teeth: it devoured and brake in pieces, and stamped the residue with the feet of it: and it was diverse from all the beasts that were before it; and it had ten horns.

I considered the horns, and, behold, there came up among them another little horn, before whom there were three of the first horns plucked up by the roots: and, behold, in this horn were eyes like the eyes of man, and a mouth speaking great things." (Daniel 7:7–8KJV)

"And I stood upon the sand of the sea, and saw a beast rise up out of the sea, having seven heads and ten horns, and upon his horns ten crowns, and upon his heads the name of blasphemy. And the beast which I saw was like unto a leopard, and his feet were as the feet of a bear, and his mouth as the mouth of a lion: and the dragon gave him his power, and his seat, and great authority." (Revelation 13:1–2KJV)

This is the description of the Beast. The Beast is complicated; when you look at the animals that make up the Beast, we have the following:

- Lion
- bear
- Leopard

We find these animals in the book of Daniel chapter 7. These are three of the four kingdoms that have risen in the earth throughout history:

- Lion is Babylon.
- Bear is Medo-Persia.
- Leopard is Grecia.

This fourth Beast is the fourth kingdom on the earth, known as "the dreadful and terrible beast." This Beast (kingdom) is powerful and will have ten kings, which represent the ten horns. These kingdoms once ruled over the Middle East.

"Thus he said, The fourth beast shall be the fourth kingdom upon earth, which shall be diverse from all kingdoms, and shall devour the whole earth, and shall tread it down, and break it in pieces. And the ten horns out of this kingdom are ten kings that shall arise: and another shall rise after them [this would be the Antichrist]; and he shall be diverse from the first, and he shall subdue three kings." (Daniel 7:23-2KJV)

These 10 kings will rule with the Antichrist and will give their kingdoms over to this man.

"The ten horns which you saw are ten kings who have received no kingdom as yet, but they receive authority for one hour as kings with the beast. These are of one mind, and they will give their power and authority to the beast." (Revelation 17:12-13KJV)

"I considered the horns, and, behold, there came up among them another little horn, before whom there were three of the first horns plucked up by the roots: and, behold, in this horn were eyes like the eyes of man, and a mouth speaking great things." (Daniel 7:8KJV)

Like I mentioned earlier, the Beast is also a king, according to the Bible.

"These great beasts, which are four, are four kings, which shall arise out of the earth." (Daniel 7:17KJV)

I believe that the four kings are:

- King Nebuchadnezzar (first kingdom: Babylon)
- Cyrus the Great (second kingdom: Medo-Persia)
- Alexander the Great (third kingdom: Grecia)
- The Antichrist (fourth kingdom: Ottoman Empire after it's is divided – modern day Middle East)

The seven heads that are attached to the Beast of Revelation 13, I believe are the 7 vain glorious nations mentioned in the war scroll, these are part of the army of Belial, which will come against Israel in the future.

The false prophet; who is this? According to the Bible, the false prophet is the one who wrought miracles before the Beast and deceived the people, who took the mark of the Beast and worshipped the image of the Beast.

"And the beast was taken, and with him the false prophet that wrought miracles before him, with which he deceived them that had received the mark of the beast, and them that worshipped his image. These both were cast alive into a lake of fire burning with brimstone." (Revelation 19:20KJV)

If we look at Revelation 13:11–18, we can see another Beast rising out of the earth having two horns like a lamb and speaking like a dragon. This is the false prophet's description. The false prophet exercises all the power of the Beast. We can see that the Beast will have power over all nations of the world. The false prophet makes the entire world worship the Beast; if we remember, the Antichrist claims to be God. The false prophet does miracles and wonders to deceive the people. The false prophet also causes the world to make an image to the Beast. In the book of Ascensions of Isaiah it talks about how Satan will be God on this earth and everyone will worship him except the true believers of Jesus Christ. They will make an image to this beast and set up his image in every city.

"And all that he hath desired he will do in the world (this is talking about the devil in the form of this king): he will do and speak like the Beloved (which is Jesus Christ) and he will say: "I am God and before me there has been none." And all the people in the world will believe in him. And they will sacrifice to him and they will serve him saying: "This is God and beside him there is no other "And they greater number of those who shall have been associated together in order to receive the Beloved, he will turn aside after him. And there will be the power of his miracles in every city and region. And he will set up his image before him in every city." Ascensions of Isaiah

Also, people who don't worship the image of the beast will be killed. The false prophet also causes all people, young or old, to take the mark of the beast on their right hand or forehead; you can't buy or sell unless you have this mark.

This mark: The name of the beast or the number of the name of it is six hundred (600) and sixty (60)-six (6); The Bible states that it's a man's number. This could be the Antichrist's name and number. As we head into the future, our society is becoming cashless. Only the future will tell us what the mark of the Beast will actually be. If it is an insert that is placed under our skins, like an RFID chip, only time can tell. However, be alert and don't take this mark. Let's say this mark does come out, and you live to see it. It will cripple you because you can't go shopping unless you have this mark; you wouldn't be able to eat or travel. Even using your car, you need petrol. It will be devastating to be a Christian at these horrific times. However, we need to stay strong and never deny our Lord, even until the death. The end result is far worse than death itself.

"And he causeth all, both small and great, rich and poor, free and bond, to receive a mark in their right hand, or in their foreheads: And that no man might buy or sell, save he that had the mark, or the name of the beast, or the number of his name. Here is wisdom. Let him that hath understanding count the number of the beast: for it is the number of a man; and his number is Six hundred threescore and six." (Revelation 13:16-18KJV)

The Bible also states that anyone who worships the beast and the image of the beast and receives a mark on the forehead or upon the hand of him will get the wrath of God poured without mixture.

"The same shall drink of the wine of the wrath of God, which is poured out without mixture into the cup of his indignation; and he shall be tormented with fire and brimstone in the presence of the holy angels, and in the presence of the Lamb: And the smoke of their torment ascendeth up forever and ever: and they have no rest day nor night, who worship the beast and his image, and whosoever receiveth the mark of his name." (Revelation 14:10-11KJV)

It's not just the mark of the beast that you need to be concerned with. It's also worshipping the image of the beast and the beast itself and receiving the mark of his name. The Bible is complicated, but this is a warning to all: read the Bible and piece together scripture with what matches.

"For precept must be upon precept, precept upon precept; line upon line, line upon line; here a little, and there a little." (Isaiah 28:10KJV)

What will happen to the Beast, false prophet, and Satan? According to the Bible, Jesus will return to the Earth with his army (his saints). He destroys the armies of the nations that are gathered together to battle him (this is at Armageddon). The false prophet and the Beast are captured and thrown in the lake of fire, and Satan is bound with a chain by an angel and thrown in the bottomless pit (hell) for a thousand years. I believe that this is when the day of the Lord takes place.

"And I saw heaven opened, and behold a white horse; and he that sat upon him was called Faithful and True, and in righteousness he doth judge and make war. His eyes were as a flame of fire, and on his head were many crowns; and he had a name written, that no man knew, but he himself. And he was clothed with a vesture dipped in blood: and his name is called The Word of God. And the armies which were in heaven followed him upon white horses, clothed in fine linen, white and clean. And out of his mouth goeth a sharp sword, that with it he should smite the nations: and he shall rule them with a rod of iron: and he treadeth the winepress of the fierceness and wrath of Almighty God. And he hath on his vesture and on his thigh a name written, KING OF KINGS, AND LORD OF LORDS. And I saw an angel standing in the sun; and he cried with a loud voice, saying to all the fowls that fly in the midst of heaven, Come and gather yourselves together unto the supper of the great God; That ye may eat the flesh of kings, and the flesh of captains, and the flesh of mighty men, and the flesh of horses, and of them that sit on them, and the flesh of all men, both free and bond, both small and great. And I saw the beast, and the kings of the earth, and their armies, gathered together to make war against him that sat on the horse, and against his army. And the beast was taken, and with him the false prophet that wrought miracles before him, with which he deceived them that had received the mark of the beast, and them that worshipped his image. These both were cast alive into a lake of fire burning with brimstone. And the remnant were slain with the sword of him that sat upon the horse, which sword proceeded out of his mouth: and all the fowls were filled with their flesh." (Revelation 19:11-21KJV)

"And I saw an angel come down from heaven, having the key of the bottomless pit and a great chain in his hand. And he laid hold on the dragon, that old serpent, which is the Devil, and Satan, and bound him a thousand years, And cast him into the bottomless pit, and shut him up, and set a seal upon him, that he should deceive the nations no more, till the thousand years should be fulfilled: and after that he must be loosed a little season." (Revelation 20:1-3KJV)

"And I saw thrones, and they sat upon them, and judgment was given unto them: and I saw the souls of them that were beheaded for the witness of Jesus, and for the word of God, and which had not worshipped the beast, neither his image, neither had received his mark upon their foreheads, or in their hands; and they lived and reigned with Christ a thousand years." (Revelation 20:4KJV)

Chapter 17

REVELATION 12

I want to look at Revelation chapter 12 regarding events that have already taken place and those that will take place, according to the Bible. I will also go through each verse from Revelation 12 and try my best to explain them.

"And there appeared a great wonder in heaven; a woman clothed with the sun, and the moon under her feet, and upon her head a crown of twelve stars." (Revelation 12:1KJV)

Who is this woman? According to the Bible, this woman is the nation of Israel. The twelve stars represent the twelve tribes of Israel, and the moon and sun relate to Joseph's dream. This is a picture of Jacob (Israel), Rebekah, and the twelve tribes of Israel.

"And he dreamed yet another dream, and told it his brethren, and said, Behold, I have dreamed a dream more; and, behold, the sun and the moon and the eleven stars made obeisance to me. And he told it to his father, and to his brethren: and his father rebuked him, and said unto him, What is this dream that thou hast dreamed? Shall I and thy mother and thy brethren indeed come to bow down ourselves to thee to the earth?" (Genesis 37:9-10KJV)

"And she being with child cried, travailing in birth, and pained to be delivered." (Revelation 12:2KJV)

This verse tells us that Israel was ready to bring forth her child. The child is the Messiah: Jesus.

"And there appeared another wonder in heaven; and behold a great red dragon, having seven heads and ten horns, and seven crowns upon his heads." (Revelation 12:3KJV)

In this verse, the dragon (who is Satan) appears in heaven. Satan gives the Beast its power, authority, and seat. He holds the seven heads, ten horns, and seven crowns.

"And his tail drew the third part of the stars of heaven, and did cast them to the earth: and the dragon stood before the woman which was ready to be delivered, for to devour her child as soon as it was born." (Revelation 12:4KJV)

Satan drew a third of the angels of heaven, and he cast them to the earth. Satan deceived these angels. Satan wanted to devour the Messiah (who is Jesus), as soon as he was born. If we look at Matthew chapter 2, we see King Herod wanting to kill Jesus by tricking the wise men into sending him word of his whereabouts.

"Then Herod, when he had privily called the wise men, enquired of them diligently what time the star appeared. And he sent them to Bethlehem, and said, Go and search diligently for the young child;

and when ye have found him, bring me word again, that I may come and worship him also." (Matthew 2:7-8KJV)

"And when they were departed, behold, the angel of the Lord appeareth to Joseph in a dream, saying, Arise, and take the young child and his mother, and flee into Egypt, and be thou there until I bring thee word: for Herod will seek the young child to destroy him. When he arose, he took the young child and his mother by night, and departed into Egypt." (Matthew 2:13-14KJV)

"And she brought forth a man child, who was to rule all nations with a rod of iron: and her child was caught up unto God, and to his throne." (Revelation 12:5KJV)

The nation of Israel brought forth the Messiah, who was and is Jesus Christ. However, he was betrayed and crucified on the cross. After three days, God raised him from the dead. Being seen by the apostles and the saints of God, he then ascended up to heaven and is now seated on the right hand of God. Jesus was given all power and authority. However, the Lord Jesus will return to rule with a rod of iron at his second coming, bringing the wrath of God upon humanity.

"And the woman fled into the wilderness, where she hath a place prepared of God, that they should feed her there a thousand two hundred and threescore days." (Revelation 12:6KJV)

The woman, who is Israel, flees into the wilderness for 1,260 days, where God takes care of her. The only other place that the 1,260 days is mentioned in the Bible is when the two witnesses or the two anointed ones start to prophesy for 1,260 days. I believe they are two prophets who stand before the God of all the earth.

"And I will give power unto my two witnesses, and they shall prophesy a thousand two hundred and threescore days, clothed in sackcloth." (Revelation 11:3KJV)

I wonder if the dates are done this way to recognised that Israel will flee into the wilderness for 1260 days. During their prophecy, the two witnesses will cause there to be plagues on the earth and no rain, as well as to turn the water into blood.

"These have power to shut heaven, that it rain not in the days of their prophecy: and have power over waters to turn them to blood, and to smite the earth with all plagues, as often as they will." (Revelation 11:6KJV)

The Beast will make war against the two witnesses. The Beast will kill them at the end of the 1,260-days. This will happen before the Great Tribulation occurs.

"And when they shall have finished their testimony, the beast that ascendeth out of the bottomless pit shall make war against them, and shall overcome them, and kill them." (Revelation 11:7KJV)

"And there was war in heaven: Michael and his angels fought against the dragon; and the dragon fought and his angels, And prevailed not; neither was their place found any more in heaven. And the great dragon was cast out, that old serpent, called the Devil, and Satan, which deceiveth the whole world: he was cast out into the earth, and his angels were cast out with him." (Revelation 12:7-9KJV)

Satan is the dragon, and Michael is one of God's angels. Satan and his angels fight against Michael and his angels. However, Satan doesn't win the war and is cast to the earth, along with his angels. They no longer have a place in heaven.

"And I heard a loud voice saying in heaven, Now is come salvation, and strength, and the kingdom of our God, and the power of his Christ: for the accuser of our brethren is cast down, which accused them before our God day and night." (Revelation 12:10KJV)

Satan is the accuser. This is clearly demonstrated in the book of Job.

"And the LORD said unto Satan, Hast thou considered my servant Job, that there is none like him in the earth, a perfect and an upright man, one that feareth God, and escheweth evil? Then Satan answered the LORD, and said, Doth Job fear God for nought? Hast not thou made an hedge about him, and about his house, and about all that he hath on every side? thou hast blessed the work of his hands, and his substance is increased in the land. But put forth thine hand now, and touch all that he hath, and he will curse thee to thy face." (Job 1:8-11KJV)

In this chapter of Job, we can clearly see that Satan wasn't cast out of heaven yet. Satan has access to enter heaven. He also is able to stand before God and his angels. I believe that the dragon, who is Satan, is cast out of heaven after Jesus had ascended into heaven. I'll try and prove this to you by looking at the rest of Revelation chapter 12 and the book of Daniel.

"Now there was a day when the sons of God came to present themselves before the LORD, and Satan came also among them. And the LORD said unto Satan, Whence comest thou? Then Satan answered the LORD, and said, From going to and fro in the earth, and from walking up and down in it." (Job 1:6-7KJV)

"And they overcame him by the blood of the Lamb, and by the word of their testimony; and they loved not their lives unto the death. Therefore rejoice, ye heavens, and ye that dwell in them. Woe to the inhabiters of the earth and of the sea! for the devil is come down unto you, having great wrath, because he knoweth that he hath but a short time." (Revelation 12:11-12KJV)

They overcame Satan by the blood of Jesus and the word of their testimony, and they loved not their lives to the death. I believe these are the true born-again Christians and Messianic Jews. They are willing to die for Jesus, no matter what happens to them. Satan is now no longer able to access heaven and is cast to the Earth. He has a short time left and has great wrath. What does he do?

"And when the dragon saw that he was cast unto the earth, he persecuted the woman which brought forth the man child. And to the woman were given two wings of a great eagle, that she might fly into the wilderness, into her place, where she is nourished for a time, and times, and half a time, from the face of the serpent. And the serpent cast out of his mouth water as a flood after the woman, that he might cause her to be carried away of the flood. And the earth helped the woman, and the earth opened her mouth, and swallowed up the flood which the dragon cast out of his mouth." (Revelation 12:13-16KJV)

We have Satan now cast to the earth; he brings on the Great Tribulation. Satan firstly tries to persecute the nation of Israel. Those who flee into the wilderness are taken care of for 3.5 years. If we look in the Bible for the phrase "time, and times, and half a time," it leads us to the Great Tribulation time period of 3.5 years or time, times, and half a time. Let's take a look at the verses below:

"And at that time shall Michael stand up, the great prince which standeth for the children of thy people: and there shall be a time of trouble, such as never was since there was a nation even to that same time: and at that time thy people shall be delivered, every one that shall be found written in the book." (Daniel 12:1KJV)

"And I heard the man clothed in linen, which was upon the waters of the river, when he held up his right hand and his left hand unto heaven, and sware by him that liveth for ever that it shall be for a time, times, and an half; and when he shall have accomplished to scatter the power of the holy people, all these things shall be finished. And I heard, but I understood not: then said I, O my Lord, what shall be the end of these things? And he said, Go thy way, Daniel: for the words are closed up and sealed till the time of the end. Many shall be purified, and made white, and tried; but the wicked shall do wickedly: and none of the wicked shall understand; but the wise shall understand. And from the time that the daily sacrifice shall be taken away, and the abomination that maketh desolate set up, there shall be a thousand two hundred and ninety days." (Daniel 12:7-11KJV)

"And he [the Antichrist] shall speak great words against the most High, and shall wear out the saints of the most High, and think to change times and laws: and they shall be given into his hand until a time and times and the dividing of time." (Daniel 7:25KJV)

"And the dragon was wroth with the woman, and went to make war with the remnant of her seed, which keep the commandments of God, and have the testimony of Jesus Christ." (Revelations 12:17KJV)

If we examine the above verse, we see that Satan's anger with Israel is now turned towards the "remnant of her seed." I believe "the remnant of her seed" are either the true born-again Christians or the Messanic Jews: those who kept the testimony of Jesus and the commandments of God.

Chapter 18

THE DIARY ENTRIES OF DANICA KED

Wednesday 12th June 2019

I've been living with schizophrenia for a few years now, and during this time demons have still been communicating to me, either through my mouth or telepathically to my mind. I know no one else can hear them, but these demons are very real. They had given me torment for many years, however, God's peace has finally entered my life through the Holy Spirit, and my health has improved a lot over the last four years. I am still taking the antipsychotic medication. However, I find that it really doesn't stop the demonic voices; but it helps my body to cope better. I think without the antipsychotics, I would've been in a worse physical state then I was currently in right now. My mind however is sound. I've even worked for many years with psychosis and was successful in keeping my position at work. I am still able to cook, clean and keep up with the housework. I believe that the Lord has helped me through these trialing times, giving me the strength to persist on and to work hard, even when I am under such heavy attacks by the demonic spirits.

Today, my friend Lisa called my phone and started to explain to me that she had set up a prayer meeting for us to receive prayer for deliverance by a pastor who had just arrived from Serbia. He was in Australia for our churches annual conference. She had asked me if I wanted to join her. Lisa has been sick as long as I have. She was originally diagnosed with schizophrenia, but now has a diagnosis of schizoaffective disorder, as well as bipolar disorder. She also suffers from arthritis; her joins in her fingers caused her pain. She told me that she had gotten sick after she was baptised. She use to take drugs when she was in her party days, but stopped when she repented and turned back to Jesus. She left her boyfriend who she was living with, with the power of the Holy Spirit and after repenting and being baptised, she was then attacked by the enemy and was diagnosed with several disorders.

I was at home, and was waiting for Lisa to get ready; I was the one that was giving her a lift to church. As I was waiting, I started to communicate to the Lord. I was annoyed and said in a firm voice, "Unless you heal me today, I will not seek after anymore deliverance through prayer meetings, so that I could be delivered from this condition." I have had enough seeking for deliverance and not being fully delivered by the Lord. I was upset at the fact that I had demons for many years now and the Lord hadn't fully delivered me from them yet.

As I got into the car, I drove over to Lisa's place and then went to church. We arrived at the church building at 11:00 a.m. and the Serbian pastor, his son and the pastor's wife were waiting for us. They greeted the both of us as we entered the building. They had a very cheerful and peaceful expression about them. We sat down with the pastor and his son. The pastor turns to us, and we chat for a while. He then speaks to Lisa, asking her to confess her sins openly to them and the Lord. She did, and they prayed over her in the name of Jesus Christ. As she was receiving prayer, I could feel the demons inside of my body as they physically tightened it. I felt lightheaded because of how they reacted to this authority. The Lord was showing me in the supernatural the power that was with these two Christians. Even the demons reacted to the Lord's name. Before Lisa received prayer, they also asked me to confess my own sins and I didn't know where to begin. I sinned alot. I explained that I was born into Christianity, and my parents were both Christians. However, my father was a message believer and he believed in the doctrines of what William Branham taught. I also told him that as a child I developed maladaptive daydreaming disorder.

I continued to tell him that I had been involved in this dream world for 22 years, and my imaginations were evil and perversion had entered me through evil sexual desires that I imagined through the walls of this world. It was a world of entertainment and lust for me, which fuelled my desire for evil. I ended up being like a Satanist, except I didn't want to serve Satan. I wanted to drink blood like a vampire and have violent sexual pleasures with these characters. Within this world I even did sacrifices like in the occult, and saw how Satan took over my world and was heavily involved with me. However, at the time my eyes were not fully opened. I was blind, and really didn't understand that I was involved with the devil. I didn't know what darkness was and truly wasn't aware that I was doing evil things. I thought that I was a good christian girl, that loved the Lord and didn't want to leave Christ as my saviour and God.

I believed in Jesus Christ, but wasn't living the life he wanted me to live. I was deep in wickedness and sin and was a servant of Satan without understanding that I was. The Lord wants us to live a righteous life and repent from our sins and not do them ever again.

In my case it meant never to re-enter the daydream state, even though I had a condition called maladaptive daydreaming disorder. The Lord wanted me never to re-enter it again and to cast it down. It might be difficult to do so because of addiction, but believe me, when you love the Lord and with his help, you can put anything down and walk away from it. No matter how bad the situation is, you have to put it down or you will end up in hell when you die due to these sins. You can't do them again and practice such things after you repent from it. You can't turn back into wickedness and a life unpleasing to the Lord.

I also told him that I was involved with a YouTube channel. Satan had trapped me again on this YouTube channel after I had repented, and I was again entangled with Satan. Again I was blinded by him, and I fell from the truth without knowing that I truly had. After being on Anne's channel, I had gotten demonically attacked and was diagnosed with schizophrenia. Satan was also causing me to enter almost every night into dreams; sometimes it was even a lucid dream I was experiencing. Satan was putting me in that position and I couldn't escape from it. However, God always helps me and I'm able to stand against the forces of darkness with his help.

After I confessed my sins, they both prayed over me. The pastor prayed over me and spoke in tongues; he drew a cross into my forehead with anointing oil. After he prayed, he told me he received a vision from the Lord. The pastor continued and said, "I saw a small bell and in steps it grew larger. This he told me represented a new life, and the lord is going to heal you slowly in stages, and the final healing will not be through a person, but by the Lord himself and you will be a new person and will have a great testimony to give and will need to share it. Your husband and children will be saved too." I was stunned by what he had just said.

We went home after saying goodbye. In the afternoon, as I sat in the car at my daughters' school. I started to look at the clouds. I started to remember when I was in psychosis, Satan was able to make clouds appear in the shape of love hearts. I was even able to take a photo of one once. It really was a real event and not an hallucination. As I was pondering this thought, the clouds in front of my eyes started turning into the shapes of love hearts. I had to turn my head away because each cloud I viewed was turning into a heart shape and I could feel Satan's presence telling me in my spirit that he was the one doing this.

A while back I had this demonic dream. A female demon in the form of a beautiful woman entered my dream. She came near me and was trying to seduce me into having sexual relations with her inside this dream state. During this dream, I was in a very deceived state of mine. When you're in a dream your eyes can be closed, and you're in a very vulnerable state and can be easily deceived by Satan. Without understanding who she was, I came up to her and for some reason, I started to rebuke her in the name of Jesus Christ. Her expression on her face changed into absolute fear and terror. She was afraid of the name of Jesus and immediately she left the dream.

Friday 14th June 2019

Again, I found myself within the walls of the dream world. I didn't realise that this was a dream. It felt so real though. In this dream fear falls over me and I become afraid of the evil spirits; thinking that they were going to kill or attack me. A demon starts to speak. He said, "This is how other people see us." Referring to how easily people become afraid of demons and the fear associated with them. Within this dream, I start demanding the Lord and tell him that Christians have power over demons, and that I wanted to show him the Bible verse of how it states that we have power over scorpions and serpents. After I spoke, Satan twists the scene and another scenario emerges,

I find myself in a very lucid dream. In a deceived state of mind, I find myself kissing a male demon (However, I feel nothing though). This demon is in a human form and I react to him and point out that this is sin. The Lord suddenly wakes me up, I'm upset at myself, and again I apologise to the Lord. Instantly, I hear the lyrics, "I have decided to follow Jesus, no turning back, no turning back."

Around that time, I had watched an ex-satanist testimony of a woman who was meant to be one of Satan's brides, but the Lord had saved her from it and the occult.

After watching this testimony, the evil lure had returned back into my heart. Satan again was tempting me to be lured towards him sexually into worshipping him. Satan is the one planting these desires and can afflict your heart and mind on an emotional level, supernaturally. He can control your feelings and desires. I again resist this feeling, wanting it to stop. As Satan was afflicting my heart, a demon in a male voice said to me, "Satan wanted you for a bride." I don't know what to believe. Are the demons lying? I'm truly not sure. They kept on saying the same thing to me again and again. However, I never desired Satan or wanted anything to do with him because I only wanted Jesus Christ as my saviour. In the reality, I actually wanted to avoid the devil and not go anywhere near him or the occult, including joining the occult. However in the dream world, I didn't avoid the devil because the way I was fantasizing led me into occult themes, and I was involved due to spiritual blindness.

This ex-satanist testimony was revealing though. Satanists have their own version of prophecy. Satan can reveal to these people hidden things which can come true too. It's witchcraft though.

This woman who was to be a bride had said that she was meant to be the 5th bride of the devil. A person in the occult had predicted this bride would fall before she would become one. She claimed that she believes Satan came to her as a beautiful Spanish man, but she could be wrong that it was truly him. On the day she was to be delivered from the demons and become a born again Christian. She met a Christian woman who would pray over her to get her delivered. This ex-satanist woman was possessed and full of demons. Her eyes were black and when she came to the house, she flung open the front door with her powers that she possessed through the involvement of Satanism (demons). This Christian woman prayed over her for 20 minutes until Jesus set her free. This Christian woman had asked this former bride to ask the Lord to fill her with his Holy Spirit because the demons left a void in her after she gotten delivered from them. She felt that half of her body was gone.

Saturday 15th June 2019

I went to a soccer game with Joshua and our two daughters. Violet was playing soccer with her local soccer club and I had spent the morning with them and decided that I wasn't going to church. I wasn't feeling up to driving to church due to my health. When I got home, I was studying the bible and the Lord decided to reveal something important from the book of Revelation to me regarding the seven seals, what will happen when Jesus returns to the Earth and the rapture.

That afternoon I had been lying on my bed resting when the Lord Jesus told me inside of my spirit to go and make a YouTube video on what was revealed to me. I got out of bed and began to write up the information.

This is what I had wrote:

Looking at the first four seals. The seals 1 - 4 from the book of Revelation. What are these seals? The first four Seals are opened and four riders on four horses are revealed; The white, red, black and pale horse.

"And I saw when the Lamb opened one of the seals, and I heard, as it were the noise of thunder, one of the four beasts saying, Come and see. And I saw, and behold a white horse: and he that sat on him had a bow; and a crown was given unto him: and he went forth conquering, and to conquer. And when he had opened the second seal, I heard the second beast say, Come and see. And there went out another horse that was red: and power was given to him that sat thereon to take peace from the earth, and that they should kill one another: and there was given unto him a great sword. And when he had opened the third seal, I heard the third beast say, Come and see. And I beheld, and lo a black horse; and he that sat on him had a pair of balances in his hand. And I heard a voice in the midst of the four beasts say, A measure of wheat for a penny, and three measures of barley for a penny; and see thou hurt not the oil and the wine. And when he had opened the fourth seal, I heard the voice of the fourth beast say, Come and see. And I looked, and behold a pale horse: and his name that sat on him was Death, and Hell followed with him. And power was given unto them over the fourth part of the earth, to kill with sword, and with hunger, and with death, and with the beasts of the earth." (Revelation 6:1-8KJV)

I believe that these riders are four spirits, which are death, famine, war and destruction. These four spirits have been given power over the 1/4 part of the Earth to kill humankind with the disasters and conditions that death, famine, war and destruction bring on the earth and humankind. Power was given to them to kill with sword, hunger, death and with beasts. According to the bible, death is also an enemy of God and Satan had the power of death.

In the Old Testament, we see something similar in the book of Zechariah chapter 6. We see four chariots with the same coloured horses (as in the book of Revelation), which are walking through out the Earth. These are also four spirits. They are called, "The four spirits of the heavens." I don't know if these are the same four spirits depicted in the book of Revelation.

"And I turned, and lifted up mine eyes, and looked, and, behold, there came four chariots out from between two mountains; and the mountains were mountains of brass. In the first chariot were red horses; and in the second chariot black horses; And in the third chariot white horses; and in the fourth chariot grisled and bay horses. Then I answered and said unto the angel that talked with me, What are these, my lord? And the angel answered and said unto me, These are the four spirits of the heavens, which go forth from standing before the Lord of all the earth. The black horses which are therein go forth into the north country; and the white go forth after them; and the grisled go forth toward the south country. And the bay went forth, and sought to go that they might walk to and fro through the earth: and he said, Get you hence, walk to and fro through the earth. So they walked to and fro through the earth. Then cried he upon me, and spake unto me, saying, Behold, these that go toward the north country have quieted my spirit in the north country." (Zechariah 6:1-8KJV)

Now, we are looking at the 5th seal of the book of Revelation:

"And when he had opened the fifth seal, I saw under the altar the souls of them that were slain for the word of God, and for the testimony which they held: And they cried with a loud voice, saying, How long, O Lord, holy and true, dost thou not judge and avenge our blood on them that dwell on the earth? And white robes were given unto every one of them; and it was said unto them, that they should rest yet for a little season, until their fellowservants also and their brethren, that should be killed as they were, should be fulfilled." (Revelation 6:9-11KJV)

This seal represents the last 2,000 year time period of all the martyred Christians. From the time of Jesus Christ walking the earth, up to the time Jesus Christ returns to rule the Earth in his second coming. This is the time that we are in right now, just before the sixth seal takes place. Within this 5th seal, the Antichrist and false prophet will reign; still martyring the Christians. In our modern day, Christians are still being martyred around the world for the Lord Jesus.

Now, we are looking at the 6th seal of the book of Revelation:

"And I beheld when he had opened the sixth seal, and, lo, there was a great earthquake; and the sun became black as sackcloth of hair, and the moon became as blood; And the stars of heaven fell unto the earth, even as a fig tree casteth her untimely figs, when she is shaken of a mighty wind. And the heaven departed as a scroll when it is rolled together; and every mountain and island were moved out of their places. And the kings of the earth, and the great men, and the rich men, and the chief captains, and the mighty men, and every bondman, and every free man, hid themselves in the dens and in the rocks of the mountains; And said to the mountains and rocks, Fall on us, and hide us from the face of him that sitteth on the throne, and from the wrath of the Lamb: For the great day of his wrath is come; and who shall be able to stand?" (Revelation 6:12-17KJV)

This seal represents the second coming of Jesus Christ. In these verses we see when Jesus returns:

- a great earthquake takes place
- the sun turns black
- the moon turns blood red
- the stars fall to the Earth
- the heaven departs as a scroll
- the mountains and Islands are moved out of place.

- everyone runs away from Jesus Christ in terror and in fear before God.

This day is called the Day of the Lord. The old testament talks about this day a lot. The book of Joel and Isaiah give us a lot of detail. This Day is darkness and not light to humankind because of all the evil and immoral human decay caused by sin. Our society is riddled with evil films, people want Harry Potter films, Monster High dolls, vampire toys for young girls to play with, new age, homosexuality, which includes gay marriage. Sexual immorality are just some examples of why Jesus is about to come to the Earth to bring the wrath of God and then set up his kingdom. Evil, immoral decay must be destroyed first for God to be able to set up his kingdom. Sinners are destroy off the earth, just like in the time of Noah. Only 8 people were saved; every other soul died in the waters.

"But of that day and hour knoweth no man, no, not the angels of heaven, but my Father only. But as the days of Noe were, so shall also the coming of the Son of man be. For as in the days that were before the flood they were eating and drinking, marrying and giving in marriage, until the day that Noe entered into the ark, And knew not until the flood came, and took them all away; so shall also the coming of the Son of man be. Then shall two be in the field; the one shall be taken, and the other left." (Matthew 24:36-40KJV)

Just before the seventh seals are opened, we see the 144,000 of all the tribes of Israel. I believe these are the old testament and new testament saints. All of the saints through-out our history, standing with Jesus on Mount Zion, these are the overcomes and are before God's throne. The 144,000 are people who are redeemed from the earth. These are the bride of Christ (his church).They follow Jesus Christ. This is when the rapture takes place and these are the raptured saints of God.

"And Enoch also, the seventh from Adam, prophesied of these, saying, Behold, the Lord cometh with ten thousands of his saints, To execute judgment upon all, and to convince all that are ungodly among them of all their ungodly deeds which they have ungodly committed, and of all their hard speeches which ungodly sinners have spoken against him." (Jude 1:14-15KJV)

Now, we are looking at the seventh seal:

"And when he had opened the seventh seal, there was silence in heaven about the space of half an hour."(Revelation 7:1KJV)

Heaven is silent because God's wrath is just about to be unleashed onto the Earth by the seven angels with seven trumpets. When the trumpets are sounded. They release plagues onto the Earth.

The following are the verses of the seven plagues that will come on the earth due to God's wrath:

"And I saw the seven angels which stood before God; and to them were given seven trumpets

The first angel sounded, and there followed hail and fire mingled with blood, and they were cast upon the earth: and the third part of trees was burnt up, and all green grass was burnt up.

And the second angel sounded, and as it were a great mountain burning with fire was cast into the sea: and the third part of the sea became blood;

And the third part of the creatures which were in the sea, and had life, died; and the third part of the ships were destroyed.

And the third angel sounded, and there fell a great star from heaven, burning as it were a lamp, and it fell upon the third part of the rivers, and upon the fountains of waters;

And the name of the star is called Wormwood: and the third part of the waters became wormwood; and many men died of the waters, because they were made bitter.

And the fourth angel sounded, and the third part of the sun was smitten, and the third part of the moon, and the third part of the stars; so as the third part of them was darkened, and the day shone not for a third part of it, and the night likewise.

And I beheld, and heard an angel flying through the midst of heaven, saying with a loud voice, Woe, woe, woe, to the inhabiters of the earth by reason of the other voices of the trumpet of the three angels, which are yet to sound!

These last three plagues will be the worst ones for humanity. These plagues are when the supernatural beings enter our world to either torment or kill a 1/3 part of humankind."

I want to explain the fifth trumpet/ plague :

An army of locusts come to the earth they are released from the abyss. Their leader is an Angel called Abaddon, Apollyon which means the destroyer; he is the king over the locust army. The locust army is called the locust army because they are vast in number, strength – it's a large army, they have wings and look like men, with lions teeth. I believe they are either the angels that are locked in hell or demonic supernatural beings led by the Angel of the abyss – Abaddon/Apollyon, which an angel from heaven releases to torment humankind for 5 months. It states people want to die, but death flees from them.

"And the fifth angel sounded, and I saw a star fall from heaven unto the earth: and to him was given the key of the bottomless pit.

And he opened the bottomless pit; and there arose a smoke out of the pit, as the smoke of a great furnace; and the sun and the air were darkened by reason of the smoke of the pit.

And there came out of the smoke locusts upon the earth: and unto them was given power, as the scorpions of the earth have power.

And it was commanded them that they should not hurt the grass of the earth, neither any green thing, neither any tree; but only those men which have not the seal of God in their foreheads.

And to them it was given that they should not kill them, but that they should be tormented five months: and their torment was as the torment of a scorpion, when he striketh a man.

And in those days shall men seek death, and shall not find it; and shall desire to die, and death shall flee from them.

And the shapes of the locusts were like unto horses prepared unto battle; and on their heads were as it were crowns like gold, and their faces were as the faces of men.

And they had hair as the hair of women, and their teeth were as the teeth of lions.

And they had breastplates, as it were breastplates of iron; and the sound of their wings was as the sound of chariots of many horses running to battle.

And they had tails like unto scorpions, and there were stings in their tails: and their power was to hurt men five months.

And they had a king over them, which is the angel of the bottomless pit, whose name in the Hebrew tongue is Abaddon, but in the Greek tongue hath his name Apollyon.

One woe is past; and, behold, there come two woes more hereafter.

And the sixth angel sounded, and I heard a voice from the four horns of the golden altar which is before God,

Saying to the sixth angel which had the trumpet, Loose the four angels which are bound in the great river Euphrates.

And the four angels were loosed, which were prepared for an hour, and a day, and a month, and a year, for to slay the third part of men.

And the number of the army of the horsemen were two hundred thousand thousand: and I heard the number of them.

And thus I saw the horses in the vision, and them that sat on them, having breastplates of fire, and of jacinth, and brimstone: and the heads of the horses were as the heads of lions; and out of their mouths issued fire and smoke and brimstone.

By these three was the third part of men killed, by the fire, and by the smoke, and by the brimstone, which issued out of their mouths.

For their power is in their mouth, and in their tails: for their tails were like unto serpents, and had heads, and with them they do hurt

And the rest of the men which were not killed by these plagues yet repented not of the works of their hands, that they should not worship devils, and idols of gold, and silver, and brass, and stone, and of wood: which neither can see, nor hear, nor walk:

Neither repented they of their murders, nor of their sorceries, nor of their fornication, nor of their thefts." (Revelation 9:1-21KJV)

"And the seventh angel sounded; and there were great voices in heaven, saying, The kingdoms of this world are become the kingdoms of our Lord, and of his Christ; and he shall reign for ever and ever." (Revelation 11:15KJV)

Then comes the white throne judgement. Everyone is judged from the books. If your name is not found in the book of life. You are thrown into the lake of fire (this is the second death).

Satan, death and hell are also thrown into the lake of fire to be tormented forever, for all of eternity by God and Jesus Christ.

The Lord God makes a new heaven and new Earth. Jesus rules forever and ever with his saints. All of the saint's through-out our history will walk in white on the streets of gold in New Jerusalem.

As I headed for bed I spoke to the Lord and cried out to him and said, "Why did you save me Lord?" Feeling unworthy to be saved and not knowing why he would still want me after everything I had done. I continued and said, I don't want to follow after Satan willingly. In front of my eyes he shows me the words, 'mercy.' He was saying that he truly had mercy over my life by saving me from Satan.

Sunday 16th June 2019

I decided to take a bath later in the day. A demon came physically close to me as I was taking off my underwear and clothes. This demon acted towards me sexually and tried to physically help me to undress. I resisted again. I decided to write about the weekend events in my diary entries on paper first before I forgot the details. My memory is sometimes bad, and I lose the detail in my memory quickly, so I need to instantly write things down or I can easily forget. It has happened many times. I went to write down something important, but a demon entered inside my body and the thought disappeared. I couldn't recall what I was going to write. I knew it was important. I asked the Lord to remind me what it was. A while later the memory comes back to me and it was about the dream I had the night before. In this dream, I happened to be at my place. I was walking in the hallway when I felt a demon approach me; I was about to be grabbed by this demon. In fury, I attacked this demon using my entire body, and as I pushed myself into this demon. I used the name of Jesus against him. I saw his invisible body manifest into a visible form. I quickly walked away and found myself at my bathroom sink. The demons came and surrounded me; I turn to them and yell out loud at them.

"What do you want?"

I awoken and find myself in the real world. I was stunned at the fact that I attacked a demon and won the fight against it. It was a lucid dream and Satan had put me inside it.

Monday 17th June 2019

Demons spoke to me all day long again. They kept telling me they just wanted me to die. It doesn't affect my mental state though. They hate me because they hate the Lord God. Words might affect other people, but I have the Lord and it really doesn't hurt me any longer. When I first started to write my diary entries the demons seem to be hating what I was writing, and each time I wrote, they would tighten my head causing me a lot of physical pain.

Friday 16th August 2019

During the time I didn't write in my diary entries. I had asked the Lord if he could give me some more work. I didn't expect him to respond instantly, and give me another assignment that day. In my spirit he told me to investigate the UFO phenomenon and post up a video for the public to view. I was surprised by what I came across. Below is the information I investigated:

When I started my investigation, I wanted to see how the devil was involved in this UFO and alien phenomenon. I could see the Lord showing me that Satan was involved. I believe these alleged alien beings are working with Satan and are part of the kingdom of darkness. I want you to continue hearing me and discover why these beings are evil, and what the UFO experts, alien abduction victims or people who have had some sort of alien encounter have claimed about what these beings have said, or what they all have experienced, and why it all points to the devil and the kingdom of darkness.

Roger Morneau spoke in an interview regarding the major deceptions in the last days. He was involved with demons and the occult. He revealed some information about what the occult leaders knew about Satan's future plans and the direction that Satan wanted the world to head towards.

Roger Morneau said these things about the future involvement of alien beings to our planet:

"Demon spirits will declare themselves to be inhabitants of far distant planets of the galaxy that are coming to warn the planet earth of the impending destruction of the planet."

I'm currently reading a book called, 'Communion' by Whitley Strieber. This is about Whitley's true story of his encounters with what he believes were alien beings. While I was investigating his story, I found how much fear these aliens had given him, as well as a vision that they had given him about the future of the earth as being catastrophic. The bible states in the book of Revelation just how much destruction and catastrophic events are really coming to the earth in the not too distant future. The earth will be in ruins, and Jesus Christ is returning with the wrath of God to destroy sinners off the earth in a very destructive way. The aliens want you to believe in a deception, that they told you first, so when you see this occurring. You'll say:

"The aliens told us the earth will go through devastation, and not God through his word, the bible, which was written thousands of years ago, and confirmed to us through his prophets and apostles, which were sent by God."

As I was reading, I started to see demons in his story instead of alien beings. I knew the demons by now through my own personal experience. Demons can bring terror and fear to a person. Christians shouldn't fear demons though. We have power over such beings by using the power and authority in Jesus name. Demons are sinful and hate God, and Jesus Christ. Many times have they told me how much they hate the Lord God. Like in these stories below, aliens are refuting Jesus Christ, the bible or anything to do with Christianity. Even to get Christians or any type of person who believes in Jesus Christ to convert into believing that he doesn't exist. Anyone who denies the Lord coming in the human body is an antichrist and is truly against God, including these alleged alien beings. Some deny the existence of God, other alien beings say God exists, but they also say Jesus was misunderstood on the Earth, like in the below story I'm going to tell you:

This is a real alien encounter story. One of the most elaborate reports of a one off conversation between a human and an alien came from Alicante, Spain on 5th July 1978. Senor Pablo, a respected local businessman, was driving home from a rural district late that evening when he saw what he thought were headlights of an oncoming car over a brow of a hill. He noticed that the beams of lights were of an orange, not the white or yellow to be expected of a car. As he crested the hill, Pablo saw an orange disc shaped object resting by the side of the road. He put his foot down on the accelerator, but the car engine spluttered and then cut out. The car rolled to a halt. To Pablo's relief the object was now out of sight. He got out of the car intending to inspect the engine. He then heard a voice calling his name. Looking around he saw a man emerging from the darkness. The stranger was over 6 feet tall and dressed in a tight one piece outfit that covered him from neck to wrist and ankles. Although he looked basically human, the man had eyes larger than usual and slanted outwards. Pablo was first alarmed, but the man addressed him again by name and opened a telepathic means of communication. Pablo became calmer at this point and later reported that he felt immediately convinced of the benign, friendly nature of the alien. The alien explained that he had come from a planet far away in another solar system. His spaceship, he said, used a method of propulsion that acted outside the concept of space and time using techniques beyond the reach of human science. Pablo then asked why he looked basically human when he came from an entirely different word. Of course was the reply, on our planet we are all human just like you. There are certain anatomical differences, but they are slight. However, what makes us so different from earthlings is not the physical matter but the inequality of our evolutions, mental and then astral and spiritual, the alien told him. The alien went on to explain that humans would one day make a similar astral, spiritual and mental evolution, not for many years yet. Pablo next asked if there were different sorts of aliens. Of course, the visitor said some come to earth in peace, others to observe you, but some are not your friends. He went on to say that there were around 120,000 forms of intelligent life in the galaxy, not all of which have achieved interstellar flight. Venus, Mars and Earth's moon had all once supported life, but not any longer. There was an advanced civilization on Jupiter's moons. There was another on Neptune, but it was of spiritual type that humans wouldn't be able to detect.

Pablo then posed a key question as to why the alien had chosen to appear on a remote country road rather than an important politician in the middle of a city. The alien seemed to find the question amusing. He explained that politicians lacked the spiritual strength to understand the message he had to impart and so the aliens sought out those with astral talent, such as Pablo. Pablo then turned to religious questions. The aliens asserted that there really was a god, but the supreme deity was not quite as humans imagined him to be. The key thing he said was to love God. He added that Jesus Christ was misunderstood during his time on Earth, but again the message of love was paramount.

The alien went on to warn Pablo that humanity was on the edge of catastrophe. Sadly, he didn't elaborate on what form this disaster would take place. Instead he reverted to speaking about his home planet. This place had been he said made uninhabitable by a terrible ice age that had covered the entire planet by glaciers. It was this he said, that had driven the evolution of his ancestors from the mere material to the spiritual so that they could now survival on cosmic energy which they called Abuchal. The alien then gave his name as Naarza Abuc before turning to walk off into the darkness. A few minutes later Pablo saw the orange disc lift into the air and fly off.

These alleged aliens talk a lot about evolution. While God states in the book of Genesis that he created the heavens and the Earth. They are contrary to God scriptures and speak against the creator and Jesus, who through the word of God created everything, whether it be invisible or visible. God created it all.

This next case was an radio interview, which was found on a YouTube channel promoting an author's book. Another case of an alien abduction was involving a Jehovah's Witness pastor and his wife. This was a case of an involuntary abduction of a man and woman taken aboard an alien craft with their car in January 1976.

"They were alone and it was about 11: 45p.m. in Brazil. They stopped for a snack down the road and were aware of the time. They pulled off the side of the road because they were drowsy. A light bloomed on above them, bright beam of bright light and as they were trying to see through the windshield were this light was coming from there was a whoosh, everything was sucked aboard that fast through this beam of light."

"It is interesting," said the interviewer. "Because the beings actually explained to these people where they were from. They were pretty open really."

"Yes, they were. They told them they came from a planet called Klermere; they said it was not too far from our sun, in our part of the galaxy. They showed the two abductees on a hemispherical map on a viewing screen. They showed their sun and our sun relation to it, and other associated suns that had intelligent life on them."

"One of the things that you mentioned yesterday," said the interviewer. "Was the fact that they spoke perfect Portuguese."

"That's right! They had their own language, but when they addressed the couple they spoke perfect Portuguese.

"These beings from this planet" said the interviewer. "They were brown, is that right?"

"Brown skin, yes!"

"And they had interesting eyes," said the interviewer.

"They had green eyes; the iris part of the eye was green. Otherwise, they had black hair and brown skin and green eyes."

"You mentioned in your book," said the interviewer. "That the lady, I believe or maybe both of them. There were two people involved, right?"

"Yes, a man and a woman."

"Someone met them" said the interviewer. "And he was living here on this planet."

"He was an alien man living as a resident on this planet, that they used as a contact. They sent messages through him. He clearly was from the alien society, because when they were all together they looked alike, but wearing Earth's clothes. The man that was abducted by the way was a Jehovah's Witness minister and was a devout religious man when he became aware that they were aboard an alien vehicle. He first tried to exorcize the alien beings by proclaiming the blood of Jesus which has power. The alien sat there and let him go. They didn't disappear, the alien sat there quietly and watch this man and when they didn't disappear with the exorcism. He began preaching to the being to convert him to Christianity. He tried hard to make them understand. The alien just sat there and looked at him. He did this for over half an hour, until his voice started to break. When he reached a quite state, the alien looked at him and said "Are you through!"

And he said, "Of course, I can't even talk." The alien carefully took all the points that he raised; in trying to convert him and explained to him his position on those points. They said, "They didn't have a God, that creation is so much beyond the concept of a God; that we are pagans in the woods with our ideas." They didn't have a bible, they didn't have money. He explained for 15 to 20minutes their position. The minister began to think about his own religion and at one point the alien mentioned that we look at our religion as a religion of love. He said, "That's not really a religion of love. You go to church because you're afraid of the devil, a victim hanging on the cross bleeding, followers are stoned to death." The man finally agreed with the alien and gave up his religion and went on to teaching yoga."

"They discussed religion and theology with them" said the interviewer, "and took the time to discuss each point with them."

"After this the alien turned to the man's wife and said, "Do all these people on Earth believe like this, Ma'am?" She replied, "Not all!" The alien being said, "Thank goodness for that!"""

In the book Prepare for War by author Rebecca Brown MD. There is a section that Rebecca wrote on look for doorways, and she spoke to a woman named Lydia.

Lydia was being attacked by whirling lights and was unable to read her bible due to this demonic presence. Rebecca looked for any doorways in her life to find the cause of this problem. it was a demonic attack, and it was linked to seeing UFO's seven years earlier. This Christian woman was fascinated by hearing about the UFO sightings in her area and wanted to see one for herself. This is her story:

"Lydia a lady in her sixties, came to me saying that she felt she surely had a demonic problem. She had served the Lord all her life, becoming a Christian in early childhood. Reading the Bible and praying was the joy of her life until about seven years prior to our meeting.

She told me that she had increasing difficulty reading the Bible until, within the last year, she had been unable to read it at all. (This is a pretty typical sign of demonic infestation.) I questioned her as to what, precisely; give her difficulty when she tried to read. "Every time I open up my Bible, I start to see whirling circles of light in my peripheral vision. As soon as I try to focus my eyes on the words, those lights come to block my vision so that I cannot see the words. I can read any other book without difficulty. I have repeatedly rebuked the demons causing those lights and commanded them to be bound and to leave me in the name of Jesus, but I have never been successful in getting them to leave. I have prayed and fasted about the problem, but it doesn't get better. It only gets worse.

When someone repeatedly rebukes demons in the name of Jesus without any results, then usually the demons have legal ground somewhere in their lives' so that they do not have to leave. I explained this to Lydia, and we started trying to find that legal ground. Finally, after about an hour of questioning, we were both getting rather frustrated. I stopped and prayed again, asking the Lord to give us wisdom in the matter. As I finished praying, the Holy Spirit directed me to ask Lydia if the lights looked like anything she had seen before.

"Why yes, they look just like that UFO!"

"What UFO?"

Well, about seven years ago, I was living on the East Coast (of America) in an area where there were a number of UFO sightings. I became fascinated with them and kept saying how much I wanted to see one for myself. Then, one night, as I was driving home along the highway I saw a strange light way over in the fields. I didn't think much of it at first, until it started moving closer to the highway. I saw then that it wasn't a plane, or even anything I had ever seen before.

It seemed to float about fifty feet above the ground, was round in shape, and had whirling lights going around and around it.

I realized then it looked just like the description of the UFO's that had been seen in the area. As it came close to the highway I put my foot on the brake to stop the car, I was so fascinated by it. The other cars were all stopping too. Just then the Holy Spirit spoke to me and told me, 'don't stop, you'll be hurt.' But I was too fascinated to really listen to him. I stopped anyway.

Just as I stopped, I realized that I was disobeying the Lord, so I tried to start my car again. As I picked up speed, the UFO moved over the highway in front of me, travelling at the same speed as I was. I pressed on the accelerator, trying to speed up, but the car motor kept cutting off and on, keeping me at an even speed. Then my silly spirit spoke to that thing saying, Just who are you and what are you doing here?

Much to my amazement, the UFO answered me by mental telepathy through my spirit, I suppose. It told me they were visitors from another planet and that they had come here to see how we lived. I had quite a conversation with it. Finally, I asked them if they worshipped and served Jesus on their planet as we did on here on earth. They started to hedge at that point, saying, well, we have a choice who we serve.' But how can you have a choice when Jesus is God, and created the entire universe including you?

At that point, they did not answer me again, and took off up into the sky and suddenly disappeared. I have seen it once since, but when it spoke to me I commanded it to leave in the name of Jesus, and it left immediately.

That was the doorway. I have always supposed that the UFO's were demonic phenomenon, especially in the light of the tremendous emphasis placed on them by the New Age Movement and other pagan religions. This was an interesting confirmation. Also, Lydia didn't realize it at the time, but she was really testing the spirits by asking them about Jesus. They flunked the test!

When the demons communicate to me, they would do it in a telepathic way also. Demons can even speak through a person's mouth, like channeling (which is really physical possession of a demon speaking through a person). There are people that channel what they believe are alien beings; which are giving them information or messages. What they don't know is that Satan is using them in a deceptive way by allowing demons to communicate these messages and give them information to pass them onto other people into believing such lies. I'll give you an example of what one person has said through these communications (he believes they are aliens). I truly believe that they are really speaking to evil spirits, and they can not understand that Satan is destroying them personally. They become servants of the devil and deceive the people.

I also have noticed that in a few abduction cases or encounters, people who are either fascinated by these UFO crafts, wanting to seek them out like Lydia and myself did, ended up seeing these UFO's around them, as well as people interested in the UFO phenomenons.

Below is an interview with an alien channeler. He believes that he is communicating to alien beings through the means of channelling.

"Hi! I'm Jonathan. I'm an extraterrestrials channel."

"Who are the Yahyel?"

"They are an extraterrestrial civilization from our future. They tunnelled through to our timeline to reproduce with us. They are actually distracting semen and eggs from females and males and mixing our genetic material with their genetic material to produce a hybrid race to help prolong their civilization."

"Do you think humans will ever have consensual sex with aliens?"

"Yes, well from what they teach we are going to be a seventh hybrid race and interbreed with all the hybrid civilizations and extraterrestrial, and we are going to be a new species formed. So yes, presumably to achieve that, we are going to be having consensual sex with these extraterrestrial."

"What do aliens make of us humans?"

"They view us as basically completely insane. When they see us worrying about things like death, they find it hilarious, and when they see us running around like chickens just to create money and to keep ourselves alive, they know it's just one big joke because you can't die anyway, even if we did die we can choose to come back from the death state."

Jonathan is deceived by Satan and by the demons that are speaking through his mouth which are portraying to be aliens. I'm against channeling and believe that it is a form of witchcraft. Demons have tried to speak through me, which was against my will, but most of the time they have succeed into doing so because they can physically possess my mouth into speaking through me. I've tried not allowing them to speak through me, but it can be difficult to stop them when you have to constantly fight them not to speak through you. The Lord God always tells me to rebuke them in Jesus name.

Another One of the Devil's agendas through the abduction process is to create hybrids by mixing the genetic makeup of humans with these evil beings claiming to be aliens.

Below are a few testimonies of real people's sexual encounters by these apparent alien beings, resulting in hybrids being created. The one behind the hybrids is Satan; he is the one producing this for his own purpose and agenda. This is a re-occurring story in many abduction cases that I've researched, as well as being told to the alien channeler that they are doing such things by the information that was given to him. Their intent is not for good but purely for an evil and disturbing purpose that Satan is planning.

As the alien channeler was sharing his information that these being had given him. You can see that Satan and the demons mix some truth with a lot of lies. He plants deception and lies by making up alien beings like the Yahyels, and posing as alien beings to fool the masses into believing a lie.

I was thinking about this man and the way he was deceived by the demons, and how he was working directly for Satan without even realizing that he truly was.

When a demon spoke to me and said, "We feed them a little bit of truth and a lot of lies."

The morning news coverage from London interviews a man from New York about his sexual act towards an alien being at 17 years of age. He claims to have lost his virginity to this female alien. This alien is called crescent and is a female. She wore a black hair wig, has large black eyes, a very pale face, body looks quite human, has also long fingernails. They said that these aliens had shown him that he had fathered a large number of alien babies. This man had said that these aliens had shown him these alien hybrid babies. They were kept in these glass cases all stacked on top of each other.

In the 1960's a woman went through a strange and shocking encounter. On her way to high school she was approached by a stranger who seemed to be familiar with her. Once the alien abducted her, she was placed in a medical scenario were the aliens tested her to see if she could get pregnant. Once the procedure was complete she reported being penetrated sexually by one of the aliens before they let her go. She didn't have her period for a full year and experienced a sudden weight loss exactly 9 months after the incident.

Two women also claimed that they had hybrid babies by aliens. They both claimed that the encounters that they had with the aliens were the most fulfilling and intense sex that they both ever had. Both claimed that they had contributed their eggs, resulting in babies of both human and alien genetic make-up being formed. One of the women claimed even though the encounters were amazing, she feels a sense of disappointment that she can't be there to raise her babies. They are always kept on the craft with the alien she mated with. They are not permitted to come onto the earth.

Another abduction testimony I found is an interview of a Christian woman.

"I'm a floral designer. I am separated from my husband. We've been separated for about 5 years. I have two children; a boy and a girl. I have nine grandchildren. One abduction we had, the both of us, the both of us remember this too. I was laying in the bed, my husband and I. I was laying on my right side. All I could see when I opened my eyes was this red light above the window. I could see my husband's shoulder, but I was paralysed. His skin looked like elephant's skin. He had the big head, with the big wrap around eyes. Whenever I went on aboard a ship. The alien got really mad at me because I have had my tubes tied after my daughter was born. He said, "Well it doesn't make any difference because I can do it." Well, I honestly believe the next morning when I woke up I was pregnant. It was about 3 months later I was abducted and they took the child. A little while later, they came again and I was on aboard a ship and one of the aliens brought a child to me. How did that come from me? How! How does that happen?

Sorry...

Once down in Coco. This was after I have just accepted Jesus Christ, they tried to come, I kept saying, "No, no! You're not doing this." I took on the empowerment of Jesus Christ and I stopped that."'"

A UFO researcher had once said, "Most of the researchers in the realm said it wasn't possible to stop an experience. Knowing that, I called some of the leading researchers in the country. So I said, "Guys I've got a very unusual case here. This man, will use the name Bill, during his experience, in fear he calls out Jesus, Jesus, Jesus, or Jesus please help me! By calling out he abruptly stops his abduction experience. These entities can be stopped in the name and authority of Jesus Christ."

Hybrids are not a new concept. In the book of Enoch and in the bible. It talks about how angels from heaven came to the earth and took wives from the daughters of men (which are the human women). As a result they had sex with these women resulting in the birth of the hybrid offspring called the Nephilim.

This is a true story. Genes of human beings will always produce another human being, not hybrids like the Nephilim. Satan is the one who drew these angels to the earth. They became the servants of the dragon, who is the devil. Before this, they were in heaven. They left their own habitation and came to the Earth to take themselves wives from the daughters of men. They are the watchers who sinned against God and are locked in Hell like the bible claims in the book of Jude and 2 Peter.

"And the angels which kept not their first estate, but left their own habitation, he hath reserved in everlasting chains under darkness unto the judgment of the great day." (Jude 1:6KJV)

"For if God spared not the angels that sinned, but cast them down to hell, and delivered them into chains of darkness, to be reserved unto judgment;" (2 Peter 2:4KJV)

"And his tail drew the third part of the stars of heaven, and did cast them to the earth: and the dragon stood before the woman which was ready to be delivered, for to devour her child as soon as it was born." (Revelation 12:4KJV)

This is ancient history and most people don't understand that this actually happened before Noah's flood came to the earth and wiped out almost all of mankind – this is not a fable, but a real event that took place at the beginning of our world's history.

God also can give us dreams and warning messages. I also went through a lucid dreaming state where you can taste, feel and physically touch things within this dream state. I was aware of my dream once and was in a very realistic lucid state that Satan placed me in. I saw a brick wall and started to hit it with my fists. I felt the bricks of the wall as I would've in reality; solid and real. Satan is able to make such places. Most times he opens my eyes into an elaborate scene to try and make me enter this world again.

Below is some information of a Christian woman who had a prophetic dream regarding UFO's, deception and Jesus' return.

I received a dream *April 28th 2008* about deception associated with UFO's.

I dreamed I was looking through a set of sliding doors. Something instantly caught my eye, descending from the sky; it was a saucer shaped UFO. There were other people in the room with me and I pointed and shouted, look a UFO! Everyone got up and ran to see it. The UFO kept descending lower, until it came into plain view. We were absolutely amazed in what we were seeing. Everyone agreed on what we saw. It was definitely a UFO. Next a second one appeared, just as clear and visible as the first one. Only this one had a triangular shape. Later I began to discuss the UFO's with someone who had seen them also. I ended up saying, "Even though we saw them, and there is no doubt what we saw, I do not believe they are real, but there is deception, a trick to make us believe we saw them." The other person agreed with me. Then I said, "Even though I do not believe the UFO's are real, I do believe that Jesus is going to return soon." She agreed with me, we both felt a great joy about this. There seemed to be a connection about the return of Jesus and also a deception about UFO's coming to the Earth at the same time. Next I saw myself standing outdoors; it was dusk dark between daylight and night. I was gazing into the sky. Soon I saw writing appear in the sky above. It was a message from Jesus and his writing was in lights and began to scroll across the sky. The message from Jesus said, "The Lord Jesus Christ will return soon." As I continued to read the lighted message given to me by the Lord Jesus Christ himself. He told me how he would return soon to gather his people. I understood all of the wonderful plans he has for us. I felt extreme joy upon hearing these things, and a great sense of peace. At times I felt total bliss as he spoke to me about our future with him. I understood that the human mind and imagination cannot comprehend what he is going to give us. I knew if I were to think of the very best dreams for myself, they would not compare with his dreams for me. I smiled with complete happiness as I continued to read. I held my hands over my heart with joy and gratitude. My mind could never fathom the incredible promises he made to me at that time. I felt euphoria as he communicated to me deep secrets from his world.

When I woke up from this dream, I could only remember the first sentence that he said, "The Lord Jesus Christ will return soon." I believe the rest of the message was speaking of secret things from heaven and only my spirit is allowed to know them. For the bible says, "The eye has not seen or the ear has not heard the wonderful plans the lord has for us." I feel my spirit has retained this knowledge, because I can still remember the joy and peace I felt when I heard these things. I began to wonder about the meaning of the UFO's Jesus gave me a bible scripture:

In the last days God will send a strong delusion and many people will believe the lie. These are those whose names are not written in the book of life.

Many deceivers are already teaching that aliens are coming to repair our broken world. And that they have our best interest at heart. They believe that aliens are going to save us. Many see aliens are super intelligent beings who are all knowing like God. They believe they intend good for us. A demon can manifest an alien, the same way they can manifest a ghost or a dead loved one. The bible says that in the end days, evil ones will work counterfeit miracles, deceiving if it were possible even the elect.

A psychic has claimed that she has had sex with an alien being while travelling into the spirit world through astral projection while she is asleep. She claims she is not dreaming, but happens when her physical body is asleep and her spiritual body travels. She says her orgasms are out of this world.

I know when the demons came to me they tried to give me an orgasm, and tried to sexually tempt me to have sexual relations with them. As a Christian, I resisted these temptations and feelings. These feeling were overwhelming, unbearable. I love the Lord and refused to sin and join the devil again. This would be a wilful sin because

I know the Lord God, he spoke to me a few times and I have his Holy Spirit. I felt his fire surrounding me and the comfort he gave me through his peace. I know Jesus Christ, he appeared to me during the most tormenting time of my life during the demonic attacks I received by the demons.

God is real, and I knew if I did this act, I will never be allowed to repent again. Some sins are unto death.

Satanists also can even have sexual relations with demons. It becomes a physical act, even if demons are a spirit, they can manifest into a physical form.

In 1969, Uniting States printing office, issued a 400 page publication entitled UFO and related subjects, an annotated bibliography the author was the senior bibliographer for the library of congress. She summaries her finding in the preface of the bibliography. A large part of the available UFO literature is closely linked with mysticism and the metaphysical. It deals with subjects like mental telepathy, automatic writing and invisible entities as well as phenomenon like poltergeist, manifestations and possession. Many of the UFO reports now being published in the popular press recount alleged incidents that are strikingly similar to demonic possession and psychic phenomenon that have long been known to theologians and parapsychologists.

A UFO researcher talks about how the name and authority of Jesus stops alien abduction experiences and a cover-up against the top researchers in the UFO realm.

"In all the research we had done we have never heard of a case where we have heard of anyone stopping an experience. All the top researchers were saying this could not be done. You couldn't stop an abduction experience, they had no record of it. Here I am with a case were a guy calls out the name of Jesus and stops an experience. Was this one case unusual, I knew I had something powerful? When God showed me to look back at this video this was something unique. If I could just confirm that it wasn't just unique in just one case. Then this could be absolutely huge in the UFO community. I contacted these top researchers in the country. I said "guys, I've got a case here and I don't know what to make of it." I shared them the case, each time I did they said, can we go off the record. I said, "Sure," I can't tell you their names but I can tell you what they said, "Yes sir, we've come across cases like these ourselves we've they've been able to stop it using prayer or Jesus's name."

I said, "Excuse me, why haven't we seen this documented. You're telling us otherwise that it can't be done, it can't be stopped." First answer they usually gave us, we didn't know what to make of it. I would have been fine with that, the second answer is what puzzled me and got me kind of angry, because it was that one I want you to hear for sure. They said, "We could not go there because it might have affected our credibility in the realm." Do I hear cover-up? Did I mention government. No! I didn't! What I'm telling you if there is a cover up of this information and has been by the top researchers that you people rely on to hear the truth about. I said to them, "You know guys, I have nothing to lose. I work for a living, I don't write books. I don't do all the stuff that you do. I just want to document this as a researcher." So I went after those cases because I knew that they were there. Over the next 10 years I have worked with over 400 cases of people that have been able to stop the abduction experience in the name and authority of Jesus Christ. This is documented evidence, okay. Documented evidence! I questioned! I had to show biblically this was relating to the bible were the authority comes from." Ephesians 6:12 states:

"For we wrestle not against flesh and blood, but against principalities, against powers, against the rulers of the darkness of this world, against spiritual wickedness in high places."

Below is an excerpt of a Christian interview of a woman who witnessed a demonic encounter with alleged alien beings.

"We're going to be talking about attempted abductions and other evil philosophies. Do you want to tell your story that happened in your home?" "Yes, well it actually started happening about 20 years ago my daughter was about two years old. And I didn't realise it when it first started what was happening, but I woke up one morning in June and my bedroom is situated on the North West corner of my home, and I have a large window to the north, on the north side. And I woke up and I had sunburn on the left half side of my face. Right down the middle, and course I went to work and we tried to figure out if I was allergic to something that has caused it. So, we came up with a lot of realistic possibilities as to how that occurred. It was a couple of weeks later and again I woke up and this time, my entire face and my arms were sunburnt. Looked like a severe burn had occurred. Again, came up with I go in some type of pesticide or herbicide was in the summer. Who knew what could have happened? Well about a month later at the end of August. I put my children down; my son was about 6 months old and my daughter a little over 2 years. I went and laid down, fell asleep, it was probably midnight, maybe one o'clock in the morning, and I wake up due to a feeling of an evil presence, so strong that it just woke me up out of a dead sleep. I couldn't move, and the first thing I did was pray to God, "Give me the strength to move." I called God, I called the angels. I asked him to come immediately and help me. Didn't know what it was, all I knew that it was the most evil presence I ever, ever experienced in my entire life.

At that point I was able to roll out of bed and walk into my daughter's room. And I saw her bed and over it she was almost encased in light like a benevolent spirit or an angel whatever was protecting her, and in the dark surrounding her bed were alien beings of different species. There were tall, reptile things, there were smaller creatures and the one closes me, right down here I reached down and touched it. And they all looked at me instantly and then they were gone. And course, I didn't sleep the rest of the night. I just kept praying to God, and thanking him for saving us from whatever evil was in this house. The next morning I called you, and had a very difficult time realising that this was something I could not protect my family against, in a physical way. This type, it was a realisation that was beyond my physical, you can bar the doors and lock the doors; they're going to get in! The only thing that saved me was my relationship with God and believing in him and asking for him to help; he came. And ever since then, whenever we experience this, we've had shadow people and creature come into the house and the first thing we do is pray to God. You live it and believe it every single day. It is with us, with myself and with my children. And they know, don't be afraid when we see this, if you pray to God it will leave. And they leave. They try, but they don't get in because we believe in God. I believe everyone needs to understand that, so they can protect themselves. It is extremely scary and terrifying when things like these happen to you. And getting a hold of that, I'm a more logical and practical person, I'm not looking for this kind of thing. And if you're like me and things like that happen, knowing God is going to be there to help you and protect you is comfort.

When I wrote the section on how people are really channeling demons and not alien beings. I felt Satan's wrath fall over me. He was extremely angry at me for writing this all down and investigating the UFO phenomenon.

This had happened twice before this incident were I felt Satan's wrath hitting my body with a supernatural feeling of fury and extreme anger.

The first time Satan did this to me was when I was studying the war scroll, from the dead sea scrolls. I read the first paragraph which talked about the Kittim of Asshur. I knew instantly this was the Antichrist himself.

The second time this occurred was when I wanted to go and buy a Menorah. Satan heard my thoughts and his wrath hit my body once again. He hated the idea of putting an Menorah into my home.

Saturday 17th August 2019

It was an ordinary day except for the demons that spoke to me all day long. There seems to be a real depth about them now. I'm seeing them in the most realistic light; so real. All week I've been confronting the demons. I seem to be spending way too much time with them. I've been asking the Lord to take them away. He told me not to listen to them a few years ago. A male demon spoke to me in a nice tone of voice, almost sweet, not in a demonic voice. This demon could fool anyone that an angel had spoken. This spirit said to me, "We show you how weak you become when you have us." He was referring to me being unable to stop listening to them. There is an addiction attached to this experience.

I spent the day with my family until I went to visit my grandmother and uncle. I had made plans with my grandmother to attend the Saturday night church service. I usually go to visit my grandmother's place before taking her and my two daughters to church. I arrived at her place and as usual we talk about the Lord Jesus, God and the demons. I talk about my experiences as well as the dreams I had seen. I decided to ask her about how the Lord had brought her family out of former Yugoslavia before the war took place. She hasn't given me enough detail regarding this event, and I just wanted more information regarding it. Grandmother May told me that my grandfather had seen a light which had appeared in front of him. May said, "He told me about it and I replied to your grandfather and said," "Why is it just you that can only see this light." "As soon as I said these words the Lord showed me the light also, and your grandfather heard words from the Lord about leaving Yugoslavia with his family."

My grandparents came to Australia and this is where I was born and raised. I became an Australian, with an Croatian/Bosnian heritage. This took place before the war broke out in the country, which was the Balkan war that took place in the 1990s. Some of my extended family had to flee from the war and came as refugees to Australia. My grandmother housed some of them in her place until they got themselves established.

I continued to ask her how did see meet my grandfather. I said, "How did you come together to get married?" I didn't know anything about them meeting, and how they had gotten married. She explained that he was a former soldier and was young. He was planning on marrying someone else. He went to the same church as her family did. He was the only one in his family that was attending the church. No one else in his family were Christians and didn't attend. My grandmother said, The Lord intervened and spoke to my grandfather to marry my grandmother instead. The church then inquired to the Lord regarding this prophecy, to see if this was true and from the Lord himself. The Lord revealed it to the church that indeed he had spoken these words and wanted them to marry. The Lord said, "I had ordained them to be married before they were even formed in the womb." My grandfather then asked her father if he could marry her.

I was overwhelmed with love for the Lord. He wanted us to exist, my family line. I was happy hearing this story. I really didn't know that this event had taken place. She had never told me this story before, and she was already in her 80s. I'm a bit sad though. I know my grandmother doesn't like to reveal too many things which the Lord has given my grandparents. My grandfather use to receive a lot of prophecies from the Lord during prayer, and she told me that she had even destroyed many prophecies that my grandfather had written down when he received a word from the Lord. She told me that they mostly had to do with their marriage, and she didn't want anyone to read them. I was so upset. I said, "Why did you do that! I could've got someone to translate them for everyone to see how the Lord speaks and works." I was annoyed by it, but there is nothing I can do now. She destroyed them after my grandfather died.

We ended our conversation and went to church. After church I came back to drop of my grandmother and went inside to have a coffee and some food that she had made. I wanted to go home but she was persistent into buying some chicken nuggets for the kids to eat and to bring it back to her place. I agreed, and I ended back inside her place again. We then spoke about the UFO that she had seen in her life. I again wanted more detail regarding this event. I asked her what exactly had she seen in the UFO craft. May said she saw people of greenish appearance sitting inside the craft, laughing to themselves. I asked what type of eyes they had, but she couldn't give me any more detail regarding these demons. The disc she told me, was like a greyish colour and we were at your place in the backyard and everyone ran to the front of the house and we saw the UFO go towards the park grounds, and it was flying low to the ground. She said, "Your mother, my sister and I witnessed it."

I recall being outside but my memory is just that bad that I truly can't remember if I saw the UFO or not. I was about 7 or 8 years old at the time. This took place in the 1990s. Our old childhood house is opposite a large park ground, and my family claimed that the UFO had flown there. I opened up to my grandmother and spoke how I also saw three UFO's in the space of a few months. My uncle walked inside and we told him about what we were talking about and he also said, "I also saw one recently myself."

It was time to leave, the children were tired and wanting to go home. It was after 9:30 p.m.

I say goodnight and return home. I find my husband waiting for me. He greets me and I put the children to bed. I was so tired that I crashed out. I didn't pray before bed. I kept on saying, "I will get up" but I fell asleep instead.

Sunday 18th August 2019

It was 3:30am. Satan had set up a nightmare for me within the walls of the dream world.

I found myself in a very beautiful and detailed hotel room. It was a five star hotel, with nice settings and expensive furnishings; very high end in appearance. It was too real to be a dream. I could no longer tell that I was not in the real world. I was being haunted by demons with insane whispers, and a feeling of worry fell over me. However, I was not in fear. I paced up and down the room hearing these voices until I was physically grabbed by the demons. A fight broke out between me and them, I fought back hard and hit the demons with my hands and wrestled with them with all my might. God has given me the ability to fight against them. It was a difficult fight. This has happened many times to me before were I've wrestled and fought with demons in the dream world. They really can attack your spirit in a very hard way. I always react and fight back though. This fight is not a small or weak fight but a full on attack on my spirit. I know God is fighting for me, but it fascinates me that I am able to stand against these spirits so well.

I woke up out of sleep and find demons around my bed. They are not amused and are angry at me. The Lord gave me the song, Softly and tenderly jesus is calling. He was telling me that he hasn't forsaken me. I got up and prayed to the Lord for help against the demonic attacks on my life. Don't go to bed without praying. Demons can attack you within the dream state.

Tuesday 20th August 2019

I had been feeling sick due to having a lack of sleep. I find if I don't sleep enough my body reacts badly, and I find myself deteriorating.

I went back to sleep and found myself back within the walls of the dream world. A demon had approached me with a gun, wanting to shoot me. However, this supernatural intervention from the Lord occurred. With his spirit I grabbed the gun out of the demons hands and disarmed the demon and his efforts against me. The Lord gives us power over the enemy. It was a very realistic dream and I know when I wake up that it wasn't just a dream but another attack on my spirit by real demons within the walls of the spirit world. When I awoke after this had happened, I quickly asked the Lord if he could send me a song to confirm if he was the one behind the help that I receive against this demon. He sent one instantly to confirm to me that he did indeed help me fight this demon. The way the Lord fought against this spirit was incredible and fast. The demon didn't stand a chance against such force and power. I found it amazing when I saw what had happened. It was like a soldier had disarmed a demon.

I went over to my in-laws place because they had just returned from their holiday from Europe. They said, "Halloween is coming up."

They were wanting to arrange to give lollies and chocolates to trick or treaters on Halloween.

My mother in law asked me to dress up the children in a costume. I replied back to her that I wouldn't dress them for Halloween because I was a Christian and Halloween goes against what we believe in.

God hates Halloween, and it's associated with the devil. I don't let them join in evil things, or let them watch evil movies like Harry Potter. They said to me, "It's just make believe and it doesn't really matter."

I hate Halloween and when people come to my door I tell them I'm a Christian and that I don't celebrate Halloween. I don't give them candy or chocolate. God really hates it.

My father in-law started to talk about how he should have died on Tuesday 18 January 1977. He was meant to be on the Granville rail train disaster which occurred at Granville, New South Wales. What happened was a crowded commuter train derailed, running into the supports of a road bridge that collapsed onto two of the train's passenger carriages. It remains the worst rail disaster in Australian history and the greatest loss of life in a confined area post war: 84 people died, more than 213 were injured, and 1,300 were affected. According to Wikipedia.

He said that he was meant to be on that train to do an exam which was to take place that day due to his studies. However, he went with a friend and did the exam on an earlier date. His schedule was changed resulting in not being killed or injured in that disaster.

I thought of the connection why God had spared his life. I thought about it and realised that my husband was not born yet. He was born in 1978. I then remembered the Lord Jesus saying to me in prayer that he was going to save my children. I thought maybe Satan didn't want them to exist either, so they won't be saved in the end.

Tuesday 21st August 2019

I had dreamt that I had heard the Lord Jesus tell me that I will never enter heaven. It was that powerful that when I awoke the words of that dream sunk deep inside my heart. I truly believed those words. I thought it was the Lord Jesus giving me a prophetic dream, and it was a very convincing dream. I started to cry with all my heart; I was in deep sorrow over this. I went to the bathtub and sat there in the hot water still crying in pain. When I heard a hymn come to me twice by the Lord. The hymns were, "Standing on the promises of God and we're marching to Zion." I couldn't accept that this was coming from the Lord. I started to doubt that I was even saved, and that a spirit was singing these songs to me, and deceiving me. I had thought maybe the Lord Jesus was truly angry with me about hearing and sometimes responding to the demons. I wanted to stop communicating with them and not hear them again. I thought I had lost my salvation.

A while back I had a dream. The Lord God spoke to me and said,"I have a place for you in my kingdom, but if you continue..."

He was talking about me continuing in my old evil ways. I thought that I must have still continued in my old ways and was now no longer saved.

Heart broken and in heavy sorrow I speak to the Lord and cried out, "I not going to leave you, even if I'm going to Hell. I'm not ever going to leave you again. I will serve you even though I'm going to Hell for all of eternity."

The demons grew angry, they were still upset that I didn't still want to leave God. They said, "We can't move you from the Lord." They wanted me to walk away from Christ in anger and follow Satan.

My entire body was overwhelmed with anger and wanting to hate the Lord for what was said in the dream. I had to pull myself together and resist the feelings of hate and resentment towards the Lord. I cried again to the Lord and said, "You're the judge, and I can't save my soul. If you want to save me, you alone can only do that." I got out of the bathtub and I heard these words, "Come to me." It felt like Jesus Christ was talking to me. He continued to say, "I will not condemn you, go and sin no more."

I went back to sleep, and I felt the Lord God tugging at my body to stop me from thinking evil thoughts against Jesus Christ. I was still fighting against those feelings of resentment.

I awoke in the morning with a heavy heart and started to feel very depressed over what I heard. I couldn't make sense of it. Two thoughts entered my mind about what was occurring. The first one was it was either from Satan to try and make me walk away from the Lord in anger to follow him. The other thought was to see if I could still stand through such trials, to show that I was not going to move from the Lord, even if I thought that I was going to go to Hell itself.

I continued hearing the hymns in the morning, but I still thought it was a spirit tricking me. As I sat on the couch I was still drifting back and forth into the dream state as I was trying to wake up that morning; Satan was giving me these deceitful dreams. I felt the Lord God still tugging at me, trying to wake me out of the dreams that were appearing in front of my eyes.

I took my children to school. I was feeling so tired and sick and I also had a cold, and my head was hurting again. I had taken some more antipsychotics in the morning because of the pain. It made me very drowsy and my head was so tight, I was feeling off and my heart was very low and sorrowful.

I stopped at a local shopping centre on the way home and brought an tuna and avocado sushi from the shop stand. I ate it in my car and then I started to talk to the Lord again. I said to him, "I wanted to thank you for giving me life and even if I went to Hell at least I was able to enjoy one life." Half way through this thought I felt forced heart breaking tears coming over me. The Lord didn't want me to say that, and he wanted me to know that he was upset over the whole situation. He showed me through these forced tears that he loved me still. I cried again and drove home.

I took a bath again; I couldn't cope. I had plans to vacuum the house and to put the washing away, but was so overly depressed that I couldn't move anymore. I drifted off while I laid in the bathtub. As I was trying to fall asleep, I suddenly felt a demon inside my head. It slowly pulled away from my body. I could feel and see it's form almost coming out of my own skin. It spoke through me causing my head to hurt; it was giving me a lot of pain. I rebuked it in Jesus name, and a voice spoke letting me know how angry he was for me not wanting to leave the Lord.

These demons were not leaving me. I continued to lie in the water and felt the power of the Lord giving me peaceful dreams. I got out of the bathtub and my head was still bad due to the demons surrounding my physical brain. I felt the pain and sat again on the couch and fell asleep. Satan gave me a dream. In this dream, I was trying to find a dress to go to a wedding, and for some reason I was on the IPad looking for a Christian song. I tried to find the song, "This is the day that the Lord has made." I awoke and all of a sudden the Lord removed from my heasd that demon that was causing my brain physical pain. I felt it leave.

My head all of a sudden improved, and hymns again flooded my mind. I had to accept that Jesus Christ still loved me and the Lord was with me still. I was in heaviness, but it was starting to lift off my mind and heart, and God started to heal the wounds that were caused this morning by the dream.

I had to believe God was still saving me, and I was saved by the blood of the lamb.

A demon spoke to me after I finished writing my diary entry for the day. He said, "The dream was harsh for a reason; you're not evil. You're meant to be saved."

Thursday 22nd August 2019

I awoke today feeling better. Last night I was in the bathroom, and I heard a spirit singing a beautiful Christian hymn. It gave me a feeling of peace. I wasn't sure if this spirit was from the Lord though.

This morning as I was in the bathroom, I heard these words and I knew it was coming from the Lord Jesus. I heard, "Thy strength indeed is small, child of weakness, watch and pray, find in me thine all in all."

I was still feeling low, I had a chesty cold on top of it all. I was unable to work much around the house this week, and left all my house work, except the washing, dishes and dinners for our family. I even made the bed this morning, but was hoping to vacuum tomorrow. I was very weak in the body.

I again tried to stop the demons from speaking all day long, thinking that they might be the cause of me ending in Hell at the end of my life. I was worried about this issue. However, the Lord was showing me otherwise, and giving me peaceful melodies inside my mind.

When I started to sing a hymn, I felt the power of God with me through the song. I felt my voice changing to a more beautiful tone.

I did my usual routine. I took the children to school, and then I went for a walk with Lisa; I walk twice a week with her. She lives about 5 minutes from my place, and we get together and talk about the Lord and mental health issues. I kept trying to explain to her that I have demons and that the devil is constantly against me 24 hours/7days a week. It's hard to live a normal life, it feels like you have this other world and understanding due to the experiences I've had with the devil, demons and God. It's not always a bad thing. At least my Christian understanding of evil demonic forces are much sharper, and I understand what true spiritual warfare is now. It's been a massive battle and I am truly tired and exhausted of it now.

After our walk, I went home and went and made some homemade ravioli with fresh tomato sauce. I went to pay the bills, grocery shopping then went home. After I came home, I was sleepy and tired and unable to move due to more head pains. I decide to take a hot bath, and I fell asleep. I wake up just before the alarm went off; it was 1:28pm. I had to get ready to go and pick up the children from school. I felt refreshed and had less pain inside my head and body. I was still mixed up inside. I was hurt from yesterday, I had cried the entire day and was very depressed by the dream. I can see God was with me and there was nothing to be afraid, but it felt like Jesus didn't love me anymore, and had rejected me. I felt lost for a moment and hate feeling like this towards him.

I was upset and spoke to the Lord about removing the rest of the demons.

I said, "Please Lord. Please deliver me from the demons. I want to spend time with you, and not constantly interact with these beings."

I tried to resist hearing them, but I noticed if you really want them to go away they do. I tell them to leave and as a Christian, I ask them to leave with the authority of Jesus Christ. On some occasions they won't, but they mostly will though. However, they return quickly and start speaking again to me. It's exhausting for me to rebuke them all day long. They are with me 24 hours/7 days a week. I feel like I can't do God's will and praise him well. I find demons want your time, taking you from the time you should be spending with the Lord.

After I spoke, I felt a tug in my arm and spirits leaving my body. My head instantly cleared up and the pain was almost gone. I just needed to take a paracetamol tablet now to reduce my headache.

I haven't done a fast for many years because of my sickness. The Lord told me years ago to do a three day fast. I wanted to finally attempt this fast again. I have failed the Lord many times trying to achieve this fast. I wasn't able to resist the temptations of food, but today I was feeling low and was hurting and my appetite was gone. I wanted the pain to go from my heart. I felt like this was the right time to try again. I started my fast today at 6:30p.m. and was planning to end it on Sunday evening, or Monday morning. Depending on how I felt.

As I started my fast, the demons inside my body started to react. They were agitated and angry, becoming physically upset at me.

I went and sat on the couch. I was listening to a Christian song on my phone when a demon emerged from my body. A voice spoke, and I felt an evil presence of a very powerful demon standing next to me. He claimed at first to be Satan, and kept on saying, "I'm going to kill you." I felt the tension and atmosphere change inside the house. My husband got affected by the demons and started to get extremely upset about something really small. This demon had caused the entire house to fall into chaos. Joshua wasn't being reasonable towards me. I know the demons were afflicting his mind. I had just sat down and it wasn't even half an hour into my fast, but I had set my heart into achieving this fast, and Satan felt this, so did the demons. Instead of being extremely angry towards him. I remembered Jesus' words to bless those who curse you. I asked the Lord to bless him instead.

During the chaos, and in anger Joshua starts blaspheming the Lord. He only calmed down after I had rebuked the demons, which had caused this disruption in our lives, things slowly went back to normal.

I decided to go to bed. I prayed, but the demons kept on interrupting my prayers. They constantly said that they can't leave me yet, and they were going to kill me. I don't believe they can unless God allows this to happen. I am protected by the Lord. They spoke a lot and once again were annoyed at me.

I fall asleep and once again I had a full on demonic nightmare by Satan. He was putting me through scenarios, and twisting my world through many different stories. I could feel myself personally fighting against him. The forces of darkness were heavily against me that morning. I awoke and I remembered I was still fasting. A demon told me, "Don't forget that you are still fasting." I got up and prayed. After I prayed the Lord sent me the song I want to see Jesus.

It was 4:30a.m. and I decided to go back to sleep. I had to soon get my children to school, and I wanted more rest. I find that if I don't sleep enough my body becomes painful, and I decline in my health.

As I was trying to fall asleep, I realised that during the dream Satan was making me eat a variety of different meals.

A demon told me, "Satan was trying to feed you within the dream." I was wondering why, and the same demon spoke again and said, "We can't tell you."

It probably had to do with the fact that I was fasting for the Lord.

It was book week again. I got to the school gates with my two daughters and I saw two teachers who came dressed up from Harry Potter, standing and greeting the parents and students at the front gate of the school.

I had enough; I couldn't just greet them and walk away. I had to tell them the truth. I would find a better school for my two daughters, but the other Christian school is a thousand dollars more and has the same morals as this school does. I can't put them in a public school because my husband doesn't like the public education in our area. He would rather them be attending the Catholic school down the road. I wanted to put them in a Christian school due to the Catholic doctrines. An example is that the Catholic's teach that Mary is the Queen of Heaven. God is king of kings and Lord of Lords. Only he reigns in Heaven. Mary doesn't reign with God. I have nothing against Mary from the Bible. She was chosen by God to bear our saviour. She is blessed and was a good and faithful woman. However, the Catholic Church worships Mary, and I only worship the Lord. He alone is worthy.

I walked up to one of the two teachers and asked her why does this Christian school allow people to dress up as Harry Potter characters? God sees this as an abomination. He hates it because it is evil and part of the kingdom of darkness.

I was concerned with my two daughters being entangled with evil, and thought that they might end up reading some of the Harry Potter books at this school.

She replied back to me and said, "Why do you think God hates it. It's just make believe! There is a line between what is real and what is not real. Harry Potter is just make believe."

I told her as a response that God wants us to avoid this type of evil. It is associated with the devil and supports the ideas of the occult. God hates witchcraft!

She continued to say back to me, "It's not really witchcraft, and I studied the occult at the university and it is not anything like the real occult."

I replied,"It's still part of the devil's kingdom, and can lead Christians into such things and God wants us to hate all evil."

I told her my background and how my family knew the Lord. I said that I come back from a long line of believers who have personally heard the voice of God, and have his Holy Spirit. I said, I've even heard from God myself.

She asked me, "Do you think you are better than a new Christian who has just come to the Lord Jesus because of your family history."

I said, "No, but we understand more than a new born again Christian due to our long family history with knowing God personally, and receiving instruction from him through prophecy and experience." I continued to tell her, "Once at this school a Christian student performed a song from the musical called Wicked, and the Lord instructed me to leave the room due to the song being associated with evil."

She said, "why is this bad? It's just a title of a musical."

I said back to her, "It has witches and wizards, and God doesn't want his people watching such things."

"What's your view on The Chronicles of Narnia?" She asked me.

"This man who wrote this book is a Christian and he wrote it to help people's imagination into understanding the Bible, and I've seen this book help people come to Christ."

I replied to her that The Chronicles of Narnia: the lion, the witch and the wardrobe is a deception that the devil has planted into the lives' of many Christians. People that believe that the Lord likes us watching these movies and reading these books, don't know him well enough."

We decided to end our conversation. I turned away into utter disappointment at the state of the apostate Christians who think they really know the Lord.

As a child, my dad showed me that The Chronicles of Narnia had a link to Jesus Christ. But when God opened my eyes, I had a shock to what I saw. I saw these books dripping in evil, and Satan was the one blinding the Christians into believing God approves of such evil things.

Remember, the fear of the Lord is to hate all evil!

Even with some of the spirits leaving my body yesterday, my health was still bad. I can see them leaving and entering my body as they pleased. My head was compressed again due to the demons. They really can oppress your body through sickness.

My husband had cooled down, and came next to me with a very repenting heart towards what he did yesterday. I forgave him, but was still deeply hurting. I was in constant agony over the persecution I was receiving by my husband due to returning to the Lord.

One night the Lord gave me a vision to buy a Menorah. I went online and brought one. I did tell my husband I was getting one, and at the time he was fine with me buying it. However, I put it up on display in my bedroom and ever since then, each time we had a fight, he has told me that he'll throw it in the bin.

At this stage of my diary entries you might be saying, "You're still being deluded due to writing about Satan or demons. You might be saying they aren't real, but a fairy-tale." If you don't believe my words at least believe in Jesus' words about demons and Satan existing. Jesus also had spoken to the demons, and the devil during his ministry on this Earth. He showed us that demons do exist. If you look on YouTube. You'll find video evidence of demonic possessions and attacks. Demons have been caught on video. There are videos of cars being smashed by a supernatural force. The car is driving along the road and suddenly, it gets smashed by an invisible force. This force is most likely a demon.

There are many testimonies out on the internet of people who have claimed to have had some sort of demonic attack happen in their lives. This is a very real event and not an Hallucination. I have felt the powers of darkness against my life and it's brutal.

The demons spoke to me all day long again, and a heavy oppression was over my body. I finally gave up my fast. I nearly did a whole day for the Lord, but it wasn't enough in my eyes. I said to the Lord before breaking my fast that I couldn't continue anymore. I was so tired due to not having any coffee.

I usually take at least three cups of coffee everyday to keep myself awake, due to the drowsiness caused by the side effects of the antipsychotic drugs. I could hardly keep my eyes open. As soon as I ended my fast. My father in heaven gave me the song down at the cross where my saviour died. He also gave me these lyrics, "If I live a holy life, shun the wrong and do the right, I know the Lord will make a way for me."

I watched a Christian testimony of a man who received a prophetic message from Jesus Christ. He said, "Jesus is coming back soon to take his people." He also said that he will only take the church that is holy and ready, a righteous people that are not in sin. He made a list of things that God revealed that he hated his people doing. He mentioned movies, television programmes, toys like Disney and Barbie. Make up, jewellery like bracelets, pants on woman, gossiping, secular music, extensions of eyelashes, hair and nail polish etc.

I was still convicted by the Holy Spirit through this preacher, and cried to the Lord to give me another chance to give up more things for him, and to be led by the Lord more. I also asked him to remove the demons, for I have had enough of them controlling my body through sickness, and trying to tempt me into following Satan. I wanted the Lord to give us power over the enemy, and it had been too long that I had suffered with these beings. As I spoke these words the demons started to release my head and my health returned. I wasn't set free fully, but the Lord intervened and helped my health return. The pain got better, and I felt whole again. I received the song, O Lamb of God. I started to not hear much from the demons after I had rebuked them heavily, in the authority and power of Jesus Christ. They were quiet, and I felt good once again. I started to hear hymns from the Lord instead of demonic voices from demons and went to bed.

When the Lord Jesus touch my body, the time that I had seen him. I forgot to write that I didn't see his face, I just saw his body and garments. His presence told me at the time that it was Jesus Christ.

In the book: Ascensions of Isaiah. I read this passage and found that it was coming to pass. It was about Jesus, and how Christians will become apostate just before the eve of Jesus' return; which is now happening to the Christian churches. Below is an excerpt of is written:

For Beliar was in great wrath against Isaiah by reason of the vision, and because of the exposure wherewith he had exposed Samael, and because through him the going forth of the Beloved from the seventh heaven had been made known, and His transformation and His descent and the likeness into which He should be transformed (that is) the likeness of man, and the persecution wherewith he should be persecuted, and the torturers wherewith the children of Israel should torture Him, and the coming of His twelve disciples, and the teaching, and that He should before the Sabbath be crucified upon the tree, and should be crucified together with wicked men, and that He should be buried in the sepulchre,

And the twelve who were with Him should be offended because of Him: and the watch of those who watched the sepulchre:

And the descent of the angel of the Christian Church, which is in the heavens, whom He will summon in the last days.

And that (Gabriel) the angel of the Holy Spirit, and Michael, the chief of the holy angels, on the third day will open the sepulchre:

And the Beloved sitting on their shoulders will come forth and send out His twelve disciples;

And they will teach all the nations and every tongue of the resurrection of the Beloved, and those who believe in His cross will be saved, and in His ascension into the seventh heaven whence He came:

And that many who believe in Him will speak through the Holy Spirit:

And many signs and wonders will be wrought in those days.

And afterwards, on the eve of His approach, His disciples will forsake the teachings of the Twelve Apostles, and their faith, and their love and their purity.

And there will be much contention on the eve of [His advent and] His approach.

And in those days many will love office, though devoid of wisdom.

And there will be many lawless elders, and shepherds dealing wrongly by their own sheep, and they will ravage (them) owing to their not having holy shepherds.

And many will change the honour of the garments of the saints for the garments of the covetous, and there will be much respect of persons in those days and lovers of the honour of this world.

And there will be much slander and vainglory at the approach of the Lord, and the Holy Spirit will withdraw from many.

And there will not be in those days many prophets, nor those who speak trustworthy words, save one here and there in divers places,

On account of the spirit of error and fornication and of vainglory, and of covetousness, which shall be in those, who will be called servants of that One and in those who will receive that One.

And there will be great hatred in the shepherds and elders towards each other.

For there will be great jealousy in the last days; for every one will say what is pleasing in his own eyes.

And they will make of none effect the prophecy of the prophets which were before me, and these my visions also will they make of none effect, in order to speak after the impulse of their own hearts.

Saturday 24th August 2019

I awoke from a horrible dream. Satan was taking me through scenarios again. In this dream I was looking up a Facebook contact who happened to be my sister. Her profile was no longer available, and I couldn't find her anymore. A thought entered my mind, my sister has died. I get extremely upset at the situation. Satan continues to show me that Jesus was going to take my sister home as well as myself before things turn bad in this world. I awoke from the dream and I open my eyes and instantly the Lord Jesus was around me. He gave me the lyrics from the song, "O lamb of God I come." After the Lord gave me this song. I was still lying in my bed when Satan gives me a slight vision of the numbers 666. Satan was telling me that I and my sister will die before he comes to rule this world. This was the message he was trying to convey with me by this vision. Again the Lord gave me another two hymns.

It was 5:50 a.m.

Years ago when I was a child a Christian man visited my cousins home. He had the gift of prophecy, and was working for the Lord. He was the one who told our family that we were all surrounded by flames, through the vision he saw. That day, I happened to be over their place and was walking into the entrance of the house when this man, and my cousin's father stopped to have a conversation. In mid-sentence this man turns to him and speaks a prophetic prophecy about Jesus' return. I overheard him say, "Jesus will return before all of your children get married." This is a family of nine children, and they are all in their mid-20s and early 30s right now, and only one of them has gotten married. It doesn't seem like any of my other cousins even want to get married. One of them even had said that she wanted to live out her life alone and doesn't want a marriage.

It might be a sign from the Lord to us that he is saying that, he is so near and returning to this earth very soon. He wants us all to be ready for his return and repent from our sins.

The end of the world will be here when Jesus comes to the Earth. It will be just like Noah's time. It will be the same when the son of man returns. Very unexpected and everyone unaware of the end that is to come.

That's why Jesus had said :

"But as the days of Noe *were*, so shall also the coming of the Son of man be. For as in the days that were before the flood they were eating and drinking, marrying and giving in marriage, until the day that Noe entered into the ark, And knew not until the flood came, and took them all away; so shall also the coming of the Son of man be." (Matthew 24:37-39KJV)

I had also received a dream once were I was hanging up my washing. I mentioned it in the first part of this book, under the chapter of dreams.

I use to wash my clothes separately in there colours, like black and blues I washed together. Red separate and so on.

When I got sick I couldn't do it anymore. I found it too hard to separate the colours. I decided to try and mix them together instead. I didn't think of the dream that I had at the time, and it never occurred to me that I was making the prophetic dream come true (which the Lord had shown me about mixing the coloured load together before his soon return.) It came to pass, and I am still mixing the washing.

Joshua and I got into a fight over my health problems. He was thinking of ending our marriage. He suddenly leaves the house and goes and watches a soccer game at a local club. I was home alone with the children. I decided that I would take them to a park and enjoy the day. I was upset. I however had a nice time with the children; they rode on their bike and scooter. At the end of the day, we had an icecream at the kiosk and decided to walk back to the car. Tina and Andrew lived in front of the park and I happened to park our car their. I decided to go and say hello. I didn't want to offend them by not saying hello. By now, they would've known that my car was park outside their place. I didn't feel like talking and wasn't wanting to speak to Joshua's parents after the fight we had.

I was feeling low.

My eldest daughter rings the doorbell and my in-laws are happy to see me and the children. We say hello and have a coffee and snacks at their place. I didn't mention the bad fight that Joshua and I had just hours earlier.

After about 10 minutes, I decide to leave my in-laws place. I take the children out for dinner and come home. I waited for Joshua to come home from the soccer club. He gets home at 10:40 p.m.

I speak to him and we reconciled our marriage. I tell him, "I wanted our marriage to work out. I want to see our grandchildren one day over at our place and we're still a couple."

I made him dinner and ask him if he wanted to come to church with me tomorrow.

He said, "I would," but I knew he would change his mind tomorrow. At least he wasn't offended by my offer.

I had a strategy, I wanted my husband to know that I was a Christian wife who can forgive my husband and not be completely hurt by the enemy that was heavily working against his life to persecute me.

Before I went to bed a demon told me, "Satan wanted you to be evil. He worked heavily in your life for you to become an evil person."

Sunday 25th August 2019

I woke in a panic. I slept in and had ignored my alarm clock. When I'm deep inside a dream, I find it hard to hear the alarm. I was going to go to church this morning. I checked the time and it was 7:37 a.m.

I was happy and had plenty of time to get ourselves ready before church started. I asked Joshua, "Did you still want to come to church? The pastor and elders can pray over you." Joshua had a very bad cold for over 11 weeks. He went on two doses of antibiotics, nasal sprays. They did blood tests, and an x-ray on his chest and nothing could be found that was causing his problem.

He thought about it and was in a very sweet and happy mood. He said, "I would go today, but I had a lot of things I had to get done at home."

I didn't want to push him. He then added to the conversation and said, "I might however come with you when you go next time."

I went to church. After the service I spoke to my cousin Jack about how Joshua nearly came to church with me today, and how the forces of darkness were heavily oppressing my marriage.

He looked over at me and said, "I once had a very powerful dream about your husband. In this dream. I saw Joshua at the front of the church, preaching, and he had a bible in his hand. I felt the power of God with him in that dream and I knew he will be saved one day and preach the word."

I was very glad when he shared with me that dream. It gave me hope for Joshua.

Jack continued to say, "Before I got married and turned to the Lord. The Lord showed my family a dream of a house which had a black flag over it. This flag represented the hold of Satan over our home and at once a light came and released us from this darkness. Shortly after that dream, I got saved, came to church and married my wife and had our son."

When Satan was over their home it was a big mess, and then suddenly everything was fine because the Lord had intervened in their lives' and set some of them free.

I came home and prayed for Joshua to be saved and for the dream to come to pass. I wanted to go to church together as a family.

Monday 26th August 2019

I was feeling well this morning. I also didn't dream last night. The Lord was healing my body and mind, freeing me from the sickness and pain. The only form of exercise that I was currently doing at the moment was walking. I had stopped any other forms of fitness. As I thought about re-organizing my life again, to do other types of physical workouts. A demon reacted to my thoughts. He started to crush my brain and body, with a crushing heavy pain of oppression. He didn't want me to improve and overcome this sickness. I went and prayed straight away to the Lord asking him to lift this demon off my body, and to set me free from the pain.

After a few hours my head was slowly released from the pain. The demons started to interact with me again. I still managed to walk on the treadmill for 30 minutes. I decided to lie on the couch when I started talking about how much I needed help with my prayer life. I felt like that I've been heavily crushed by the demons, and my prayer life was withering away slowly because of it. I didn't always have a deep desire to pray. I thought about how my grandmother and our relatives, who were Christians, had a meaningful and intercessory prayer life. They pray with all their hearts, and with the power of the Holy Spirit. As I lied there the Lord touched my heart to cry out to him, and I asked him to help me be a better Christian towards him.

Tuesday 27th August 2019

My alarm went off at 4:00 a.m.

I got out of bed to help Joshua get ready for work. I've been waking up around 4:00 a.m. at least four days a week to make him breakfast, coffee and a packed lunch for work.

This morning I had finished helping, so I decided to sit down on the couch and have a coffee. Without realising it, I had sat down on Joshua's work tie. Joshua was rushing to get himself dressed and didn't realise I had sat on his tie. His a supervisor at a large security company, and works in a large building in the city of Sydney. I thought maybe he might have had a meeting to attend to today. I hear a voice in my head, but it was so soft that I ignored it. The Holy Spirit had told me to move and I didn't. I was enjoying my coffee that much that I couldn't be bothered to move to another position. I had failed to hear the Lord's instruction. My husband gives me a kiss good bye and leaves for work. I get a sms from Joshua and he wrote:

"Honey, you were sitting on top of my tie, and now I left it at home."

I replied, "Will it be ok to work without it?"

Joshua texted, "Not really. I'm the supervisor. Plus I maybe having a meeting today, to make things worse."

I sat down and got upset. I was thinking the worst things. I thought maybe he might lose his job, like I had a few months before. The reason why I had lost my job in the month of February 2019, was because the Chiropractic building that I was working at was not maintained properly over the years, and the roof above the yoga studio had collapsed to the ground. It was a blessing to my boss that it had happened overnight, because the area that the roof had fallen down happened to be where the yoga classes were practising yoga. People in the public could have been killed. I wanted to leave anyway because of the yoga classes. I had asked the Lord to help me leave a few months before. I asked the Lord to make it possible for me to walk away from this job. I was so sick at the time, I was working, but I didn't want to stay any longer. However, we needed the money and my wage was good. The local council decided the building was unsafe, and they closed that business site down for now. My boss told me that we have no more positions available, that they will tell us if things change. I had been working there since 2008.

My husband was the only one working now. I was worried that if he lost his job and couldn't find another job fast enough, that we would eat into all our savings, and then we would have to sell our property to be mortgage free. As I pondered these thoughts. I heard the same soft voice enter my mind. The Holy Spirit told me to ask a night shift worker to lend Joshua a tie. I realised that Joshua could return it to the night shift worker when he finished his shift at 6:00 p.m.

I texted him and wrote, "Why don't you ask one of the night managers to lend you their tie?"

He texted back a while later and said, "It's okay honey. The night shift guy lent me his as he is returning tonight."

I texted to Joshua and wrote, "That's a relief. The Lord told me to tell you to lend it off a night shift manager. That's where that idea came from, and as soon as I heard these words talking to me, I texted you straight away to get one of the workers to lend it to you, so you don't get into trouble."

Joshua texted back and wrote, "Thanks Honey. I would rather be working night shift, and relaxing during the day with you and spending more time with the kids. I'll see what I'm going to do in the next month regarding a new job."

After dinner, I started to think of all other significant events that had occurred to me as a child. A demon started speaking to me about how they were watching me as a child. He said "Don't worry angels were around." It sounded like the demon was mocking me. I thought of one event that had happened to me. I use to suffer from night terrors as a young child. I recall my mother trying to wake me out of this nightmare I once had. I was sitting on the bathroom sink with my mother desperately trying to snap me out of that dream. What I was seeing at the time was a dream unfolding inside my mind as I was trying to wake up. I could hear my mother calling me, but I couldn't wake up. I know now that Satan was the one giving me this night terror. I was unable to come out of the dream, and it took my mother a while to snap me out of it. Eventually, I awoke and found myself sitting on the bathroom vanity, and my mother trying to comfort me from crying or screaming uncontrollably.

Wednesday 28th August 2019

Last night I prayed before going to bed, but once again I had ended up inside of a dream. I was feeling a spirit causing my lower parts of my body to react with a sexual pleasure. It felt like the spirit had put his male genitals inside of me. I awoke inside the walls of the dream world, and reacted to this. I got very angry at the spirit. It was portraying to be Satan again. While inside this dream I started to rebuke the spirit in the name of Jesus. I even tried to throw an object that I found inside my hand towards the spirit. I awoke and found the feeling still affecting my physical body. As I laid on the bed a demon kept on saying, "I can't touch you, I can't touch you!" The spirit was upset and reacted to my resistance.

I felt defiled by this spirit, and felt unsaved for a moment. I was thinking is God truly with me, and saving me. A little while later, as I drifted almost back to sleep. I could hear the song, "You are my hiding place." I somehow manage to type the song on YouTube, letting it play as I fell back asleep.

I drifted again into the dream world. I happened to be standing in front of a small outdoor shop, there was a window, and I looked through this window and started to view all the different things that were available for purchase. I saw this unusual shell object. I wanted to buy it, but another customer (who was a demon) had beaten me to it.

I heard the shop attendant say to me that it was a swordfish sword. As I viewed this object, a symbol of a dragon appeared on a metal disc on the shell object. I react and say, "I didn't see that before. I'm glad I didn't buy it." This dragon symbol represents the devil. The dream changes course and another scene appears. I found myself in a bedroom. I had an occult book with me, for some reason I wanted to read it, but a voice of a spirit urged me to put it on the bookshelf instead. This spirt was trying to stop me from wanting to read the occult material. In response to this voice, I start trying to hide the book. The spirit again spoke and said, "She is not going to read it."

At lunch time, I happened to be heading into the kitchen when I had a quick glimpse of the Lord Jesus. I started hearing these words from him, "For a thousand generations the covenant will stand. Great is your loving kind words towards me."

The Lord was referring to the covenant God gave to me when I had that dream. I believe the covenant was about saving my soul and helping me stand against Satan, so I wouldn't lose my soul and go to Hell. I had fallen away unwillingly twice from the Lord already. I don't think I can ever fall away from him again. I'm that strong now for him, and I am no longer blind.

In my heart and mind I didn't want to leave the Lord. I always loved him from a child. I would lift up my hand when the churches I use to visit had ask people if they wanted the Lord to save them. I would say the sinner's prayer at these churches on more than one occasion, but I felt nothing, and I knew in my heart that I wasn't saved yet. However, I knew I would be saved one day and go to heaven when I died. The Lord was telling me that he was going to save me one day. Even when I was in darkness, I knew I would be saved one day. I believe that I felt nothing because I was blind. I didn't really truly repent from my evil ways, or was even thinking of repenting from them when I wanted the Lord Jesus to save me. When I did repent, I felt the Lord's power fall over me. I got on my knees in an instant when I felt that power, repenting with fear and trembling. I knew from that moment on that I never wanted to go back to my old evil self again.

Thursday 29th August 2019

Lisa and I went for another walk to the lake. As she was driving, she told me that she felt like she was going to have a delusion soon. I asked her, "What do you feel like when you go through psychosis or a delusion?" She replied to me and said, "I have a thought enter my mind and I start to believe I am the devil." I asked Lisa and said, "Do you really think when you're in that state of mind that you are really the devil, or can you still tell that you're Lisa." Lisa replied, "No, I can still tell that I am myself, but my thoughts tell me that I am the devil. Also I feel something inside of me, like it's going to possess me." I told her, "That's a demon!" Satan or that demon is the one planting these thoughts into your mind making you believe the lie.

Lisa responded and said, "I don't want to talk about the demons because I don't want to go through a delusion."

We start to walk around the lake and Lisa says to me that she would love for it to rain after the walk.

At the moment Australia is going through a drought. It wasn't raining. I said to Lisa, "I don't mind if it rained. It's a blessing from the Lord if it rains."

We walk for 45 minutes. She drives me home and we depart our separate ways.

2 hours later it starts to rain.

I messaged Lisa and texted, "Hi Lisa, it rained just like you wanted. The Lord heard your request."

She replied back, "Hi Danica, Yes it did, but had to drive Dad to Mount Druitt hospital for tests."

I texted Lisa and wrote, "God can give you what you ask for even if we don't see exactly what we will be doing in the future. We are all going through trials to see if we can stand. Have faith! God will help you. Just hold onto him always. Have a good day otherwise."

Lisa texted back, "You too. Thanks for the encouragement."

I texted back and wrote, "Take care and don't stress about things. Give your burdens to the Lord."

When I was a child a girl a bit older then myself used to come with her mother to church. It was a small church and the only children attending were my siblings, and on occasion this girl. She also was mentally challenged. She would flick a piece of paper with her fingers and make noises. She loved us though, and when she attended the services I would always sit next to her during church. I felt sorry for her. Her mother was a widow and had two children. Her mother liked my father because they both lost their partners and had been attending the same church. She wanted to marry him, but my father wasn't interested in her. She decided to give him a card to show her feelings to him, but he mocked her words because of what she had written inside this card. My siblings and I happened to be in the same car when I heard him laughing and provoking my eldest brother Paul to mock her too.

I was hurt by it and couldn't understand how he could laugh at her. They were both Christians. Once my dad took a homeless man into our house. This man was staying overnight in the park and my dad had brought him home so he could sleep out of the cold. I didn't know who this man was, and didn't understand at the time what he was doing. He was trying to be a good Christian by helping the less fortunate. However, when we drove pass a homeless man years later in our car, my dad was mocking him instead, and didn't stop to help him or show us what God's love was towards those that are without.

The reason why I wrote this was not to mock or make fun of my father but because the Lord was urging me to reveal this to every other Christian. You can't be double minded in the things that you do for God. No matter if you got a reward at first from the Lord for doing good, but if you change your ways you can lose your rewards as well as your soul in Hell.

I again ask Joshua if he would like to come to church tomorrow. He said that he would go but I was still was not sure if he really would. I wanted him to go and hoped that he would attend.

Saturday 31st August 2019

I had spent the morning with Joshua. He again wanted to go to the soccer club. He was part of their organisation and is in the committee.

I was happy for him to go but I asked him to meet me at my grandmother's place after he was done to attend church with me and the children. I still wasn't sure that he really would attend. I arrive at my grandmother's place and grandmother May greets me at the door. She is getting older and I could see just how much she was aging. She is 81 years old now and the great-grandmother to my two girls. She loves to spend time with my children and was happy to see me again. I was over to take her to church, and to spend some more time with her. She is still strong though and always has some Slavic traditional cakes on hand for everyone to enjoy. She always bakes sweets from scratch and loves her cakes.

I make a coffee and text Joshua to come around to grandmother May's place. I told him that I was already over. He texts me back and says that he'll be over in about 20 minutes, for the soccer games had finished.

After about 20 minutes the doorbell rings. I open the door for Joshua to come in. I couldn't believe he was really going to come to church with me.

Joshua talks for a while with both grandmother May, and uncle James until it comes for us to go to the church service. We drive over to church, Joshua is slightly annoyed at the fact he was at church. He was thinking about all the work he wanted to finish at home. I asked him to relax and to enjoy the service. The service begins, I feel the presence of the Lord over me through song, and I could feel the Holy Spirit helping me sing in the spirit. It was nice, but I wanted the Lord to save Joshua as soon as possible. I was hoping for a miracle tonight, but I knew in my heart that it was not in God's plan at the moment. One of the preachers, preached on the message of Jesus' Christ, and I was hoping it would touch his heart to move him to surrender his life to Jesus Christ. He didn't though. The service ended and we stay back, speaking with our family and the preacher.

As we head home, Joshua is still upset at the amount of time he spent at church. I had also noticed that the demons had almost stopped talking today. I had a sense of normality, and was feeling like my old self again. I did ask the Lord if he could make my life normal again. I wanted to go back to my normal life. I had enough of this spiritual fight, and was so tired by the battle. He was answering my request today.

Sunday 1st September 2019

It was Father's Day today. Our children got Joshua a gift to say thank you to their father for being there for them.

I was meant to be at church today for the Holy Communion or the Lord's Supper, but I didn't attend because of Father's Day. Joshua's family had organised a picnic at the local park grounds.

My grandmother May doesn't take the Lord's Supper due to a prophecy that was spoken by a Christian person. The Lord said in this prophecy that he wanted everyone to partake using one cup for everyone to drink from, not little cups individually to drink from. He was upset at the Church for their own fear of germs between the church members. He was not happy with them partaking of the body and blood of Christ using individual glass cups.

My grandmother refuses to go on this day to the church because the Church members didn't listen to the prophecy, and were still practising using individual glasses. I didn't know what to do though. I still went to church for the Lord's Supper, but deep down I wasn't sure what the Lord wanted me to do.

Did he want me to boycott the church and not participate with them like some of the Church members were already doing, or do I stay with the church and get involved instead?

I couldn't decide what to do, and I didn't want to upset the Lord either, but I was tired of making a fuss.

I had told the Pastor and several members of the church that I was having a very severe demonic battle against the demons and Satan. It had almost crippled me, and it felt like I was going to die sometimes.

Some prayed for me, but I didn't get a great deal of help. One person fasted for me. My aunt who is a born again Christian didn't want to talk about what was happening to me. The pastor listened, but I felt neglected sometimes by the church. They do ask to put your hand up for prayer requests, but if it wasn't for the Lord himself personally helping me with the demonic situation that plagued my life I wouldn't have been able to cope. I was tormented, crushed physically by demons, I felt insanity. The Lord was always with me, and was holding onto me. I wanted help from the church and wanted them to respond as Christians, to help me seek the Lord as a church for me to be delivered from the demonic forces of Satan. I'm not trying to write these things to annoy everyone, but to show you and teach you just how bad schizophrenia really is, and just how much of a spiritual battle is really occurring in the lives' of those people. It's not just a sickness, but a demonic attack on your life. I find that If you don't get much support from the church and family members who really don't get it, especially when you're saying, "demons are attacking you, and your own body is deteriorating due to your physical body being very sick from the demonic attacks." It can be very hard to cope. I found no one truly understood what was occurring in my life, and I found many weren't even interested in what you said or wrote.

Voices are the demons. They can control you if Satan blinds you into listening to the demons, or the so called "voices" instructions. People with demonic voices have hurt, or even killed people when under such a state. I found that when I was under this blindness, Satan wanted me to do something bad, but I refused and resisted the devil. I know I don't want to harm a fly, and won't hurt anyone. I have love in my heart for my children, family and husband. I love people and can't imagine even lifting my hand against anyone. Most people who have schizophrenia really don't harm others; it's just the few cases that make every other schizophrenic person look like a murder or violent human being.

Demons can even take possession of people, taking control of sinful people who haven't surrendered their lives' to the Lord Jesus for protection against such evil. Jesus Christ is the only one keeping me from truly going into an insane state of mine, and I always have believed that believers have a sound mind in Christ Jesus.

For God hath not given us the spirit of fear; but of power, and of love, and of a sound mind. (Timothy 1:7KJV)

Tuesday 3rd September 2019

What a nightmare! I had one of the worse nights fighting the demons and Satan. I went into at least two different dreams. In the first dream I was talking to the devil. I was telling him that I did not want to spend time with him. I had also asked him to leave me alone. Soon after I said these words I grew very angry at the demons and started to attack one of the demons within this dream state. I again called upon the name of Jesus. During this attack I asked the devil if he could please let me go? He reply back in anger and said, "No! I will not."

In the second dream I was in my current bedroom and I saw how a demon was being cast out of my body and leaving my house. It was a bit disturbing at least. This demon was like a white smoke of essence and it had no form. When it was cast out, I saw it went quickly into Violet. I was concerned about this demon being inside of her. It was meant to be the spirit of Maladaptive daydreaming disorder and I saw a hand come near my daughter. I didn't see a body or face, just an arm and this male's hand reaching down and pulling out this spirit from her. After it was pulled out of her, it then left through the bedroom window. I saw it return and go back inside of me. I then asked the Lord to cast it out again. I woke up from the dream and found a very loud demon talking to me. He was saying, "You're not a normal human being." He continued to say, "You're not going home." Referring for me not to go to heaven when I died. When he said these words, I felt that dream hit me again. The one about when Jesus had told me that I would never enter his kingdom. It started crushing my heart. I was getting upset at what the demon had said. I then heard another spirit which spoke to this very evil demon. He said to the demon that he can't tell me that I couldn't go home. He turns to me and says, "You're going to go home." He was telling me that this wasn't true, and not to worry about these words. I ask him if the Lord came in the flesh and he said, "Yes."

I get up and pray to the Lord. The Lord guides my words supernaturally through prayer. The Lord gives me the song, "Surely goodness and mercy shall follow me all the days of my life and I shall dwell in the house of the Lord forever." I climb back into bed and again drift off to sleep. I'm not even fully asleep when Satan again makes the scenarios of the dream world appear. In the last dream, I found myself at the shop and I had a broomstick in my hand. I was about to ride it like a witch when I felt the power of the Lord remove the broomstick away from my body to stop me in the act. He then made the broomstick disappear from the dream.

I was watching videos of demons caught on camera to see how I would react to them visually. Most times the demons only speak to me, or show me an invisible form. I can feel their presence and sometimes they touch my body, and physically crush my brain with pain. However, I only saw them manifest a few times and it was very quick. As I watched the video's on YouTube, I realised that it was so real, the whole thing that was occurring to me. It all made a lot of sense to me now.

As I viewed the spirits in the clip, I said, "I'm not scared of them anymore." I know that demons can give you a lot of fear and there is a very great fear that falls over people when they are seeing spirits. I wondered if I would be able to stand if I really got to see one manifested fully to me. I wasn't asking to see this though, but wondered as a Christian if we can really stand without complete fear. I also said, "I would probably be afraid at first because of the fear that is associated with seeing the demons." After watching the video, a woman demon appeared in my vision and her long black hair covered her face, unable to see her appearance just her pale death like skin, and she wore a long white dress. I knew this was a demon that I had just seen in the spirit world through my eyes; I dismissed it and showed that demon that I wasn't afraid of her.

A few days later, I was on my bed when I looked up and Ruby, my youngest daughter was standing inside the room. She climbed on the bed and stood staring at me. I didn't see her enter the room and I called out her name as I'm feeling a climbing level of fear rising inside of me, "Ruby, Ruby," I called. She didn't move and wasn't responding to her name. A thought entered my mind, I knew Satan wanted to grab hold of me, and I couldn't escape the psychosis again. I slipped into a fearful state because I really thought I had seen a demon, and not Ruby staring back at me. I tried to dismiss the feeling, but Satan took hold of me, and I fell back into a fearful state of mind. I felt a shock ran through my body, and I stood up in fear and started shouting out, "I rebuke you in the name of Jesus." She breaks the silence and starts laughing at me. I come to my normal self and realise that I had just slipped back into psychosis. Satan had just shown me a lie again. However, I knew it was a lie and I was aware this time that Satan was trying to drag me back into a false reality through psychosis. I felt it though, the power of darkness behind my child and because I let fear inside my heart. Satan had taken hold of me again. I looked at Ruby and I knew it was her again. I said to myself, "Satan just used my child against me. He had made Ruby come into the room to scare me." I asked Ruby, "Why did you not say your name when I asked if it was you?" She said, "I wanted to scare you!" I told her, "It wasn't a good idea to go and scare people." She didn't understand that people can be triggered by the devil and go into a psychotic episode like I had just experienced.

A few more days later, I went to my cousin's place and Violet was jumping over me, trying to play around with me, when her eyes started to pierce my eyes seeing her as a demon and the fearful state of psychosis was trying to re-enter me again. I closed my eyes. I didn't let the fear consume my heart again this time. Satan kept on trying to put me back into psychosis, and I just kept on resisting the fear and false reality that he was trying to put me into again.

At least the feeling fled and I won the victory over Satan.

Saturday 28th September 2019

I had slipped into another demonic scene with the demons. In one scene, a spirit was writing these words along this wall. He wrote it four times. It said, "BEAST IS HERE." Referring to the book of Revelation and how the beast will ascend out of the abyss. I grew annoyed and reacted, telling the spirit with force to flee.

The other day, I had a few spirits talking to me. I decided to say to them, "The Lord Jesus had crushed Satan's head." Referring to the prophecy found in the book of Genesis against the serpent. These spirits grew very annoyed and in anger they had stopped speaking to me and retreated back inside my body.

I went out with my husband and children for dinner. We had just celebrated an early 13th year wedding Anniversary. It was nice to sit and relax with the children and my husband. Yesterday, my head pain returned and it ruined my entire day. I find that when demons talk to you sometimes their presence brings with them torment and insanity. I find myself in a lot of pain when this happens. My body reacts to these demons and it makes me feel like I'm slipping into an insane state of mind. However, I'm aware that they are truly demons, and I am not truly going to go insane due to them. God has set me free from the insane state of mind I had experienced at the mental health hospitals. When that Angel spoke to me I was sent free mentally by the Lord God. I became aware of the deceptive nature of the devil, and knew I was being deceived by him as well as being infiltrated by the demons.

While we had dinner I started to hum the song quietly, "In the name of Jesus." I didn't want Joshua hearing me though. He gets upset at this song because it was the same song I sung on the balcony when

I went through the psychosis during our brief holiday stay. It was a nice Christian song. As I hummed the tune I felt the Lord Jesus' presence, and felt his power over my voice. He helped me hum this song. The demons reacted and kept on saying back to me, "Shut up, shut up, shut up."

Joshua starts talking to me, so I stopped humming and we continued our conversation and dinner.

We ate and then allowed the children to play at the outdoor park area which was part of the restaurant.

Soon after we returned home I went to bed. I was tired and just laid on the bed. I said, "I'll get up to pray soon." I just needed a few minutes to recover. As I'm drifting, the Lord urges me to pray. I try to sit up on the side of the bed, but couldn't get myself to pray. I was too tired to move. I decide to go back to bed and fall asleep.

The devil again sets up another scenario. I see Joshua and sister-in-law Jade speaking to themselves about me. They got into a car and I tried hard to meet up with them, but the car slowly takes off and I'm unable to catch up with them. These again weren't my family members but demons tormenting me again within this dream. I thought to myself,"They didn't want me near them." They park the car but I was already offended by them. Joshua and Jade show me that I could hop into the car now. I refused. Hurting, I walk away from Joshua and Jade.

As I'm walking the scenario changes, and I find myself in a very difficult setting. I'm naked and I'm in front of a large group of people. I noticed that they had cameras and I'm covering my body with my hands. I desperately try looking for the exit. All the gates were locked and I couldn't leave the scene.

I wake up and the Lord gives me a song. He usually does when I wake up in the mornings. Sometimes the demons can put Christian hymns inside my mind too. I notice that sometimes they even change the lyrics to the song.

Demons kept on entering my dreams and portraying themselves as people like Joshua and Jade. They portray themselves as people so they will not be noticed by the dreamer that demons are inside their dreams and deceiving them. I think they just like tormenting me and having fun with me at my own expense.

Like in my dream, the demons want us to become very angry at the people who have hurt us. In my case it was my husband Joshua and sister-in-law Jade. The Demons can really cause people to drift into resentment towards that other person. They are truly hurt by that person within that particular dream scenario. When I woke up, I felt the hurt inside my heart and I just had to tell myself that this is the demons that have cause the pain, and not Joshua and Jade. They had done nothing wrong to me.

Joshua had the same thing happen to him. Satan gave him dreams where I had left my husband and wasn't going to return back to him. He thought that our marriage was over. He awoke and was hurt and upset at me due to the dream. I told him that Satan had infiltrated his dream to plant resentment between us.

Sunday 29th September 2019

I hadn't gone to church for a number of weeks due to family visiting, and other family plans that have risen through-out the weeks. I was desperate to go to church, and even though I was trying to worship the Lord at home. I had failed to praise the Lord well due to demons talking through my mouth and hindering my praise to God. I was longing to attend church by now. I finally went today. As I was praising the Lord. A demonic oppression fell over me and I was in so much pain that I had to take more antipsychotic medication to ease my pain in my head. The pain feels like rawness and an inflammation that takes hold of my head. Paracetamol helps but the only cure for the pain to ease off is the antipsychotic medication. After church I went home. I was upset at something that had caused me a world of grief. I didn't want to say what it was exactly, except Satan was behind it again. I ended up in the bathtub crying. I began to speak to the Lord when he suddenly pulls out, with force, two demonic spirits out of my body. I really did feel better physically after the Lord had pulled out these demons from me.

Tuesday 1st October 2019

My children are on school holidays at the moment. I decide to take the children and myself to the shopping centre. We walked around the shops looking at stuff and decided to have a snack at the food court. We sit down, I looked over and saw this woman pointing at the air and talking to herself. I knew that look! She must be suffering from a form of schizophrenia. I felt my heart breaking for her because I knew she was really talking to a spirit, and it had blinded her. She was in a state of psychosis. I decided not to approach her, and left the food court with my two girls. However, I had a longing to go back and to speak to her. I asked my daughters if it was ok with them if I went and spoke to that woman at the food court. Violet approves, and I repent to the Lord for not doing his will and went back to see if she was still there. I went to the food court and found that she was gone. I walked away with my daughters and Violet shouts to me, "Mum, that woman is over there!" Violet was right, she was over in the distance still pointing in the air talking to herself. I walk over to her and ask her if she was ok, trying to explain to her that I also suffered from schizophrenia.

She reacts and moves away from me in fear and says in a sweet anxious tone of voice, "I'm fine, I'm fine." I really wanted her to know the truth and to tell her that she was speaking to an evil spirit. I didn't though, because she didn't allow me to approach her. Only the Lord can wake people out of psychosis. I again approached her and said, "Would you like prayer? Would you like Jesus?" I was upset at what Satan had done to her. She kept on walking away in fear saying, "No, I'm fine, I'm fine" and pointing to the air and continuing to talk to herself. In defeat, I leave and walk away from a hopeless situation. As I walked away, I turn again towards her, and quietly rebuke the demons in Jesus' name, praying for her state of mind to return. That's all I could do for her. Only the Lord can truly help those people.

Thursday 10th October 2019

"You have been chosen to do something for the Lord," I heard these words as I was waking out of sleep. I don't know who spoke these words. I was pondering if this was from the Lord or from Satan.

There is this prophecy in my family that had been given to us by a prophetess from the Lord. It's about how the Lord will give one person in my family a gift from the Holy Spirit, so the Lord could bring more people into his house.

I went to my Great-Aunt Fiona's place and she showed me what was written down, as well as many other prophecies that was said to the church members. One prophecy stated that the Lord will give his people various sicknesses within the church. I think this was to trial those within the church, to see if they can stand. The Lord said to the church to be careful because those who think they are standing, might end up falling instead. This prophecy was given many years ago, and many people including myself had gotten sick.

Friday 11th October 2019

I went to the shopping centre with my children to buy a gift for Ruby's school friend. I had been boycotting a lot of popular toy brands because of their involvement with producing evil and immoral toys that go against the Lord. I was rushing to get home before Joshua came from work and went to a toy shop and bought the gift. This was a Barbie product brand toy of Chelsea and a treehouse. I was at the checkout to buy the toy when I saw two masks on the picture of the toy box. I was next in line, but I was in a rush and bought the product anyway. I took it home and was upset at myself for buying this product. In the morning, I was thinking if I should go and get a refund on the toy when the Lord urged me to return it to the toy shop. I felt the tug on my arm and knew the Lord was telling me to take it back. I go back to the toy shop and I get a refund.

After I let my children play at the shopping centre playground. As they played, I turned around and saw this new age shop full of dreamcatchers, and new age products. The worse product was of a cow skull with a symbol of a cross attached to it's forehead. I was upset, and said to the Lord in faith, "Please Lord, close down this shop so it doesn't succeed." As soon as I had said this demons sent a compressing searing pain inside my head. They were angry at my words. I wondered how many demons were inside of that shop to begin with. One time, I was walking around the shops when I walked into a section dedicated to Halloween. I felt the demonic oppression against my body, and felt the demons amongst the objects. I know demons enter into objects. People in the occult can curse objects, put them up for sale and the general population of people end up wearing or buying them. The Lord has always shown me not to enter into the new age shops and to avoid them completely. I'm warning you not to buy anything from these types of stores. You don't know how many demons and curses you'll end up bringing on yourself and your household.

Monday 14th October 2019

School holidays had just finished. I took the children back to school. During the school holidays I've been sleeping in and taking regular paracetamol tablets to reduce my headaches. These headaches are so crippling that it hingers my ability to perform basic tasks sometimes.

The lack of sleep this morning played a toll on my mind. I was tired due to the antipsychotic medication making me drownsy. I'm usually unable to hear my alarm clock sounding. I stay awake instead from 4:00 a.m. after helping Joshua get ready for work. I don't go back to sleep. I'm scared I'll sleep in and not get the children to school on time.

During the day the demons once again spoke to me the whole day long.

In the evening I was depressed. I called out to the Lord for help and said, "This was too much for any person to bear." I was upset at the whole situation. I wanted to be free and was hurting inside. I couldn't understand why the Lord allowed this much pain and torment to come upon me. I could see other people who have come out of Satan's kingdom being instantly delivered, but I was in pain for over four years. I love the Lord and I didn't want to speak against the Lord in anger. I just cry instead and tell him I'm in pain. People just think schizophrenia is just a mental disorder, but I'm physically in pain over the anguish caused by the disease. It hurts when people tell you it's just a mental problem.

In all the distress the Lord's power falls upon my head and silence comes over me. I'm refreshed and can hear the birds singing in the background. The noise of the surrounding environment is soothing to my mind. I miss what everyone else hears and feels. I've stepped out of the normal reality of life. I've forgotten what that feeling felt like now. However, the demons still were inside of my body. I knew that they hadn't been cast out of me. The Lord is faithful to his word and I believe one day he will set me free and heal me completely.

Friday 18th October 2019

I'm in a dream and I'm mixing up alcoholic beverages. I can see demons posing as people interacting with me within this dream. I came up to a demon (who was in a human form.) He was behind a bar. I asked him to serve me a sweet alcoholic drink. He gave me the drink, but the whole time I wasn't allowed to drink any of appealing drinks. I don't know if it was because the Lord was holding me back or because the demons were trying to torment me with the idea of having a drink, but they were withholding me from ever being allowed to taste any of it. The scene changes, and I find myself strapped on a chair aboard a UFO craft. I call out to the Lord and tell him, "I don't want to be aboard a UFO." I wake out of sleep and knew instantly once again that Satan was behind the whole dream.

I want to talk about testimonies and the power behind these type of stories. Christian testimonies not only help us know that Jesus is real, but it also gives us understanding of what God does and how he works in people's lives. When I want to know something about the Lord's kingdom or the Devil's kingdom I turn to testimonies. They are a great source of information and can help you're understanding. Beware though, Satan also can use a testimony to show lies. He can cause someone even in a near death experience to report a lie about eternity. I've seen this in only a few testimonies that I have came across, but most of them lead to the Lord and can show you a glimpse into the spiritual world like heaven, hell and ex-satanist testimonies, ex-new age testimonies, near death experience testimonies. Testimonies of Jesus Christ appearing to people. You'll have to use discernment though because Satan can use people too.

Monday 21st October 2019

My health had started returning again after taking some electrolyte tablets. I had been rehydrating myself and the results even amazed me. My body goes into cycles. Somedays, I feel good. Other days my health declines and I deteriorate. I had even stopped drinking soft drinks because of the sugar content and my weight issues. While at the supermarket the lord kept on putting the word, "electrolyte" inside of my mind. I've been wanting to see if taking this would make any difference to my health and it made the biggest change to my overall health. I also find if I go outside and have lots of vitamin D that my health improves, making me feel great.

On a different topic. A few years ago, I had watched a YouTube video of a man who lived in Australia as a false Jesus. He was an cult leader and lived in Brisbane. The Lord had opened my eyes to how Satan had twisted his mind. This man would receive these memories of him being our Lord Jesus Christ. His memories consisted of Jesus Christ's life 2,000 years ago. He claims that he can remember being Jesus Christ because of these memories that he was seeing, and his partner claims to be Mary Magdalene.

They are both deceived by Satan and have been given false memories. Which the devil has implanted into their minds, so they can truly believe that they are Christ and Mary Magdalene. They are really believing a lie and are now luring away people who should have been the Lord's children.

Beware of false Christ's! Jesus will only come back in the air and every eye will see him. You will not miss the way the Lord Jesus Christ will return to the Earth because it will be in a very drastic way.

The Lord was urging me to point out something interesting in the book of Matthew, regarding the parable of the wise and foolish virgins.

"Then shall the kingdom of heaven be likened unto ten virgins, which took their lamps, and went forth to meet the bridegroom.

And five of them were wise, and five were foolish.

They that were foolish took their lamps, and took no oil with them:

But the wise took oil in their vessels with their lamps.

While the bridegroom tarried, they all slumbered and slept.

And at midnight there was a cry made, Behold, the bridegroom cometh; go ye out to meet him.

Then all those virgins arose, and trimmed their lamps.

And the foolish said unto the wise, Give us of your oil; for our lamps are gone out.

But the wise answered, saying, Not so; lest there be not enough for us and you: but go ye rather to them that sell, and buy for yourselves.

And while they went to buy, the bridegroom came; and they that were ready went in with him to the marriage: and the door was shut.

Afterward came also the other virgins, saying, Lord, Lord, open to us.

But he answered and said, Verily I say unto you, I know you not.

Watch therefore, for ye know neither the day nor the hour wherein the Son of man cometh." (Matthew 25:1-13KJV)

In this parable the bridegroom is Jesus Christ, and the story is about Christ's return and the rapture of his church. Jesus has delayed for 2,000 years, and when the midnight cry was made. Only the righteous and ready church was taken, and once the door is closed, no-one can enter it again. You'll be cast out of the kingdom of God and not enter into the rapture and the resurrection; life eternal. The door will be closed to these foolish Christians forever.

Jesus' return is the day of the Lord, and Matthew 24 says that it will happen after the tribulation of those days. The Antichrist comes first.

"And then the lawless one will be revealed, whom the Lord will consume with the breath of His mouth and destroy with the brightness of His coming. The coming of the lawless one is according to the working of Satan, with all power, signs, and lying wonders, and with all unrighteous deception among those who perish, because they did not receive the love of the truth, that they might be saved." (2 Thessalonians 2:8-10KJV)

After the tribulation, Jesus Christ will send out his angels to gather up his elect; which are his ready and righteous people (his church). The 5 foolish virgins are foolish because they hadn't been made ready to meet Jesus at his return and was rejected by Jesus Christ due to their unrighteousness and sins. These are the apostate Christians. These are those who have not prepared their oil in their lamps, and are not the light of the world. Just because people confess Christ doesn't mean you are saved. They will never enter eternity with Jesus Christ. They end up in outer darkness for all of their eternity.

Remember! for many are called, but few are chosen.

"Not everyone who says to Me, 'Lord, Lord,' shall enter the kingdom of heaven, but he who does the will of My Father in heaven. Many will say to Me in that day, 'Lord, Lord, have we not prophesied in Your name, cast out demons in Your name, and done many wonders in Your name?'

And then I will declare to them, 'I never knew you; depart from Me, you who practice lawlessness!" (Matthew 7:21-23KJV)

One time at the mental health facility, a demon came to me and said, "You're an elect." I started to realise that even the demons and Satan know who the elect of God are.

Tuesday 22nd October 2019

I ran a bath for my children and sat on a chair next to them. Supervising them as they played with their toys. I was talking to the lord and speaking to him. Thanking him for what he had done for me, when a demon was suddenly pulled out of my frontal lobe by the Lord's power. This pressure in my head eased off and I felt good inside. As the demon emerged from my body, I could hear him in the distance and he said to me, "Don't go back into sin." He left and I was happy, but I was left pondering why a demon would warn me not to go back into sin. Was he an evil spirit that was sent by the Lord?

In the bible, King Saul had an evil spirit which tormented him:

"But the Spirit of the LORD departed from Saul, and an evil spirit from the LORD troubled him."

(1 Samuel 16:14KJV)

Sunday 27th October 2019

I dressed Ruby into a pretty dress for her primary school friend's birthday party. Her friend was turning 6, and was having a pony theme party with real horses to ride and brush. I met the school parents and mingle with a few of them. These parents are Christians and they start a conversation about tooth fairies. Everyone shared an opinion about if they do or don't leave money for the tooth fairy. One parent is a school teacher named Mia. She told a story of how she had left a coin for her daughter and forgot to take out the tooth. When the child had woken up, the tooth rolled to the back of the container and her daughter didn't see the tooth and thought that the tooth fairy had taken it away. Other parents gave their opinions. When it was my turn I responded and said, "No, I don't leave a coin for my child." I didn't get into the details why I didn't. When my daughter had lost a lost a tooth once. Joshua wanted to put a coin under her pillow. I asked him not too because I didn't want Violet to believe a lie and in fairies. Fairies are part of the devil's kingdom, just like mermaids, unicorns, dragons, witches and wizards. I went to sleep that night and the Lord suddenly wakes me up out of sleep. I realised I just witnessed Joshua placing a coin under her pillow. I wait for him to leave and then go in after him to remove the coin because the Lord had woken me up to remove that coin from underneath her pillow. Joshua was angry about it in the morning, but I was trying to do God's will and sometimes it can be a very hard decision that a Christian has to make to please the Lord.

I also didn't want to judge this teacher or the other parents because I could hear from their conversations that they were trying to boycott certain things too with the understanding that God had given them at the time. Only God should judge a person. We shouldn't judge others on what they do because we don't know a person fully, and only God knows them completely in both their hearts and minds. I had an evil mind once, and no-one ever thought that I was evil in my thoughts. I acted sweet and innocent on the surface, and no-one could see the poison underneath.

I don't know why God had given me a lot of understanding regarding certain things. I believe it's because God wants me to write and share the information in order to try and teach others what God has given me.

As we are packing to leave the party. I get into a conversation with Mia. She tells me about how God had pulled her out of the new age movement and witchcraft. During the conversation, Mia tells me how a spirit had put her into a sleep paralysis state. She would be fully alert and unable to move any part of her body, except her mind. She would try to talk, but no words would escape her mouth. She rebuked it in the name of Jesus and this spirit never returned again to haunt her. She described that the spirit made a lot of noise, like the buzzing of wings on a bug. She had asked the Lord what the noise was, and the Lord gave her a glimpse of a very small mosquito. Mia said that the Lord was telling her that it was a lot of noise and it was nothing, meaning that we don't have to fear it because it was nothing (this mosquito represents those demonic spirits that had cause Mia to go into a sleep paralysis state).

I find it funny that the Lord kepts putting me into different situations, or conversations like I had with Mia, so that I can write about these things and share them with you.

Wednesday 30th October 2019

Last night as I was drifting off to sleep. I spoke unconsciously and said, "I don't want to share any more information with anyone." Suddenly, the Holy Spirit's anger fell over me. I felt the Lord's anger. He didn't like what I had just said, he wanted me to reveal everything that I had written down. The truth is, I really didn't mean to say these words too. They came into my mind as I drifted off to sleep.

He wants me to share this book, and he was the one who urged me to re-write it, and to re-publish it again. My first book, "The Traps That Satan Laid: Overcoming the devil and other demons with the power of Jesus Christ" wasn't a perfect copy in my opinion; I made a few doctrinal errors when I wrote it and the Lord wanted me to fix my mistakes. I wrote it when I was at my worst and studying the Bible was hard work at the time. Everything seems to be making more sense now.

The Lord is saying through his word that when Jesus returns to the Earth, the world will end.

That morning, I took the children to school and felt just how great my body was feeling. I had continued to rehydrate myself and it made a massive difference to my headaches. However, another cold had returned last week due to Joshua. He was ill from a chesty cold, and was on his third dose of antibotics. He was on and off sick for 7 months and he wasn't getting any better too. I wasn't up to working or cleaning and decided to head down to the local shopping centre to buy something small that I needed for the house. It was an excuse for me to leave the house and go out. I liked going out. It makes me better mentally too. I arrive at the shops and walk around looking at the items on sale.

Halloween was tomorrow, and the shop was filled with Halloween products. I walked over to the party section of the shop and I overheard a young child with her mother. This child had been yelling at her to buy her a costume for halloween. She said, "I want a witch costume for Halloween!" My heart sunk deep inside and I walked away crying, thinking, why? Everyone now wants to be a witch or wizard. It starts off with simple costumes of witches or wizards for Halloween, but do you know what real witches in the occult really do for Satan? They do human or animal sacrifices in occult rituals. Do you really want your child to be a witch or a wizard and talk to demonic spirits and get involved with the devil or demons and end up in an occult with real satanists who practise these things. Read Dr. Rebecca Brown's books and you'll see what the occult does. As I was in the party section (before I walked away), this oppression once again hit my mind and body, with a real heaviness which weighed me down. Demons were once again oppressing me. I realised that it was because most people were out in the shops buying these Halloween products; so they can celebrate Halloween tomorrow. I could see them putting chocolates and lollies inside of their trolleys, buying halloween costumes for their children. I bought what I needed for the house and left feeling depressed over what I had seen, felt and heard.

Thursday 31st October 2019

It was Halloween today and the neighbours had put out halloween decoration of the Grim Reaper on their front door. Both of my children are afraid and close their eyes as we leave to go to school. After school a couple of children knock on my front door with their bags opened ready to receive lollies or chocolates. I approach the door and say to these two boys, "We don't celebrate Halloween because we are Christians." They looked confused and soon realised that I wasn't going to give them any sweets, they leave and another little girl who was dressed as a witch comes to my door with her mother. Once again I told the mother that I wasn't celebrating Halloween. They apologise to me for knocking and leave too. My children don't go trick or treating, and they don't feel like they are missing out because they too don't like this holiday because of all the scary masks and objects that people are wearing, as well as the shops being filled with these type of products. My eight year old niece Olivia doesn't even want to go shopping at that time of year because she is that afraid of the Halloween products being sold. My children would cling on me, as they close their eyes so they wouldn't see all of the scary halloween products that the shops are selling. Not every child wants to be involved with evil, and not every child will be afraid to speak their mind. On one occasion just after Halloween, Joshua's friend told him on facebook that her son called her a devil worshipper because she was decorating the house for Halloween.

Saturday 2nd November 2019

The Lord usually gives me a song first thing in the morning after waking from sleep. I found that I have days were I find myself not being able to talk properly. I want to say a certain thing and I find that my voice is being held back by the demon who is afflicting my brain. It makes me sound dumb to others. Other times as I'm speaking, a demon helps my voice sound intelligent and I'm able to speak very well. My voice seems to change as I speak, depending on the demon who is afflicting my voice and mind. I do ask the Lord for it to stop. It is affecting my life and I found myself saying a certain word that I wasn't going to say due to being possessed by a demon who speaks through me.

Sunday 3rd November 2019

I dressed both of the children for church and headed out the door to make the 35 minute drive. I ate some carbohydrates this morning, and didn't take a snack in-between meals due to the church service starting at 10:00 a.m.

I sat at church trying to sing, when my blood sugar levels dropped and I became hypoglycemic. I felt like I was going to faint; I felt dizzy and hungry.

The church was holding a dedication for a baby and were going to serve food afterwards. I was grateful because I couldn't drive home in such a state. I ate some food, but it took me a long time to return to normal. I realised later that I should have had a soft drink to bring up my blood sugar levels. I didn't because I was avoiding these soft drinks due to my diet changes. I've never experienced this before. I was pre-diabetic and had been reducing my sugar intake a lot over time. I had decided to walk more and eat better.

Wednesday 6th November 2019

My grandmother was getting these prophecies from a man she was in contact with overseas. This man she believes is getting prophecies from the Lord, and I wanted to know if he was a true or false prophet. I've been fearful regarding prophecies because of Anne's Channel. I'm truly testing every spirit, like the bible teaches. Don't believe everyone that gives prophecies, no matter how real they sound to you. Grandmother May gave me some of these prophecies. It was in the slavic language but I can't read it well enough. However, I still tried to read this prophecy. I suddenly find myself reading bits and pieces with the Lord's help. The Lord was making me read the words supernaturally with the gift of the Holy Spirit. However, even with the Lord's help I still struggled. What the Lord wanted me to read was a part which stated that their was not much time left. This prophecy was a scenario of the Lord Jesus with the Lord God; his father.

The Lord Jesus continued to say in this prophecy, "The Father will give just a little bit of more time. Only the Father knows the timing when the Lord is coming." The prophecy mentioned America, but I couldn't make out what it was about. I know of a man who was given a prophecy about America being a type of Mystery Babylon, and the Lord had told him that America will burn with fire. I believe that the Lord will judge America, and many prophets have spoken these words and received visions against this country.

Thursday 7th November 2019

I've been crying to myself and felt thankful to the Lord for saving Ruby from a near accident. I've had this fear inside of me about cars pulling out of driveways and crushing my children. I've trained both my children to watch out for the cars that pull out of driveways, and

I've told them and shown them many times that if you see a light on the back of the car. Stop!

Usually, I keep Ruby close to me when we go for a walk or scooter ride but Violet took off on her bike and Ruby wanted to catch up to her. I called her to wait for me, but she didn't and a car pulled out of the driveway. I quickly in fear, shout to the man to stop his car. He just heard me and Ruby was right behind the car. I ran to her and asked her if she was ok. "Did the car hit you?" She said, "No."

The man said to me, "If you didn't shout out to stop, I would have continued to reverse the car." My heart sunk and I felt numb inside. I just told myself 10 minutes earlier not to worry too much. I had to let go of that fear. I said, "God will protect my children with his angels." I wanted to let go of that fear, but Satan made it worse for me. He knew I was walking to help my pre-diabetic state, and I felt better inside my body when I walked. I was struggling to walk everyday and had only been walking two days a week and it wasn't enough to improve my health. He was trying to stop me from walking and deter me from leaving the house with my children. Satan and the demons can place you in certain positions to cause a person's death or accident. He had done it to me several times. However, the Lord had always saved my life in the end.

Sunday 10th November 2019

I arrived at church before 10:00 a.m. and sat down for the service. I found that the demons come around me, causing my body to feel sick. I can hear them speaking while the preaching is happening. I ask the Lord for help. I never had a good day at church for many years. I enter the building and I fall sick. As I'm singing, the Lord is with me and I can feel his Holy Spirit helping me sing the words in the slavic language with power. I have the gift of the Holy Spirit.

It is amazing to experience, and I know the Lord's presence is with me, especially at church.

Tuesday 12th November 2019

I awoke this morning wondering if my children are going to go to school today. The school had send an email to all the parents on Monday about if the school will be opened today due to the bushfire dangers in NSW. It was going to be a very hot day, and they predicted that it will reach up to 35 degrees celsius and the weather will only get hotter during the week, reaching 42 degrees celsius in NSW. Bushfire's are common in Australia, and every year firefighters and residents fight these fires to protect their homes. We are blessed that it has never affected us personally. I open the email and the letter reads:

Dear Parents and Caregivers,

A Catastrophic Fire Danger has been forecast for tomorrow, Tuesday 12 November. This is the first time since the new Fire Danger Ratings were introduced in 2009 that the Catastrophic Fire Danger has been forecast for Greater Sydney.

After discussions this morning with the Rural Fire Service and local evacuation centres due to the School being in a bushfire risk area, the following has been decided:

- The School will be open. However, some staff will be absent due to the fire weather warnings and the impact on their personal situation. This will have an impact on normal lessons and classes may be reduced to accommodate changes to staffing and class sizes.

- The School strongly advises any family that lives in a bushfire risk area to implement their Bushfire Survival Plan. Families living in these areas should not send their children to school on Tuesday.
- Due to the School's general location, if a bushfire occurs in the Blacktown / Hawkesbury district, the School will work with all Emergency Services to keep students and staff safe. Evacuation of the School is a possible outcome and will be implemented if required under the direction of Emergency Services.
- Local road infrastructure will be severely impacted if fires occur in our general area, meaning afternoon travel to school to collect your child will be affected. Please consider this in your decision making.
- Parents should consider the air quality and the health needs of their child before sending them tomorrow. Classrooms will be open at lunchtime to provide spaces off the playground during recess and lunch.

Thank you for your support in this situation.

Kind Regards

Principal David

I didn't know what to decide on, to send them or not. As I laid on the couch after having a cup of coffee. I closed my eyes and an alien looking demon runs toward me with full speed. It shocked me, but I wasn't allowing myself to get frightened. The demon was bronze and had an alien looking head and features. It was ugly to look at. I again rebuked it in the name of Jesus and knew Satan once again was involved.

I check the emails again for any more updates and received another email from the principal:

Dear families,

You will undoubtedly be aware that a catastrophic fire alert has been declared over the Greater Sydney area.

As a result a number of schools who are at significant risk have decided to close their campus today, Tuesday 12 November. Following consultation with the local RFS decided to leave it's campus open for minimal attendance.

However, wherever possible families are encouraged to make alternative arrangements for their children today.

The school will provide minimal supervision and limited activities for any students whose family situation may still require them to attend.

I'm sure you join me in praying peace and protection for every member of our community and for anyone exposed to threat or risk today, especially those working in so many ways to combat the fires.

Thank you for your assistance and God bless.

"That decided that" I thought. I'm not taking them to school today. I will spend the day with my children.

As the day progressed, the heat soared and the sky became a reddish colour. It was a horrible day. You could feel the danger in the air. Most people stayed inside because of the air quality and so did I.

Friday 22nd November 2019

I've tried to reduce my carbohydrate intake and found it made the biggest difference to my health too. My head hurts when I eat too many carbohydrates. I feel physically sick and my head pain gets worse. When I eat a high protein, low carbohydrate diet with lots of fruit and vegetables my head is no longer in severe pain.

Sunday 8th December 2019

I haven't been writing for a while again. It took me a while to return and complete the book. Today, Joshua, our children and myself are off to Port Stephens for a five day break from life in general. I had decided to go to church last Friday afternoon with my grandmother because the Saturday service was now changed to Friday nights, due to a low number of Christians attending the Saturday night services.

I loaded our car with the luggage and Joshua drives us to the holiday destination. I had been hearing the demons again, and now I knew I was also slightly possessed on occasion by them.

When I read a book I didn't have to even pay much attention to the words on the page and I can read the words almost without looking at them. I could feel the possession in my body, and knew I wasn't fully being controlled by them because I was a Christian, but I knew the demons were using my hands, mouth and voice sometimes, and I had caught them doing so.

We check and settle in. It was going to be the usual holiday fun that we have together while we are away. I was grateful that our marriage wasn't over and we were still together as a family. It was hard at times living in a marriage when your the only one living for Christ. Joshua doesn't understand why I do the things I do sometimes for the Lord. The Lord has said in his word that he will bring a sword to the earth and your own households will be your own enemies. The people you love will end up persecuting you for Jesus Christ:

"Think not that I am come to send peace on earth: I came not to send peace, but a sword. For I am come to set a man at variance against his father, and the daughter against her mother, and the daughter in law against her mother in law. And a man's foes shall be they of his own household.

He that loveth father or mother more than me is not worthy of me: and he that loveth son or daughter more than me is not worthy of me. And he that taketh not his cross, and followeth after me, is not worthy of me. He that findeth his life shall lose it: and he that loseth his life for my sake shall find it." (Matthew 10:34-39KJV)

Wednesday 11th December 2019

We had a day of fun with my children at Tobbogan Hill Park. That night I went to sleep and a demon came and said, "If you publish this book, I will kill you." I had just pondered that I needed to finish and publish this book for the Lord like he wanted me too. I was delaying the process now.

Thursday 12th December 2019

We went to the beach with the children and watched them play on the sand with their sand buckets and shovels. They were running towards the water and filling up their buckets to tip the water into the sandpits and sandcastles that they had made. Violet suddenly starts screaming really loud with joy. She had just seen one of her bestfriends from school who had ran up to her to give her a big hug. We are two and an half hours away from Sydney and she met her friend from her primary school on this beach. I see her parents and they approach to greet us both. It's a small world when the Lord arranges you to meet someone for his own plans and purpose. I realised instantly that the Lord arranged this meeting. My daughters friend reads Harry Potter books and the Lord urged me to talk to her parents about this problem. At first, I didn't want too. I didn't want to come across strong and speak about this subject to them without an opening. We spent three hours talking and I finally had the nerve to tell her mother about Harry Potter and how I didn't allow Violet to read that type of material or watch the films due to the evil nature of the books heavily involved in the ideas of witchcraft. The woman responds positive and agrees with me about the issue. I even said, "I don't take my children to the movies due to most films not being pleasing to the Lord."

She replies,"Peoples imaginations aren't clean, and you can see them in the films that they project." She continued,"I know that the missionaries over in America had made a big deal about not going to the movies. It was a big issue over in the states."

However, she expressed that she was still going to take her children to the cinemas to watch the latest film that had come out.

During the conversation and after staying in the hot sun for over three hours. I had gotten badly sunburnt. However, I felt extremely happy that I had repented and did the Lord's will, and had spoken to this woman about this issue.

We said our farewells and leave to go to our hotel room to freshen up. I was dehydrated and feeling overheated from the sun. It was a hot day, and I was glad I was out of the Australian sun. It gets really hot over here. I have a shower and we go out to dinner for the night with the children and relax for the evening.

Friday 13th December 2019

We check out and go to the cafe for our breakfast before returning home from the few days away. We had dinner plans today with Joshua's family, so we wanted to get back to Sydney to make it to the dinner. We drove home and met his family and a few other guests and had a nice night together. I look back at the past few years and realise I had come a long way. I wasn't entirely free from the demons, but the Lord had freed my life and soul from Satan. I believe the Lord's words when he said, "I will deliver you." However, it will be in the Lord's time.

Sunday 26th January 2020

It is Sunday morning, and I was currently away in Melbourne with our family. We decided to go away for Joshua's soccer club tournament. I decided to listen to a YouTube video from Omegaman radio. I was listening to John Ramirez who was speaking on the topic, "You are never too small for Yehovah to use you." It was a very powerful message, and inspiring to hear a true Christian telling people the truth.

Thank you John for such a message.

I started to think about my book, and to finally get it finished for publishing when I was directed by the Lord to send a copy to John Ramirez.

I wasn't sure why the Lord wanted him to receive the information, but the Lord was still directing me to give it to John. When I got home I found an address for his ministry and I said, "I will send him a copy after I have published the book." The demons were angry about this. I could feel their presence as they were directing their outrage to me through a tormenting feeling of wrath against my own body. However, I was going to send it to him either way, and I was hoping that he would read it and understand that the Lord was wanting him to receive the information that I had written down.

On a separate day, I heard, "What do you want?" a demon had spoken to me in a very serious tone of voice. I replied to the demon and said, "I want nothing. I just want to serve the Lord." This demon wanted to find out if I would accept anything from the devil, like materialistic things in exchange for my soul. Satan does give people fame and money in exchange for your service to the devil, and for you to ultimately end up in Hell.

Our Lord Jesus once spoke these words:

"And when he had called the people unto him with his disciples also, he said unto them, Whosoever will come after me, let him deny himself, and take up his cross, and follow me. For whosoever will save his life shall lose it; but whosoever shall lose his life for my sake and the gospel's, the same shall save it. For what shall it profit a man, if he shall gain the whole world, and lose his own soul? Or what shall a man give in exchange for his soul? Whosoever therefore shall be ashamed of me and of my words in this adulterous and sinful generation; of him also shall the Son of man be ashamed, when he cometh in the glory of his Father with the holy angels." (Mark 8:34-38KJV)

I had entered into another demonic dream. At the end of the dream before waking up I found myself on what looked like my bed. Demonic spirits again were trying to grab me with force. I kept on pushing them off the bed and wrestling with them to leave me alone. I heard a voice and thought it was Satan. I told him, "I don't like you." He responded and said, "You have ruined all the wonderful plans we had planned for you." I felt the Lord Jesus' presence and knew he was with me. I suddenly wake up and find myself lying on the couch. I must have fallen asleep. I look at the clock and it was around 10:00 p.m. I also had looked at the clock before I fell asleep and knew that it was around 8:30 p.m. when I had laid down on the couch. I had slept for about an hour and a half, but it felt like seconds had only gone by.

On another day, I woke up and heard these words directed to Joshua.

"He will not come out until he pays the last farthing."

I don't know who spoke. I was wondering who it was. It came out of my voice. I didn't hear any demons speak, only my voice. It wasn't me saying these words. I know it wasn't from me, but was it from the Lord? Joshua had been speaking a lot these last few years against the Lord. I wondered if this was the Lord, his Holy Spirit. I wasn't sure because I know my cousin Jack and the pastor from Serbia had spoken that Joshua will be saved by the Lord. I was a bit confused and didn't know now if Joshua was going to be saved after all. I was hoping for our household to be saved by the Lord, but I wasn't sure anymore.

The voice was referring to this verse:

"Verily I say unto thee, Thou shalt by no means come out thence, till thou hast paid the uttermost farthing." (Matthew 5:25-26 KJV)

It means, if this truly was the Holy Spirt. Joshua will not be saved by the Lord God.

I wasn't sure, I didn't want to say anything against it. I also didn't want to say this was God because demons can give a person, even a Christian, a false word. I didn't know who spoke these particular words, and I couldn't figure out who had given them to me.

Chapter 19

SIN

All unrighteousness is sin. However, sin not only affects human beings, it also affected angels as well as the kingdom of darkness.

As a result the angels that had sinned are in hell like the Bible mentions.

"And the angels which kept not their first estate, but left their own habitation, he hath reserved in everlasting chains under darkness unto the judgment of the great day." (Jude 1:6KJV)

For if God spared not the angels that sinned, but cast them down to hell, and delivered them into chains of darkness, to be reserved unto judgment; (2 Peter 2:4KJV)

These angels that are kept under darkness are the angels that left heaven and came to the Earth to take themselves wives from the children of men. They sinned and now are locked in hell with everlasting chains. These angels fathered, The Nephilim, they sinned against God.

"And it came to pass, when men began to multiply on the face of the earth, and daughters were born unto them, That the sons of God saw the daughters of men that they were fair; and they took them wives of all which they chose." (Genesis 6:1- 2KJV)

There were giants in the earth in those days; and also after that, when the sons of God came in unto the daughters of men, and they bare [children] to them, the same [became] mighty men which [were] of old, men of renown. (Genesis 6:4KJV)

The devil sinned from the beginning. Anyone who commits sin is of the devil.

"He that committeth sin is of the devil; for the devil sinneth from the beginning. For this purpose the Son of God was manifested, that he might destroy the works of the devil." (1 John 3:8KJV)

Sin entered into the Earth by one man, this man was Adam. He disobeyed God by eating the fruit from the tree of the knowledge of good and evil; as a result, death passed upon everyone.

"Wherefore, as by one man sin entered into the world, and death by sin; and so death passed upon all men, for that all have sinned." (Romans 5:12KJV)

If we willingly do wrong, it is sin. For the strength of sin is the law, and by the law we know what sin is.

"All unrighteousness is sin: and there is a sin not unto death." (1 John 5:17KJV)

Sin lies at the door and has a desire to rule over you. However, we have to rule over sin and not let it rule over us.

"If thou doest well, shalt thou not be accepted? and if thou doest not well, sin lieth at the door. And unto thee shall be his desire, and thou shalt rule over him." (Genesis 4:7KJV)

The Bible teaches that all have sinned and fall short of the glory of God.

"For all have sinned, and come short of the glory of God." (Romans 3:23KJV)

The word of God (Jesus) came to the Earth in the form of sinful flesh. Jesus committed no sin and was a spotless lamb to God: perfect and without blemish. He was the ultimate sacrifice and was offered once to bear the sins of many.

"For what the law could not do, in that it was weak through the flesh, God sending his own Son in the likeness of sinful flesh, and for sin, condemned sin in the flesh." (Romans 8:3KJV)

"So Christ was once offered to bear the sins of many; and unto them that look for him shall he appear the second time without sin unto salvation." (Hebrews 9:28KJV)

"But with the precious blood of Christ, as of a lamb without blemish and without spot." (Peter 1:19KJV)

By Adam, many were made sinners. However, because Jesus was obedient, by him, many are now made righteous and are given eternal life through our Lord Jesus.

"For as by one man's disobedience many were made sinners, so by the obedience of one shall many be made righteous." (Romans 5:19KJV)

"That as sin hath reigned unto death, even so might grace reign through righteousness unto eternal life by Jesus Christ our Lord." (Romans 5: 21KJV)

This is why it is important to repent from all our sins and to live a righteous life. We can only renew our minds by the help of the Holy Spirit, who lives in us. We choose to either obey God or disobey him.

God wants to save the world. If you believe in Jesus, then there is no condemnation. However, if you do not believe in him, you're already condemned. The end result is that you will spend the rest of your eternity in the lake of fire. The Bible teaches that people like darkness rather than light because of their evil deeds, so expose your sins and repent. God is faithful and just to forgive us of our sins.

"For God so loved the world, that he gave his only begotten Son, that whosoever believeth in him should not perish, but have everlasting life. For God sent not his Son into the world to condemn the world; but that the world through him might be saved. He that believeth on him is not condemned: but he that believeth not is condemned already, because he hath not believed in the name of the only begotten Son of God. And this is the condemnation, that light is come into the world, and men loved darkness rather than light, because their deeds were evil. For every one that doeth evil hateth the light, neither cometh to the light, lest his deeds should be reproved. But he that doeth truth cometh to the light, that his deeds may be made manifest, that they are wrought in God." (John 3: 16-21KJV)

"If we confess our sins, he is faithful and just to forgive us our sins, and to cleanse us from all unrighteousness." (1 John 1:9KJV)

Conclusion

Our Lord is gracious and merciful. The key to a good relationship with God through Jesus Christ our Lord is to truly repent and turn away from all evil and worldly involvement. Confess your sins and asked the Lord for forgiveness. Most of all don't be a hearer of his word only, but a doer. God wants to save the lost. Seek God and read the Bible on a daily basis and meditate on what you read. Jesus is the truth, and there is no other way to God but through him.

"Jesus saith unto him, I am the way, the truth, and the life: no man cometh unto the Father, but by me." (John 14:6KJV)

He is the road to salvation. There is no other way.

I wrote the following poem during my time of extreme torment; it describes how the Lord set me free:

Set Free

I was deep in darkness.

No light I saw.

Many years I spent behind closed doors.

I turned myself away from him,

Christ Jesus,

my risen King.

Deep in sin,

I was stained.

No one else but me to blame.

The devil tried to take my life.

He set me on a course.

He had absolutely no remorse.

It wasn't until God stepped in,

removing all these hidden sins,

that I'm now sanctified, justified, and called.

Eternal life is now my great reward.

Printed in the United States
By Bookmasters